DISCOVER THE
WORLD WIDE WEB

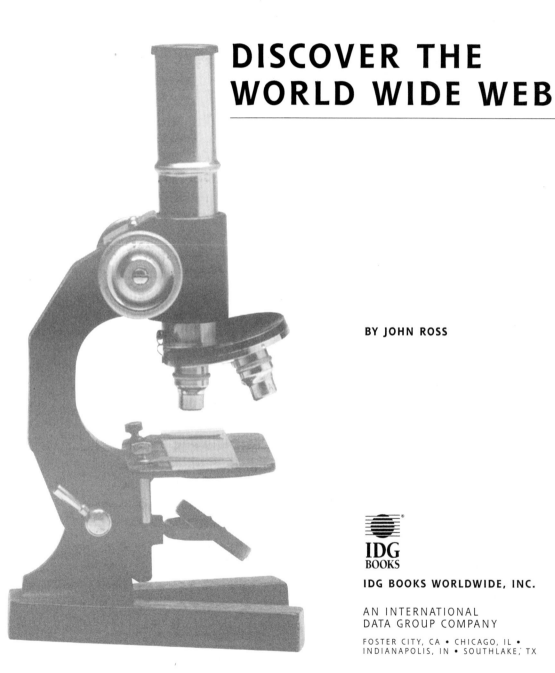

DISCOVER THE WORLD WIDE WEB

BY JOHN ROSS

IDG
BOOKS

IDG BOOKS WORLDWIDE, INC.

AN INTERNATIONAL
DATA GROUP COMPANY

FOSTER CITY, CA • CHICAGO, IL •
INDIANAPOLIS, IN • SOUTHLAKE, TX

Discover The World Wide Web

Published by
IDG Books Worldwide, Inc.
An International Data Group Company
919 E. Hillsdale Blvd., Suite 400
Foster City, CA 94404

http://www.idgbooks.com (IDG Books Worldwide Web site)

Library of Congress Catalog Card No.: 96-70939

ISBN: 0-7645-3060-7

Printed in the United States of America

10 9 8 7 6 5 4 3 2 1

1EC/ST/QU/ZX/FC

Distributed in the United States by IDG Books Worldwide, Inc.

Distributed by Macmillan Canada for Canada; by Contemporanea de Ediciones for Venezuela; by Distribuidora Cuspide for Argentina; by CITEC for Brazil; by Ediciones ZETA S.C.R. Ltda. for Peru; by Editorial Limusa SA for Mexico; by Transworld Publishers Limited in the United Kingdom and Europe; by Academic Bookshop for Egypt; by Levant Distributors S.A.R.L. for Lebanon; by Al Jassim for Saudi Arabia; by Simron Pty. Ltd. for South Africa; by Pustak Mahal for India; by The Computer Bookshop for India; by Toppan Company Ltd. for Japan; by Addison Wesley Publishing Company for Korea; by Longman Singapore Publishers Ltd. for Singapore, Malaysia, Thailand, and Indonesia; by Unalis Corporation for Taiwan; by WS Computer Publishing Company, Inc. for the Philippines; by WoodsLane Pty. Ltd. for Australia; by WoodsLane Enterprises Ltd. for New Zealand. Authorized Sales Agent: Anthony Rudkin Associates for the Middle East and North Africa.

For general information on IDG Books Worldwide's books in the U.S., please call our Consumer Customer Service department at 800-762-2974. For reseller information, including discounts and premium sales, please call our Reseller Customer Service department at 800-434-3422.

For information on where to purchase IDG Books Worldwide's books outside the U.S., please contact our International Sales department at 415-655-3172 or fax 415-655-3295.

For information on foreign language translations, please contact our Foreign & Subsidiary Rights department at 415-655-3021 or fax 415-655-3281.

For sales inquiries and special prices for bulk quantities, please contact our Sales department at 415-655-3200 or write to the address above.

For information on using IDG Books Worldwide's books in the classroom or for ordering examination copies, please contact our Educational Sales department at 800-434-2086 or fax 817-251-8174.

For press review copies, author interviews, or other publicity information, please contact our Public Relations department at 415-655-3000 or fax 415-655-3299.

For authorization to photocopy items for corporate, personal, or educational use, please contact Copyright Clearance Center, 222 Rosewood Drive, Danvers, MA 01923, or fax 508-750-4470.

is a trademark under exclusive license to
IDG Books Worldwide, Inc.,
from International Data Group, Inc.

ABOUT IDG BOOKS WORLDWIDE

Welcome to the world of IDG Books Worldwide.

IDG Books Worldwide, Inc., is a subsidiary of International Data Group, the world's largest publisher of computer-related information and the leading global provider of information services on information technology. IDG was founded more than 25 years ago and now employs more than 8,500 people worldwide. IDG publishes more than 275 computer publications in over 75 countries (see listing below). More than 60 million people read one or more IDG publications each month.

Launched in 1990, IDG Books Worldwide is today the #1 publisher of best-selling computer books in the United States. We are proud to have received eight awards from the Computer Press Association in recognition of editorial excellence and three from *Computer Currents'* First Annual Readers' Choice Awards. Our best-selling *...For Dummies*® series has more than 30 million copies in print with translations in 30 languages. IDG Books Worldwide, through a joint venture with IDG's Hi-Tech Beijing, became the first U.S. publisher to publish a computer book in the People's Republic of China. In record time, IDG Books Worldwide has become the first choice for millions of readers around the world who want to learn how to better manage their businesses.

Our mission is simple: Every one of our books is designed to bring extra value and skill-building instructions to the reader. Our books are written by experts who understand and care about our readers. The knowledge base of our editorial staff comes from years of experience in publishing, education, and journalism — experience we use to produce books for the '90s. In short, we care about books, so we attract the best people. We devote special attention to details such as audience, interior design, use of icons, and illustrations. And because we use an efficient process of authoring, editing, and desktop publishing our books electronically, we can spend more time ensuring superior content and spend less time on the technicalities of making books.

You can count on our commitment to deliver high-quality books at competitive prices on topics you want to read about. At IDG Books Worldwide, we continue in the IDG tradition of delivering quality for more than 25 years. You'll find no better book on a subject than one from IDG Books Worldwide.

John Kilcullen
CEO
IDG Books Worldwide, Inc.

Steven Berkowitz
President and Publisher
IDG Books Worldwide, Inc.

Eighth Annual
Computer Press
Awards ≥1992

Ninth Annual
Computer Press
Awards ≥1993

Tenth Annual
Computer Press
Awards ≥1994

Eleventh Annual
Computer Press
Awards ≥1995

Welcome to the Discover Series

Do you want to discover the best and most efficient ways to use your computer and learn about technology? Books in the Discover series teach you the essentials of technology with a friendly, confident approach. You'll find a Discover book on almost any subject — from the Internet to intranets, from Web design and programming to the business programs that make your life easier.

We've provided valuable, real-world examples that help you relate to topics faster. Discover books begin by introducing you to the main features of programs, so you start by doing something *immediately*. The focus is to teach you how to perform tasks that are useful and meaningful in your day-to-day work. You might create a document or graphic, explore your computer, surf the Web, or write a program. Whatever the task, you learn the most commonly used features, and focus on the best tips and techniques for doing your work. You'll get results quickly, and discover the best ways to use software and technology in your everyday life.

You may find the following elements and features in this book:

Discovery Central: This tearout card is a handy quick reference to important tasks or ideas covered in the book.

Quick Tour: The Quick Tour gets you started working with the book right away.

Real-Life Vignettes: Throughout the book you'll see one-page scenarios illustrating a real-life application of a topic covered.

Goals: Each chapter opens with a list of goals you can achieve by reading the chapter.

Side Trips: These asides include additional information about alternative or advanced ways to approach the topic covered.

Bonuses: Timesaving tips and more advanced techniques are covered in each chapter.

Discovery Center: This guide illustrates key procedures covered throughout the book.

Visual Index: You'll find real-world documents in the Visual Index, with page numbers pointing you to where you should turn to achieve the effects shown.

Throughout the book, you'll also notice some special icons and formatting:

A Feature Focus icon highlights new features in the software's latest release, and points out significant differences between it and the previous version.

Web Paths refer you to Web sites that provide additional information about the topic.

Tips offer timesaving shortcuts, expert advice, quick techniques, or brief reminders.

The X-Ref icon refers you to other chapters or sections for more information.

Pull Quotes emphasize important ideas that are covered in the chapter.

Notes provide additional information or highlight special points of interest about a topic.

The Caution icon alerts you to potential problems you should watch out for.

The Discover series delivers interesting, insightful, and inspiring information about technology to help you learn faster and retain more. So the next time you want to find answers to your technology questions, reach for a Discover book. We hope the entertaining, easy-to-read style puts you at ease and makes learning fun.

Credits

ACQUISITIONS EDITOR
John Read

DEVELOPMENT EDITOR
Barb Guerra

COPY EDITOR
Kerrie Klein

TECHNICAL EDITOR
Ken Welch

PROJECT COORDINATOR
Ben Schroeter

QUALITY CONTROL SPECIALIST
Mick Arellano

GRAPHICS AND PRODUCTION SPECIALISTS
Laura Carpenter
Christopher Pimentel

PROOFREADER
Mary C. Oby

INDEXER
Elizabeth Cunningham

BOOK DESIGN
Seventeenth Street Studios
Phyllis Beaty
Kurt Krames

About the Author

When **John Ross** is not trying to explain computers and telecommunications to non-technical audiences, he spends his time making apple cider and restoring antique toy trains. He has written almost a dozen books about computers and the Internet.

PREFACE

*D*iscover the World Wide Web is a book for people who want to learn how to use the Web without becoming data communication engineers in the process. First time visitors to that strange, new place called the Internet can use this book as a guide.

The Web contains millions of documents, movies, sound recordings, and other forms of information. Where do you start exploring? What kind of equipment do you need to get there? And where do you go when you want to find something specific? That's what this book is about. It tells you how all that information is organized and how to use search engines, directories, and other online tools to move quickly to the specific item you want to find.

This book has four major sections:

Part One, "Introduction to the Web," describes the internal structure and organization of the Internet and tells you about the computer and connections you need to use the World Wide Web.

Part Two, "Navigating the World Wide Web," explains the specific tools — browser programs, Web search services, and directories — and skills you use to move around the Web.

Part Three, "World Wide Web Destinations," contains pointers to specific Web sites, including places that track the latest news and weather, and sites that contain more specialized information. It also tells you how to use the Web to obtain free and low-cost computer programs, and how to find many kinds of businesses on the Web.

Part Four, "Beyond Browsing," provides information about the other ways to use the Web and the rest of the Internet, such as viewing movies, listening to radio stations and other audio services, exchanging messages with other people, and joining virtual communities of people who share your interests.

The Web is out there all around you, just waiting for you to come and visit. Most of the natives are friendly, and they have almost every imaginable kind of treasure and trinket on display. Use the instructions and examples in this book to find your bearings, but beware: Once you get there, you may never want to leave.

Acknowledgments

Thanks to all the people at IDG Books Worldwide who helped convert this from a half-baked idea into a book: Acquisitions Editor John Read, Development Editor Barbra Guerra, Copy Editor Kerrie Klein, Tech Editor Ken Welch, and all the design and production people who put an attractive frame around my words. They've all helped make this a much better book.

Thanks, too, to the network folks at Northwest Nexus and the Microsoft Network, who provided my connections to the Internet. This book would not have been possible without them.

CONTENTS AT A GLANCE

PART FOUR—BEYOND BROWSING

CONTENTS

PART THREE—WORLD WIDE WEB DESTINATIONS, 127

WORLD WIDE WEB QUICK TOUR

To demonstrate the kind of information you can find on the World Wide Web, here's a trip from San Francisco to Boston and the Maine coast, entirely planned and arranged through the Web.

First, a flight across the United States. To make airline reservations, jump to the Travelocity Web site (http://www.travelocity.com) and select Travel Reservations. Several other Web sites offer similar services, but this one works as well as any. After you enter your itinerary and the dates you want to travel, Travelocity consults the airlines' reservations system computer and returns a list of flights that meet your needs, as shown in Figure T-1. When you decide which flights you want, you can make your reservations through the Web site.

Choose a flight by clicking the button next to it. Then click Select Flight. If you've requested more than one destination, we'll show you those flights next.

Availability for SAN FRANCISCO, CA (SFO) to BOSTON, MA (BOS)
Thursday, April 10

Select	Airline	Flight	Departing		Arriving		Stops	Meal	Plane
			City	Time	City	Time			
○	UA	22	SFO	7:00 am	BOS	3:26 pm	0	BS	320
○	UA	24	SFO	8:00 am	BOS	4:28 pm	0	BS	757
○	UA	26	SFO	8:50 am	BOS	5:18 pm	0	BS	757
○	UA	28	SFO	12:00 pm	BOS	8:28 pm	0	L	757
○	UA	30	SFO	1:30 pm	BOS	9:58 pm	0	L	757
○	UA	32	SFO	4:15 pm	BOS	12:43 am+1	0	D	757
○	UA	34	SFO	10:05 pm	BOS	6:27 am+1	0		757
○	DL	1886	SFO	6:30 am	BOS	4:35 pm	1	L	757
○	US	76	SFO	7:20 am	BOS	5:45 pm	1	B	757
○	NW	928	SFO	1:15 am	BOS	11:14 am	1	B	757
○	AA	1210	SFO	1:33 pm	BOS	11:56 pm	1	S	S80
○	NW	356	SFO	3:00 pm	BOS	12:59 am+1	1	D	757

Select Flight

Document: Done

Figure T-1 Travelocity's airline reservation system.

For the lowest fare, you can use Travelocity's low fare search engine to sort through all possible options and give you the best available deals it can find. Of course, these low fares may not be the most convenient times or connections.

If you can travel on very short notice, several airlines offer special deals for last-minute reservations on selected routes that are lower than the ones Travelocity may report. For example, Figure T-2 shows some typical Hot Fares from TWA, such as coast-to-coast for $179 round-trip. You can find TWA's Web site at http://www.twa.com. Northwest Airlines has similar deals at http://www.nwa.com. Other airlines distribute weekly bulletins with last-minute fares through e-mail.

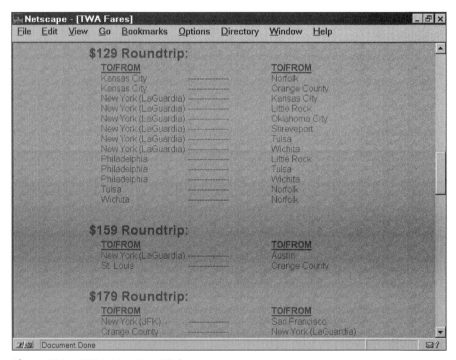

Figure T-2 TWA's Hot Fares Web page.

When you're ready to leave, many airlines can tell you about departure and arrival delays through their Web sites, such as the United Airlines Flight Status page (http://www.ual.com). The Trip.com Web site (http://sapphire.thetrip.com) can keep your friends and family apprised of the progress of your flight (Figure T-3).

Arriving in Boston, how do you get out of the airport and into the city? Massport, the Massachusetts Port Authority, has a Web site at http://www.massport.com/logan/toandfro.html that provides schedules and fares for buses, mass transit, and a water shuttle. For more information about the Boston subway and bus system, visit the MBTA's Web site at http://www.mbta.com (Figure T-4).

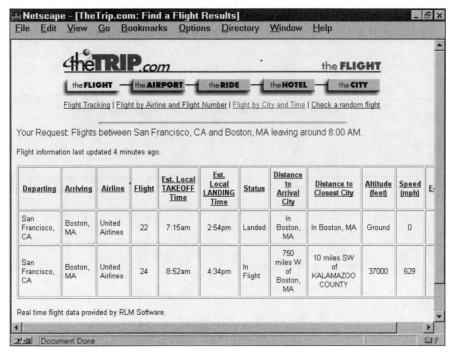

Figure T-3   The Trip.com Flight Tracking Web site.

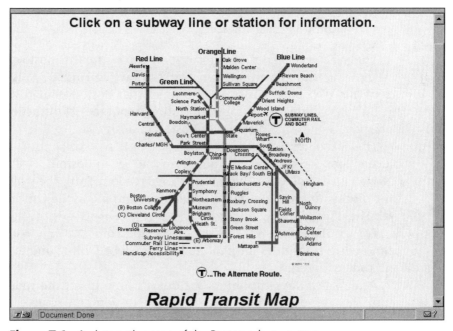

Figure T-4   An interactive map of the Boston subway system.

You'll need a hotel in Boston, and you have many choices. Fodor's Hotel Index (`http://www.fodors.com/hi.cgi`) is an interactive directory of hotels that will recommend hotels fitting your choice of location, price range, and facilities. Figure T-5 shows Fodor's Trip Planner.

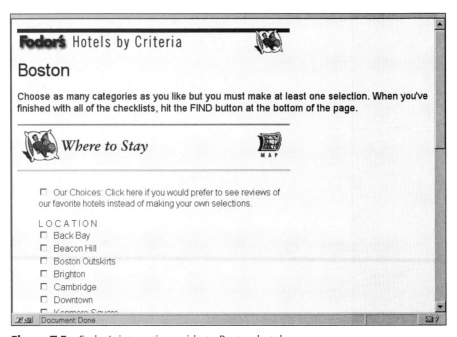

Figure T-5 Fodor's interactive guide to Boston hotels.

The Web has plenty of information for visitors to Boston. Boston Online (`http://ftp.std.com/NE/boston.html`), shown in Figure T-6, is a good place to start. This Web page has links to many other Boston-related Web sites. Follow the link to Visiting Boston for information about tourist attractions, places to eat and shop, and even a glossary of Boston English.

The Boston Insider (`http://www.TheInsider.com/boston`) is another good place to look for tips about things to do and see in Boston.

No visitor to Boston should miss the Freedom Trail, the walking tour of historic places. You can preview the sights by jumping to the Official City of Boston Web Site at `http://www.ci.boston.ma.us/freedomtrail.html` (Figure T-7).

For local news, the Web site at Boston.com (`http://www.boston.com`) is unmatched. It includes links to the Boston Globe Online and to several local TV and radio stations.

After a few days exploring Boston, it's time to hit the road. All the major rental car companies have Web sites where you can reserve a car and learn about special offers. For example, National offers discounts and free upgrades to customers who visit their site (Figure T-8).

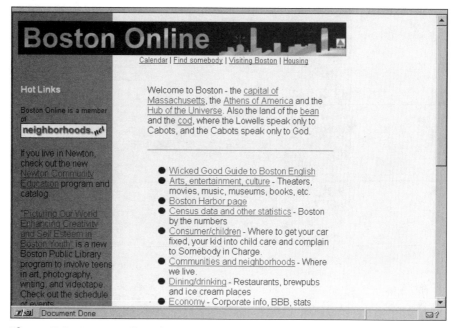

Figure T-6 Boston Online's home page.

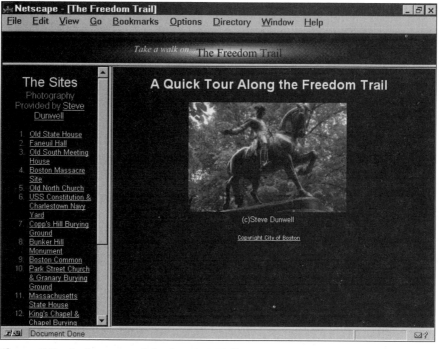

Figure T-7 A photo tour of the Freedom Trail.

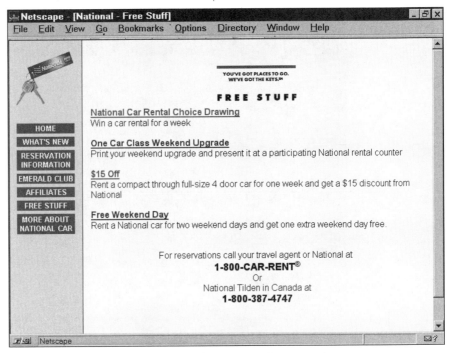

Figure T-8 Discounts and upgrades from National Car Rental.

On to Maine. AutoPilot (`http://www.freetrip.com`) is one of several services on the World Wide Web that will provide detailed highway routing for automobile travelers. To obtain routing information for your trip, enter your origin and destination points in the Web page. You can select a direct or scenic route and instruct the system to avoid toll highways. In a few seconds, you will see a new page with complete directions, like the one in Figure T-9.

Driving out of Boston is almost always an adventure. For current traffic reports, jump to the SmartTraveler Web site (`www.smartraveler.com`).

Congestion isn't the only problem you may face on your way to Portland. The Speedtrap Registry Web site at `http://www.speedtrap.com/speedtrap` (Figure T-10) lists known speed traps in each state. Best to stay under the posted speed limit.

Now that you've reached Maine — without any speeding tickets, of course — Lobster.net (`http://www.chickadee.com/lobster`) can tell you about attractions along the southern Maine seacoast. For a guide to Greater Portland, go to the TravelMaine site at `http://www.sourcemaine.com/TravelMaine`.

You can't come to the Maine coast without eating lobster. The Lobster Institute (you just knew there had to be one, didn't you?) has a Web site at `http://www/lobster.um.maine.edu/lobster`, where you can find recipes, lobster lore, and a lobster chat area. Figure T-11 shows the Lobster Institute's cookbook.

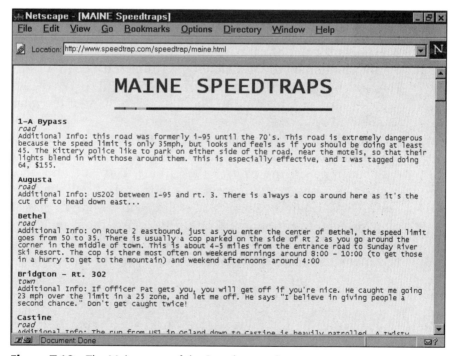

Netscape - [Your Personalized Trip Itinerary!]

File Edit View Go Bookmarks Options Directory Window Help

ORIGINATION : Boston , MA
DESTINATION : Portland , ME
PREFERENCES : All Scenic , Do Not Avoid Tolls
Total Trip Distance: 106 mi.
Total Trip Time: 1 hours 53 minutes

Accumulated Miles / Time		Directions / Enroute Information	Remaining Miles / Time	
0 mi	0:00	Starting at: I-93 & I-93 Tun Ramp	106 mi	1:53
		Start North on I-93 for 0.5 mi		
1 mi	0:01	Junction With US 1 Adamski Hwy	105 mi	1:52
		Cont. North on US 1 Adamski Hwy for 4 mi		
2 mi	0:02	Approaching US 1 Tobin Brdg (Toll)	104 mi	1:51
4 mi	0:05	Junction With US 1 Northeast Exwy	102 mi	1:48
		Cont. North on US 1 Northeast Exwy for 2 mi		
6 mi	0:07	Junction With US 1 Bennet Hwy	100 mi	1.46
		Cont. North on US 1 Bennet Hwy for 1.8 mi		
8 mi	0:09	Junction With US 1 Broadway	98 mi	1:44
		Cont. North on US 1 Broadway for 5 mi		
13 mi	0:15	Junction With I-95	93 mi	1:38
		Cont. North on I-95 for 28 mi		
17 mi	0:19		89 mi	1:34

Document: Done

Figure T-9 An AutoPilot route from Boston to Portland.

Netscape - [MAINE Speedtraps]

File Edit View Go Bookmarks Options Directory Window Help

Location: http://www.speedtrap.com/speedtrap/maine.html

MAINE SPEEDTRAPS

1-A Bypass
road
Additional Info: this road was formerly I-95 until the 70's. This road is extremely dangerous because the speed limit is only 35mph, but looks and feels as if you should be doing at least 45. The Kittery police like to park on either side of the road, near the motels, so that their lights blend in with those around them. This is especially effective, and I was tagged doing 64, $155.

Augusta
road
Additional Info: US202 between I-95 and rt. 3. There is always a cop around here as it's the cut off to head down east...

Bethel
road
Additional Info: On Route 2 eastbound, just as you enter the center of Bethel, the speed limit goes from 50 to 35. There is usually a cop parked on the side of Rt 2 as you go around the corner in the middle of town. This is about 4-5 miles from the entrance road to Sunday River Ski Resort. The cop is there most often on weekend mornings around 8:00 - 10:00 (to get those in a hurry to get to the mountain) and weekend afternoons around 4:00

Bridgton - Rt. 302
town
Additional Info: If officer Pat gets you, you will get off if you're nice. He caught me going 23 mph over the limit in a 25 zone, and let me off. He says "I believe in giving people a second chance." Don't get caught twice!

Castine
road
Additional Info: The run from US1 in Orland down to Castine is heavily patrolled. A twisty

Document: Done

Figure T-10 The Maine page of the Speedtrap registry.

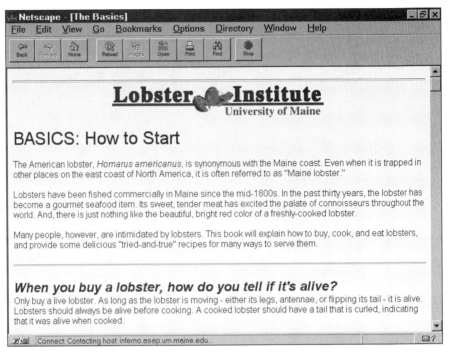

Figure T-11   The Lobster Institute's cookbook.

If you don't want to cook your own lobster, there are plenty of restaurants that will do it for you. Mabel's Lobster Claw in Kennebunkport (`http://www.lamere.net/kpwebpages/htdocs/mblstclw.htm`) is just one of many with its own Web pages.

Information on the Web about the Maine coast doesn't stop at the waterline. The National Weather Service has a Web page (`http://www.nws.edu/buoy`) that supplies current data from an automated sea buoy at the mouth of Casco Bay (Figure T-12).

Eventually, it's time to go home. Return your car to the airport and fly back to San Francisco. You're running low on cash, so you should find a bank with a cash machine on the way to the airport. You can find an ATM Locator at `http://www.visa.com` that provides a map and a list of the three closest ATMs to any address. Figure T-13 shows an example in Portland.

This demonstration could go on for many more pages, but you can now begin to understand how much is out there on the World Wide Web. You will find many more interesting Web sites in the rest of this book.

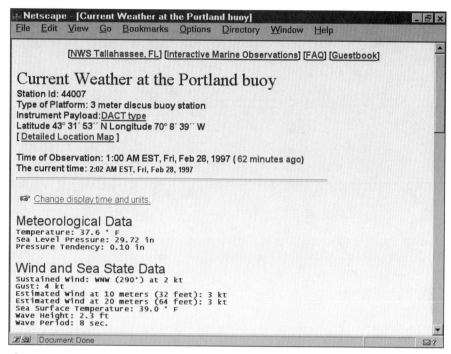

Figure T-12 Data from the Portland weather buoy.

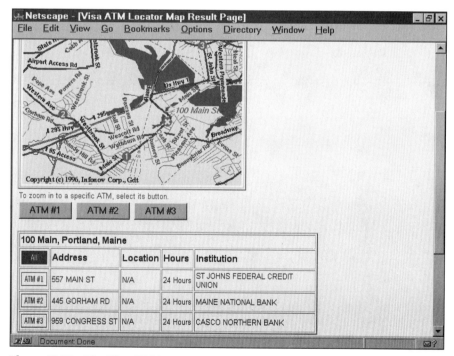

Figure T-13 The Visa ATM Locator.

INTRODUCTION TO THE WEB

THIS PART CONTAINS THE FOLLOWING CHAPTERS

Before you start any journey, you should understand where you are going and make sure that you have the proper equipment. This section tells you how the World Wide Web works and what you need to get there.

5/1/85: What a disaster. Karen finally agreed to go out with me tonight, but it may as well not have happened. Thought I'd impress her by making dinner (chicken with Bearnaise sauce) but couldn't find the recipe. Finally called mom for the recipe and an HOUR AND A HALF later (thanks, Mom!) left for the market. Found all the ingredients, except something called "tarragon." Decided it can't be that important if it only needs ¼ teaspoon. Forgot to buy the newspaper to check the movie times. Called the cinema, but it was busy for over an hour. 5:00 — the sauce tastes terrible. Probably needed that tarragon. Added some oregano to the sauce for flavor instead. 5:15 — Yuck! Dumped the sauce and decided we'd eat out instead. 6:00 — Karen arrived on time, but the restaurant had an hour wait and the movie started at 8:30. We grabbed a slice of pizza at the local pizzeria instead. Found out the tickets had sold out for 8:30 show, so we went to some sappy love story. Karen woke me when it was over. On the drive home, we ran out of gas. She was not happy. Doubt she'll ever go out with me again.

5/1/95: Crazy day. I was so nervous last night I couldn't sleep. I'd finished reading my book, so I logged on and downloaded excerpts of King's new one and settled in for the night. Great story, but I was out in 10 minutes. Asked Karen to marry me tonight, 10 years from that disastrous first date. I wanted it to be perfect, so I logged on to the Web when I got up, ordered flowers, downloaded her favorite chicken recipe, and placed an order at the Market's site for delivery this afternoon. Before logging off, I read some theater reviews, reserved tickets for the most talked-about play, and ordered that new King book. Enjoyed a leisurely lunch, then e-mailed my buddy to tell him the news. Got e-mail from Karen, reminding me to get gas, and one from mom wishing me luck. Wrote back and told mom I'd call her tonight. Spent the rest of the afternoon browsing for the best 'honeymoon' airfares to Greece. Dinner was superb and the show dynamite. Later, when Karen and I logged on to play the trivia game, I pointed the browser to a poetry site, recited a quote from her favorite poem, and popped the question. She said yes. Thank God for the Web.

HOW THE WORLD WIDE WEB WILL CHANGE YOUR LIFE

IN THIS CHAPTER YOU LEARN THESE KEY SKILLS

The Internet and the World Wide Web are either this year's answer to Citizen's Band radio and the Hula Hoop or a major advance in the way people communicate with one another. Or maybe both.

You can use the Internet to gather information from hundreds of thousands of sources, exchange messages with millions of people, and participate in *virtual communities,* whose members share your own interests — all without leaving your own home or office. With a few mouse clicks and keyboard commands, you can widen your horizons, meet new people, and keep up with the world. Like the telegraph, telephone, radio, and television before them, the Internet and the World Wide Web are communications media that you can use to obtain information and exchange ideas quickly and efficiently.

People who pay attention to such things believe that the growth and wide use of the Internet is having a huge impact on modern society. A hundred years ago, telephones (along with elevators and streetcars) made modern cities possible because people no longer had to live and work within walking distance of their suppliers and customers. Today, the Internet connects millions of computers and enables them to exchange information. As a result, you can use computers located almost anywhere in the world as easily as you can use the one on your desk.

The advantages of immediate computer communication are obvious for scientists and researchers who want to collaborate with colleagues in other cities (or other countries) and for businesses who want to share information among their branch offices. But these user groups are not the only ones who can take advantage of the Internet; grandparents can exchange electronic mail with their grandchildren, would-be travelers can find descriptions of routes and destinations, investors can obtain the very latest stock market reports, and hobbyists can share information about everything from needlework to genealogy to model trains. If you know where to look, there's practically no limit to the things you can find online.

But will the Internet change your life? Maybe not today, but give it time. If you're old enough to remember when your family got its first television set, you know that it took a while before you treated it as part of your regular routine rather than as a new and compelling novelty. But looking back, you can see that it has made a difference to the way you live. Now you probably use television every day to obtain news and entertainment.

The Internet will be very much like that: after using it a few weeks or months, you will begin to expect an answer to an e-mail message within just a few minutes of sending it, and you will treat your computer as an "information appliance" that provides all kinds of specialized information upon request. Reading newspapers in electronic form from half a dozen cities around the world and learning about current events through the Internet long before you hear about them on radio or television will become perfectly normal to you.

Using the Internet probably won't help you lose twenty pounds in a month or improve your golf stroke (though you might find someone online who wants to help you try). It may help expand your interests, however, keep you closer to friends and family, and put you in closer contact with the rest of the world.

Widen Your Horizons

Because everything on the Internet is connected, you can obtain information from Singapore or Sweden as easily as from next door. If you're interested in news, you can use the World Wide Web to download material that never appears in the local newspaper or the evening news on television.

Not all the information on the World Wide Web appears in English. Figure 1-1 shows the *Aftenposten Interactiv*, from the largest daily newspaper in Oslo, Norway.

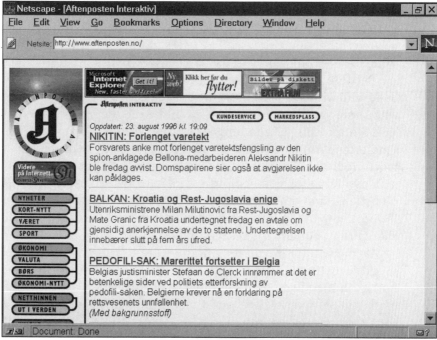

Figure 1-1 *Aftenposten Interactiv* provides the day's news from Norway — in Norwegian.

The World Wide Web can also offer you a way to find out about people, places, and things completely separate from your day-to-day life. You may not want to take the time to actually visit the North Alabama Railroad Museum or the Hockey Hall of Fame, but you can get them to come to you with a few keystrokes. You can also eavesdrop on discussions of hobbies, lifestyles, and politics that you might not find elsewhere and go to places you might be uncomfortable visiting in person. For example, the Web can be a great place to learn something about other religions or politics without becoming the target for hard-sell evangelists.

In general, if you can think of a topic, you can probably find something related to it on the World Wide Web. From recipes and stock quotations to descriptions of tourist attractions in Nepal and library catalogs from around the world, a huge amount of material is out there.

Meet New People

The Internet is much more than information archives. It's also an extremely effective channel for one-to-one and one-to-many communication among users. When you have an Internet connection, you can exchange electronic mail (e-mail) with millions of people around the world and participate in a huge variety of ongoing public and private discussions.

This communication takes several forms. Some modes require special software programs called *clients* to connect your computer to the conversation, whereas other discussions can be accessed through the World Wide Web with the same browser program you use to visit Web pages.

Because most newsgroups, chat sessions, and mailing lists are open to anybody who wants to join, these forums are easy ways to make contact with people who share your interests — you might be the only person in your town who collects Staffordshire China birds or restores antique gramophones, but when you send a question to a group devoted to those birds or gramophones, you may be reaching hundreds or thousands of other enthusiasts. Online support groups are also available for homebound mothers of two-year-olds, people with diseases, addictions, and other problems, and just about anything else you can think of. If you know how to find it, you can probably connect with other people who share just about any interest you have.

Before you try it, you may find it hard to believe that you can develop close friendships through your computer, but as you begin to recognize the same names in messages, you will quickly assign personalities to those names. And after you start answering questions from other people and contributing your own opinions to ongoing discussions, you will be on your way to developing a reputation as a *net.guru,* or online expert.

Newsgroups

Newsgroups are public spaces on the Internet (and similar spaces on some online services) where anybody can place a message. Other users post replies to the original message that may contain answers to questions or comments on the original message writer's opinions. A series of messages that includes an original message, replies to the original message, and replies to the replies is called a *thread.* Some threads may continue for months or even years, with thousands of separate messages.

More than 15,000 separate newsgroups are available on the Internet, each devoted to a specific topic. Some of these topics are of a very wide interest, such as jazz or cooking, whereas others have a more limited appeal, such as large-format photography or politics in Nebraska.

It's safe to say that nobody can keep up with every new message in every newsgroup, but following two or three groups can be a good way to get started. After *lurking* for a week or two, you may want to add your own thoughts to the conversation or ask a question of your own. With a few exceptions, you will find that most newsgroups are pretty friendly, and nobody will bite your head off unless you do something especially awful. In general, if you read other messages before you post your own, you should get a pretty good idea about the local customs and traditions followed by regular members of a group.

To read articles in newsgroups, you need a program called a *newsreader* or a subscription to an online service that includes Internet newsgroups along with its own proprietary content. For example, Figure 1-2 shows a newsreader called Free Agent. A list of newsgroups that you can join appears at the top of the screen; in the center, the screen displays a list of current messages in a specific newsgroup; and at the bottom, the text of an individual message appears. You can select a new newsgroup or a new message by double-clicking the description.

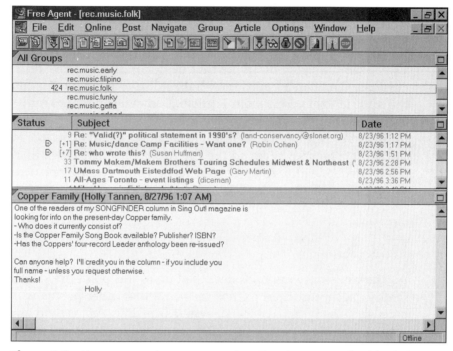

Figure 1-2   Use a newsreader program such as Free Agent to read articles in Internet - newsgroups.

Mailing Lists

Like newsgroups, *mailing lists* are ways of distributing messages about a specific topic of interest to a specific group of people through the Internet. Messages are distributed to members of a mailing list via electronic mail through a central computer called a *list server,* or *LISTSERV*. Some mailing lists work automatically — every message that anybody sends to the LISTSERV goes back out to the list — whereas others are moderated, which means that a human reviews every message to make sure that it fits the objectives of the list. Some mailing lists are open to anybody who wants to join, but others are limited to people who meet some qualification, such as membership in the sponsoring organization.

Mailing lists are available for people with all kinds of interests — radio drama producers, people who make their own apple cider, alumni of the same college, and even people who write books about the Internet.

To join a mailing list, you must send a request to the LISTSERV. But how do you find out that a list exists in the first place? You may find a description in a magazine or newsletter or hear about it from a friend. You can view a "directory of directories" of e-mail mailing lists at the Web site `http://www.curnet.com/ml.html` and a similar listing at `http://ifrit.web.aol.com/mld/production/index.html`.

Conferences

Conference is a catch-all name that describes several other forms of online discussions. Conferences are somewhat similar to newsgroups, but they don't use the same kind of access tools. Participation in a conference may be open to anybody who wants to join or limited to only subscribers. Some conferences operate through the World Wide Web, whereas others require you to connect directly to a distant computer by using the Internet tool called *Telnet* (remote login) or a direct telephone link. A few conferences offer more than one access method.

While you're connected to a Telnet host, it treats you as if you were typing directly into a local terminal.

Live Chat

All the conference methods described up to this point are *store-and-forward* systems — each participant sends messages that other people will see when they connect to the system. Live chat systems are different: as soon as you type a message, all the other people currently connected see a copy of the message on their screens. Live chat feels very different from other types of conferences because communication is immediate — it's more like a telephone conversation than an exchange of letters.

On the Internet, the most common use of live chat is a service called *Internet Relay Chat* (IRC) that connects users in many parts of the world. You might not find the conversations that take place on IRC all that exciting, although there are exceptions.

Another use of live chat is more promising. Online information services such as America Online and The Microsoft Network organize regular schedules of appearances by special guests who answer questions from other participants. These guests may be journalists, celebrities, or experts in specialized fields. Similar guest sessions occasionally take place on IRC, but they're not as common.

Join Virtual Communities

Just as the regulars at a neighborhood tavern get to know each other and eventually organize softball teams, picnics, and parties, the people who frequent Internet newsgroups and conferences also develop online friendships that may extend beyond their keyboards. Although the members of a *virtual community* may never meet face to face (or f2f, as the abbreviation-happy world of online typists calls it), they can be as close as any other kind of social group.

Dozens of stories exist about romances that have bloomed by e-mail, authors who collaborate on a book or magazine article, and communities who provide encouragement and moral support to online friends who need help. In at least one case, the users of a conference service spontaneously raised enough in small donations to pay for a young member's school tuition when the family fell on hard times. When another member of the same community died, her online friends rapidly mobilized to find a new home for her dog.

You won't become part of one of these communities by just subscribing to a mailing list or reading a newsgroup; you have to become an active participant in the group. If you're a "lurker" who never adds anything to the conversation, nobody will pay much attention to you. But once you start contributing, you'll probably be made welcome.

Keep Up with the World

In most parts of the United States and Canada, you have just a few places to find the day's news: one or two local newspapers, a handful of radio and TV stations (which probably get most of their news from the same wire services), and the national media, such as CNN, the *New York Times*, *USA Today*, and *The Wall Street Journal* (and in Canada, *The Globe and Mail*). If you're looking for the results of an out-of-town election or scores for a minor league team (or worse, a foreign sport such as Italian football), you're probably out of luck.

The Internet, however, can bring news from all parts of the world to your desktop within seconds. Dozens of radio and television stations and hundreds of daily and weekly newspapers, magazines, and industry newsletters make their content available through the World Wide Web. To follow the results of an Irish election, you can listen to newscasts from Radio Telefis Eireann in Dublin or read the latest from the *Irish Times* or the *Galway Advertiser*. Or if you're interested in the Midlands Open Squash tournament in Lusaka, Zambia, you can find a daily update on the *Zambia Post* Web site.

When you hear a two-sentence news report on the radio, finding more details through the World Wide Web is a simple matter. Many of the world's major news wire services, including the Associated Press, Reuters, Canadian Press, ITAR-TASS, and the British Press Association, provide news summaries that are revised every few minutes. Several other news services also maintain their own Web sites with frequent updates, including CNN, MSNBC, and Time magazine.

Trade magazines and newsletters are another great source of timely information. The editors of *Hotel-Motel Management*, *Pacific Fisheries*, *Credit Card News*, or any of a thousand other publications spend all their time reporting the latest developments in their own specialized areas. Not uncommonly, a story that was previously reported in the trade press makes huge headlines in the *New York Times* six months later. If you're interested in developments in a particular industry or if you're an investor looking for early warning of new opportunities, you can use the World Wide Web to keep up with trade publications in many fields.

(More or Less) Instant Communication

Exchanging messages with someone located thousands of miles away is no more difficult or costly than communicating with people in your own town. Electronic mail combines the speed of telephone calls with the economy of written mail. Unlike postal mail, which forces you to wait a few of days (or more) between sending a message and receiving a reply, e-mail is almost immediate. If the recipient of your message is online when you send it, you might get an answer within five minutes or less, even if your messages are traveling thousands of miles.

Internet services can be fascinating, useful, and entertaining. But will they change your life? They might, but you probably won't notice until after it happens. In the meantime, a tremendous amount of material is available at the other end of that wire. Whether you treat it as an information appliance or an entertainment system, the Web can provide you with immediate access to the rest of the world. In another five or ten years, that access will be as commonplace as radio and television are today.

BONUS

A Tour of the Web

The Web has more than 50 million separate pages, so you won't be able to visit all of them. But to introduce you to the wonders of the Web, we take a look at a handful of more or less representative sites here. You will learn more about the mysterious `http://www.something.xyz` codes that identify individual sites on the Web in later chapters.

The sites in this tour are not the most popular spots on the Web, nor are they necessarily the ones that you will want to visit first — look for those sites in Part Three. But they will give you an idea of the huge variety of stuff you can find online. Some of the Web sites described here are obscure, odd, or just plain strange: the site for the last feudal fiefdom in Europe, and another site with a recording of people laughing in 1922, for example. But you can bring them all to your own computer with a few mouseclicks.

Ready to start exploring? Let's go . . .

Finding Greenwich Mean Time

To begin, we can check the exact time from the "home of the world's time," the Greenwich Royal Observatory in England. Figure 1-3 shows the Observatory's Web site (`http://greenwich2000.com/time.htm`).

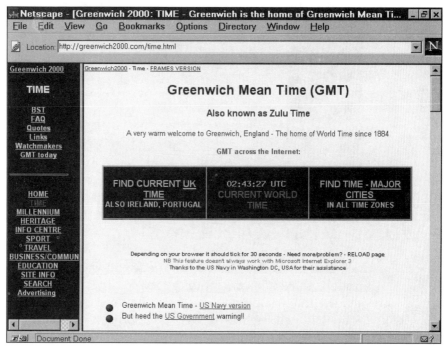

Figure 1-3   What time is it? The Greenwich Royal Observatory's Web page.

Pick a Flag, Any Flag

Next stop, a database of the world's flags. This site is maintained by The Multimedia Corporation at `http://flags.mmcorp.com/`. Select the name of the country, territory, or international organization whose flag you want to see and click the link. For example, Figure 1-4 shows the flag of Sark, one of the Channel Islands off the coast of France.

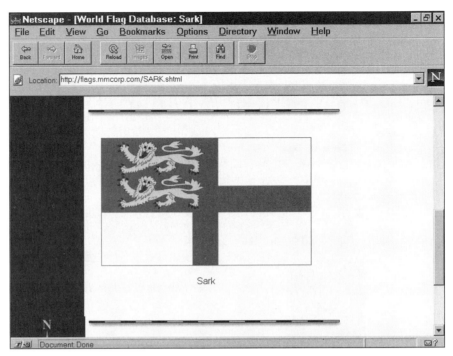

Figure 1-4   The Flag of Sark, from the World Flag Database Web site.

A Quick Visit to Sark

Sark is a pretty obscure place. What else can we find out about it? A search through the Net for *sark* produces several links to pages about the famous ship, the Cutty Sark, and one from the tourist bureau in Guernsey — the next island over, which has a Web page with a couple of pictures of Sark (`http://www.guernsey.net/~tourism/sark.html`) and the fascinating information that Sark is the last feudal state in Europe. The Lord of Sark is the only person on the island allowed to keep doves.

Other pages related to Sark include descriptions of half a dozen hotels on the island and a business that forms offshore corporations and trusts that take advantage of Sark's unique tax status.

Finding the Perfect Rubber Chicken

Now that you're leaving Sark, how about some shopping? Everybody needs at least one rubber chicken, and Archie McPhee's rubber chickens are the best you can get. Archie's Web site (`http://www.halcyon.com/mcphee/products/RubberChicken.html`), has all the details.

Finding Your Way

E very tourist needs a map. The U.S. Geological Survey's Geographic Names Information System is a database that includes the names of every airport, island, arroyo, atoll, basin, bay, beach, bridge, canal, and millions of other natural and man-made landmarks in the United States.

To find a map that shows the location of a particular site, follow these steps:

1. Jump to the Geological Survey National Mapping Information home page (`http://www-nmd.usgs.gov`), shown in Figure 1-5.

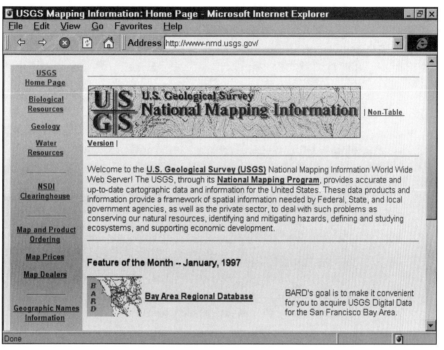

Figure 1-5 The U.S. Geological Survey home page.

2. Follow the links to Geographic Names Information and then to the GNIS Online Data Base. You will see a query form like the one in Figure 1-6.

3. Type as much information as you can about the feature you want to find — in this case, a stream called College Creek in Annapolis, Maryland. You can just as easily search for Hat Island in Washington state or the Oregon Trail as it passed through Nebraska, Wyoming, and Idaho.

4. Click the Send Query button to send your request to the database server. After approximately a minute, you will see a description of the place you requested, similar to the one in Figure 1-7.

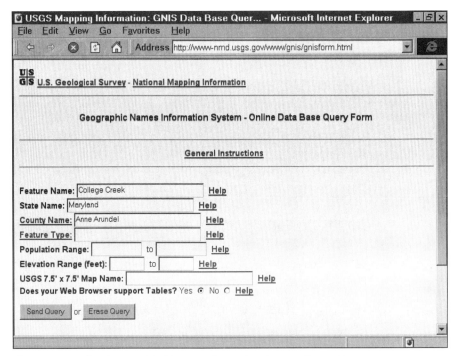

Figure 1-6 The Geographic Names Information System Query Form.

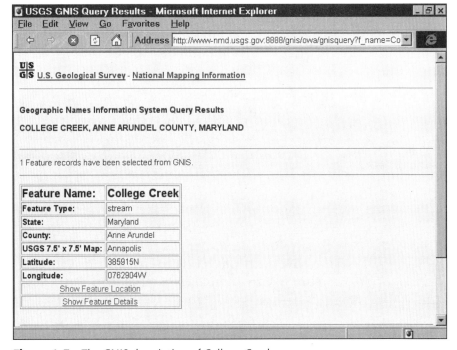

Figure 1-7 The GNIS description of College Creek.

5. Click Show Feature Location to see a map of the region surrounding College Creek like the one in Figure 1-8. For more detail, click Zoom In.

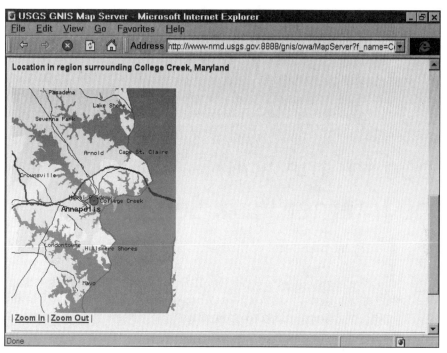

Figure 1-8 The GNIS map showing the location of College Creek.

Laughing All the Way

To fully appreciate this site, you need a sound card in your computer. In addition to all those words and pictures, the Web has all kinds of sounds, including radio broadcasts, sound effects, and music. For example, here's a link to the Wolverine Antique Music Society's Web site (`http://www.teleport.com/~rfrederi/rafiles`), shown in Figure 1-9. Along with recordings by Bix Beiderbecke and Stuff Smith, you can use a system called RealAudio to listen to the original Okeh Laughing Record, recorded in 1922. What *were* those people laughing at?

Figure 1-9 The Wolverine Antique Music Society logo.

Food for the Soul — The Internet Pizza Server

Finally, here's one of the silliest sites on the Web: the Internet Pizza Server, at `http://www.ecst.csuchico.edu/~pizza`. You can use this service to choose the toppings you want: traditional things like sausage and olives, or weird stuff like kittens, hammers and basketballs. Then wait just a few seconds for a piping hot digital pizza to appear on your screen. You're responsible for cleaning the cheese off your own disk drive.

With any luck, this quick description of some of the more obscure sites on the World Wide Web has whet your appetite for more (no, not for pizza). As you read the rest of this book, you will find the detailed instructions you need to explore other parts of the Web and a batch of pointers to more serious and useful Web pages and services that you can visit.

Summary

The Internet in general, and the World Wide Web in particular, make information and services in all parts of the world accessible through your computer's keyboard and screen. You can use them to reach hundreds of newspapers, broadcasters, and other sources of news; visit museums; obtain the very latest stock quotations from just about every exchange in the world; look up telephone numbers; and consult library catalogs. You can also exchange messages with millions of other users and participate in thousands of discussion groups dedicated to just about every imaginable topic.

In the chapters that follow, you learn a little about how the Internet works, with special emphasis on the World Wide Web. You also find information about setting up a personal computer to connect to the Web, and where and how to obtain the special (and usually free) *Web browser* software you need to display the wonders of the Web on that computer.

WHAT THE WEB IS AND HOW IT WORKS

2

IN THIS CHAPTER YOU LEARN THESE KEY SKILLS

A t this stage in its development, the Internet is more complicated to use than it ought to be. It's almost like you had to tell the people who run Grand Coulee Dam to let some extra water through the dynamo before you could use an electrical appliance. If the telephone system worked the way the Internet does today, you'd have to understand everything that goes on inside the telephone companies' central offices and switching centers to place a long distance call.

This is likely to change within a few years (or possibly sooner), but for the moment, knowing something about the structure of the Internet can be very useful. In this chapter, you learn a little about the way the Internet is organized and how data moves through it.

What the Heck Is the Internet?

T o use the Internet and the World Wide Web, you should understand two very basic concepts: (1) everything is connected together, and (2) every computer or other device connected to the Internet has a unique address. These two facts make it possible for you to use your computer to exchange data with any other computer on the Internet. Everything that happens on the Internet is some form of data transfer from one computer to another.

Most network diagrams show the Internet as a big cloud, with data going into the cloud in one place and coming back out in another place. It may be convenient to think about the Internet as one big network, with each individual computer connected directly to the network as shown in Figure 2-1, but that's not completely accurate. In fact, as Figure 2-2 shows, the Internet is made up of hundreds of thousands of separate networks, each connected in some way to a *backbone* that moves data from one network to another. There are about a dozen major backbones in the United States and more backbones in other countries.

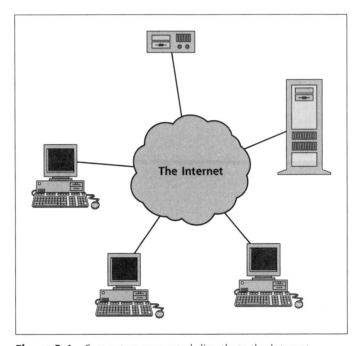

Figure 2-1 Computers connected directly to the Internet.

Every backbone has at least one place where it exchanges data with another backbone. Everyone in the system has agreed to pass messages along to other backbones, even if they don't involve their own customers or users. Therefore, when a local network connects to any backbone, the people using that network have access to the entire system. Thus, you can send a message from a computer on any network that has a backbone connection to any other computer on a connected network.

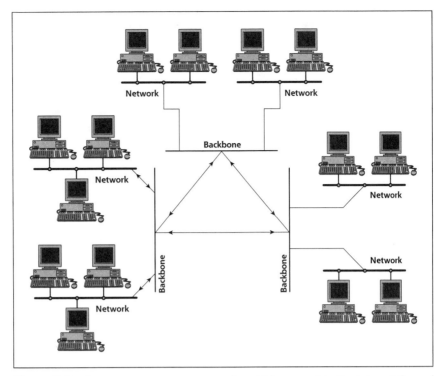

Figure 2-2 Computers connect to networks, which connect to the Internet through backbones.

This worldwide system of **inter**connected **net**works makes up the Internet. That's why the Internet is sometimes described as a "network of networks." Most of the time, you won't have to worry about backbone connections and all the internal switching and routing needed to move a message across the Internet, as long as you know the address of the distant computer with which you want to communicate. Your Internet access provider should take care of the internal details.

Working With Internet Addresses

very computer connected to the Internet has a unique name. That's the www.*something*.com you see on television and in newspapers. This address format is called the *Domain Name System* (DNS).

A DNS address has at least two parts separated by a period (called a *dot*). On the right side of the dot is either a three-letter major domain name identifying the type of organization that owns the address or one or more two-letter geographic codes.

The most common major domains are as follows:

Domain Name	What It Represents
.com	Commercial businesses
.edu	Educational institutions
.net	Network support centers
.gov	Government agencies
.mil	Military activities
.org	Miscellaneous organizations

As the Internet continues to expand, you will probably see other major domains added.

Outside the United States, many Internet addresses use geographic domain names, such as .fr for France or .hk for Hong Kong. In some countries, the two address schemes are combined, so you may find an address such as www.computer.com.uk for a business in England (uk indicates the United Kingdom) or www.travel.com.sg for one in Singapore.

The portion of a DNS address that appears to the left of the dot is a name that identifies the business, agency, or other organization using the address. For example, the DNS address for Washington State University is wsu.edu, America Online's address is aol.com, and IDG Books Worldwide's address is idgbooks.com.

Some companies and organizations divide their addresses into smaller *subdomains*. Thus, a university might have separate subdomains for different departments, such as physics.huxley.edu and history.huxley.edu. A business may create subdomains for branch offices, such as newyork.bigcorp.com and denver.bigcorp.com.

The other common use of subdomains is for indentifying multiple servers on the same system. The next section of this chapter explains servers in more detail.

Domains and subdomains identify computers, but each computer may have many users. Therefore, e-mail addresses have one more element: the user's name with an "at" symbol (@). Every e-mail address on the Internet is in the form *user@computer.xxx*, which you would read as "user at computer dot xxx."

You will also see another address format that identifies each address on the Internet with a four-part number called an *Internet Protocol (IP)* address. An IP address looks like this: 23.206.14.3. Each of the four parts of an IP address may be any number from 0 to 255.

The internal switching equipment that moves messages and data around the Internet could operate quite well with nothing but numeric addresses, but most users prefer using addresses made up of words rather than numbers. When you request a connection to a DNS address, the local Internet access service uses a database called the *Domain Name Server* to convert the DNS address to the numeric IP address that the Internet uses to route the message to its intended destination.

Who or What Are Servers and Clients?

In general, the Internet is run by cooperative agreements among the people who use it — there is no central authority that dictates how things will be done. This may not be the most efficient possible way to organize things, but it works. When somebody wants to create a new type of Internet service, he or she invites other people to comment on the proposal, and eventually all the interested parties agree to adopt a new standard.

Commonly accepted methods exist for many different kinds of data exchange through the Internet, including electronic mail, news, file transfer, remote access to distant computers, the World Wide Web, and several others. Each service has its own set of rules, but these and all other online services have a similar structure: a program on one computer called a *client* requests some kind of action from a program on a second computer called a *server*.

NOTE Because all clients and servers are supposed to follow the rules for their type of service, you can mix and match programs from different software developers. For example, any file transfer client program should work with almost any service provider's file servers. Just because the server is from IBM doesn't mean that you need to use an IBM client. It should work just as well with a server made by Apple or Data General, or, for that matter, on a server made by the Chinese People's Long March Water Pump Collective and Computer Works.

Why is this important? Most of the things you will do on the Internet are not much more than sending an instruction from a client on your own computer to a server that actually performs the work. That instruction might be "send me a copy of the file called XXXX," or "please perform this command," or "here's some data; please do something with it," or possibly even "send me the output of some existing process." Because there are millions of computers connected to the Internet, made by many different manufacturers, it's essential that all those systems speak a common language.

A client program can communicate with any server offering the same type of service, but it can't talk directly to another client. You can send messages from your mail client program to your daughter's mail client program through a mail server located on a third system, but you can't connect directly to her computer unless she's running a server program.

About a half dozen types of services account for almost all the activity on the Internet:

* **Remote access to a distant computer.** When you send commands to a Telnet client, the client treats them as if they were typed into a local terminal. The client may echo your commands to your Telnet client program or it may return the results of a command.

* **Electronic mail.** When you use a mail client program to send a message to a mail server, the server passes along the message to a second server that contains a mailbox for the recipient, who uses a mail client program to read the message.

* **File transfer.** You can instruct a *file transfer protocol* (ftp) server to send you a copy of a file stored on the server or to accept and store a copy of a file that you send to the server.

* **News.** When you send an article to a news server, the server relays it to every other server that supports the newsgroup to which you posted the message. Your news client program first obtains a list of newsgroups from the server, then a list of articles within a newsgroup, and finally the individual articles that you want to read.

* **Continuous data.** A server that supplies continuous data — such as the audio from a radio station, the output of a video camera, or information from a stock ticker — receives the data from an outside source and relays the data to all client programs currently connected to it. The client program converts the incoming data back to its original form and reproduces it. Each type of continuous data uses a different kind of client and server, but the basic process is similar for all of them.

* **Live chat.** When you send text to an *Internet Relay Chat* (IRC) server, the server passes that text to every other client currently connected to the server, and to other IRC servers. IRC is a specialized form of continuous data.

* **The World Wide Web.** A World Wide Web server uses a set of rules called *HyperText Transfer Protocol* (HTTP) to move text files encoded with a page description language called HyperText Markup Language (HTML) to a client that adds pictures and other graphic elements located in other files to the text in the original file. Web pages can also include links to other files that allow a user to jump directly to them from the original page. Many Web browsers also recognize other file types and automatically open application programs that can display them. (The next section of this chapter describes the World Wide Web in more detail.)

To connect incoming access requests to different servers at the same site, many system administrators use a subdomain address for each server. Even if all the server programs are running on the same computer, the address provides the information needed to connect an incoming message or command to the correct server program. So, the Web server at server.net might be www.server.net, and the ftp server at the same site would be ftp.server.net.

Even if more than one server program is running on the same physical computer, it's convenient to think about each server as a separate device. Like your own computer, a server may contain files that are organized into directories and subdirectories (Windows 95 calls them *folders*, but they work the same way). Unless your client program does it automatically, you must specify a directory and filename when you request a file from a server. For example, if you want to obtain a copy of a file with the name program.exe, located in the "software" directory of a server called ftp.software.com, you would tell your ftp client or Web browser to get ftp.software.com/software/program.exe.

Notice that this address uses forward slashes (/) instead of the backslashes (\) used in a DOS or Windows address. Computers connected to the Internet use many different operating systems, and they don't all use the same file structures. Unfortunately, that means that some addresses contain forward slashes and others use backslashes (and others are probably out there someplace on the Internet that use other, even more obscure symbols). When you specify a file address, you must make sure that you're using the right kind of slash, or the server won't recognize the file path.

And Why "The World Wide Web"?

If you know exactly what kind of server contains the information you want, using the specific, single-purpose client program that works with that client is simple enough. But in most cases, you're more interested in content than in form. What you really want is an all-purpose client that accepts data from many different server types. That's where the World Wide Web comes in.

The World Wide Web (WWW) started out as a tool that placed links to other files into text. It was used in scholarly papers to allow a reader to jump directly to another document, illustration, or other resource. For example, if a document contained a footnote or a reference to some other document, or possibly a graph or illustration, you could retrieve a copy of the second document by selecting the link in the first one. The link's destination could be anywhere on the Internet.

As long as Web pages were limited to text, the Web was an interesting tool, but it wasn't very widely used. But in 1993, software developers at the University of Illinois-Champaign/Urbana created a graphic Web browser program called Mosaic that added graphics to Web pages. More recent programs, such as Netscape Navigator and Microsoft Internet Explorer, have their roots in that original Mosaic program.

Using a graphical Web browser, you can view text, pictures, background images, and other elements on a single Web page, such as the one shown in Figure 2-3. Because a link in a Web page can be any kind of file located on any server anywhere on the Internet, your Web browser doubles as a client that will work with many types of servers. If the browser does not support a particular file type, it can open some other client program that will recognize that file. For example, if you select a link from a Web page to a Telnet server, your Web browser will automatically open your Telnet program and connect it to the specified server.

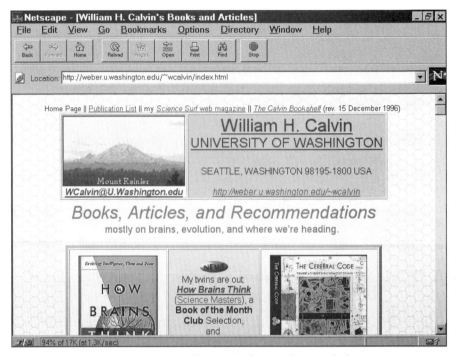

Figure 2-3   A typical Web page with text, background art, and pictures.

The World Wide Web is a huge step toward making the Internet easy to use. It enables a user to jump from one file to another, regardless of the type or actual location, simply by clicking a link. As more and more content providers have created pages that take advantage of HTTP, related page description languages, and *plug-in* programs, a tremendous number of Web sites now offer pictures, animated cartoons, sounds, and interactive services along with text.

Hundreds of thousands of information providers are using the World Wide Web to distribute information on the Internet. If you know where to look (and if you don't, you can find pointers later in this book), you can find hundreds of daily, weekly, and monthly newspapers, magazines, and newsletters, illustrated tours of museums, thousands of free or inexpensive software programs, recipes for everything from oatmeal cookies to gumbo, and even a collection of scorecards from golf courses around the world. If you can think of a topic, you can probably find Web pages or other files devoted to it.

So, how does the Web work? Figure 2-4 shows part of the Web page in Figure 2-3, encoded in HyperText Markup Language (HTML). In addition to the text of the document, the page also includes codes enclosed in angle brackets (< and >).

These codes are instructions to your browser to import and display other files along with the page, and to display parts of the text as links to other Web sites and files.

```
<html><a name="top"></a>
<head>
<title>William H. Calvin's Books and Articles</title>
</head><body background="./img/hexagon.gif" link=blue alink=red vlink=brown>

<center><FONT face="Technical" SIZE=-1>Home Page || <a
href="quicklist.htm">Publication List</a> || my <a
href="scisurf.html"><i>Science Surf</i> web magazine</a> || <a href="http://www.well.com/~wca

<TABLE WIDTH=600 BORDER=1>


<TR><TD bgcolor=#f0f0f0 VALIGN=top align=center><A HREF="http://www.washington.edu/cambots/
src="./img/mtr-label.jpg"></A><br clear><a
href="mailto:WCalvin@U.washington.edu">
<b><i>WCalvin@U.washington.edu</i></b></a></i></TD>
<TD  bgcolor=#C0D9D9 ALIGN=center VALIGN=center>
<FONT SIZE=6 color=blue><a href="http://weber.u.washington.edu/~wcalvin">William H.
Calvin</a></font><br>
<a href="http://www.washington.edu"><FONT SIZE=5 color=blue>UNIVERSITY OF WASHINGTON
</FONT></a><br>
SEATTLE, WASHINGTON 98195-1800 USA<P>

<a href="http://weber.u.washington.edu/~wcalvin"><i><font face="Technical">
http://weber.u.washington.edu/~wcalvin</i></a></font></TD></TR>
</TABLE>
<TABLE WIDTH=600><TR><TD bgcolor=F0F0F0 VALIGN=top align=center>

<CENTER>
<FONT SIZE=6 COLOR=fuchsia><i>Books, Articles, and Recommendations</i></font><br>

<font size=4 face="Technical" color=fuchsia>mostly on brains, evolution, and where we&#0146;r
<p>

<TABLE BORDER=5 width=580 cellpadding=10>
<TR><td bgcolor=white>
<A HREF="bk8.html"><img border=1 width=145 height=222 hspace=6 src="./img/xbk8.jpg"></A><
```

Figure 2-4 Source code for a Web page.

Web browsers can display files from many types of servers and they can use *file associations* to open others. So, for example, if you transfer a spreadsheet file from a distant server to your own computer, your browser can automatically open Microsoft Excel and load the imported file. If you're using Windows, some browsers use the same file associations that you use with files located on your hard drive.

In the end, you don't really want to think about all this stuff. You want to find the score of an out-of-town football game, a recipe for oyster stew, or a description of a new computer accessory. Why should it be more difficult to use the World Wide Web than to change the channels on a television set? It shouldn't, but to be brutally honest, it's not quite there yet.

Five years from now, using the Web will almost certainly be a great deal easier than it is today. But for the moment, you still need a trained native guide to help you cut through the underbrush. In the rest of this book, we step through the procedures you need to connect to the Internet, find and install a Web browser, and start finding things online.

BONUS

Special-Purpose Internet Clients

A Web browser is the closest thing you will find to an all-purpose Internet client program. But you may also want to install one or more specialized clients to obtain specific kinds of information, such as weather forecasts, news headlines, and stock quotations. This bonus section contains descriptions of some of these special-purpose programs.

Many of these programs are shareware. In other words, their developers make them available for anybody to download and try, but they expect people who use them beyond an initial trial period to register with the developer and send a (usually small) one-time payment to support the product.

All of the programs described here are for Windows 95. However, many similar programs exist for the Windows 3.1 and Macintosh platforms. For pointers to these programs, look at the TUCOWS (The Ultimate Collection of Winsock Software) Web site at http://www.tucows.com.

Checking the Weather Online

W etsock is a client program that obtains current weather forecasts through the Internet and displays them on your computer. It places an icon in the Windows system tray that shows the current local weather (for example, Figure 2-5 shows the cloud icon for overcast skies next to the current time). When you click the icon, it displays more detail about the current conditions in a box like the one in Figure 2-6. For full text of the local forecast, click the Forecast button.

Cloud icon for
overcast skies —• 6:13 PM

Figure 2-5 The icon in the system tray shows the current weather.

Figure 2-6 The WetSock information window.

Wetsock is available for free download from `http://www.locutuscodeware.com`. Registration costs $12 for individuals and $25 for businesses.

Their Time Is Your Time

World War II commando movies always have a scene where the leader tells everyone else to synchronize their watches to ensure that their grand plan to blow up the crucial bridge and capture the enemy general goes according to schedule. You may not be planning to blow up a bridge, but many Internet servers support a time-synchronizing protocol that enables client programs to connect and download the exact time. This service is especially important for computers configured to perform specific network tasks at specific times, but it also provides a convenient way to ensure that your computer's internal clock hasn't gained or lost time.

SocketWatch, from the same developers as the Wetsock weather client (`http://www.locutuscodeware.com`), is a simple program that automatically finds and connects to a time server, obtains the precise time, and sets your clock.

NOTE The same folks from SocketWatch also have a slick little program that tracks the phase of the moon, but it doesn't use the Internet yet...

This simple program calculates the transmission delay between the server and your own system, so your computer should report the exact time within a few hundredths of a second of the U.S. Bureau of Standards' atomic clock. It checks for an Internet connection every ten seconds and runs a new time synchronization once an hour.

All of this takes place in background whenever you connect to the Internet. If you don't connect for 24 hours, the program automatically sets up a new connection on its own. Figure 2-7 shows a SocketWatch status report.

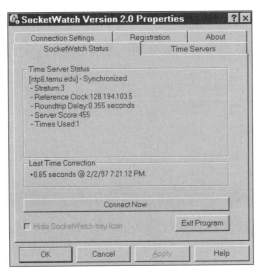

Figure 2-7 The SocketWatch status report window.

News While It Is Hot

As you will learn in Chapter 7, hundreds of newspapers, wire services, and other sources of news are available on the World Wide Web. Each organization has a Web site where you can find many of the same news stories that will later appear in print or on the air. HeadLiner is a free news client program that extracts current headlines from one or more of these sites and displays them on your computer, in either a separate, "news ticker" window, a screen saver, or in the Windows title bar of the currently active program. You can obtain HeadLiner from `http://www.lanacom.com`.

When you install HeadLiner, the program asks you which specific topics and geographic regions you want it to track. The choices range from Arizona Central Golf News and Classical Music Online to *USA Today* and the *Straits Times* from Singapore. You can also add or remove sources after installation is complete.

Figure 2-8 shows the HeadLiner ticker that runs in its own window. To see a complete story, double-click the headline.

Figure 2-8 The HeadLiner ticker window.

If you prefer, you can put the HeadLiner ticker in the title bar of any active Windows application, as shown in Figure 2-9. The HeadLiner controls also appear in the title bar, to the right of the buttons that control the window size.

Figure 2-9 HeadLiner in a Windows title bar.

HeadLiner is a neat way to get a continuing stream of news, but the crawling text can be awfully distracting. You can, however, use HeadLiner as a screen saver that only appears when no other activity has taken place for a while. As Figure 2-10 shows, the screen displays the lead paragraphs of individual stories, along with the headline ticker across the bottom.

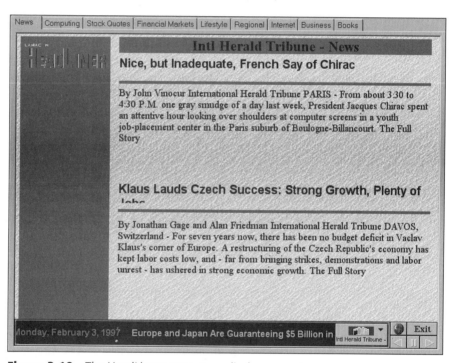

Figure 2-10 The HeadLiner screen saver display.

HeadLiner can automatically check the news sites you requested whenever your computer is connected to the Internet, or set up a new connection on a regular schedule. It holds each story in the computer's memory after you disconnect, so you will continue to see the headlines until you shut down the ticker.

Net Gains and Losses: Tracking Your Investments

If you've ever visited a stock broker's office or watched one of the cable TV finance channels, you've seen the stock ticker that shows the current prices of individual stocks and other securities as transactions take place. WinStock is an Internet client program that obtains stock quotations through the Internet and displays them on your computer screen. You can obtain the latest version of WinStock from `http:www.teleport.com/~magoldsm/winstock/index.html`.

Unlike the tickers that stockbrokers use, which show every trade on every exchange, WinStock updates itself every few minutes and displays the current prices at the time of the most recent updates. Most *quote servers* operate on a 15-minute delay. Figure 2-11 shows the WinStock ticker window.

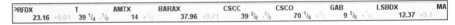

Figure 2-11   The WinStock ticker window.

WinStock also displays the most recent updates for all the stocks that you have requested in more detail, in a separate window. You can enter the details of your portfolio and let the program calculate the current value of your investments, as shown in Figure 2-12.

Ticker	Shares	Avg Price	Total Cost	Curr Price	Curr Value	Profit/Loss
AMTX	200.000	18.500	3,700.00	13.875	2,775.00	-925.00
BARAX	531.380	33.910	18,019.10	37.960	20,171.18	2,152.09
CSCC	100.000	70.000	7,000.00	39.250	3,925.00	-3,075.00
CSCO	100.000	57.438	5,743.75	70.375	7,037.50	1,293.75
GAB	1,000.000	9.250	9,250.00	9.250	9,250.00	0.00
LSBDX	1,303.740	12.190	15,892.59	12.370	16,127.26	234.67
MACR	200.000	15.250	3,050.00	11.250	2,250.00	-800.00
MKIE	1,000.000	6.625	6,625.00	7.375	7,375.00	750.00
NYN	200.000	46.000	9,200.00	50.625	10,125.00	925.00
PRFDX	904.510	22.195	20,075.70	23.160	20,948.45	872.75
T	500.000	38.625	19,312.50	39.250	19,625.00	312.50
Total			117,868.64		119,609.40	1,740.76

Figure 2-12   The WinStock Portfolio window.

None of these programs is a replacement for a general-purpose Web browser, but each offers specialized information in a more convenient format than you might find on a Web page. They can also do their work in background while you're concentrating on other, more productive or interesting activities.

Summary

Millions of computers around the world are connected to local networks, which are themselves connected together through backbone services. We know the sum of these interconnected networks as the Internet. Any computer connected to the Internet can exchange files and data with any other connected computer. Each computer with an Internet connection has a unique identity, called an address, that can appear as a name (such as idgbooks.com) or as a four-part number.

The Internet offers many different kinds of information transfer, but all of them are based on a *client/server model*, where a client program on one computer sends an instruction to a server program on another computer, which returns the product of that request to the client. The World Wide Web is specialized for client/server transactions. A client, called a *Web browser*, uses a set of rules called HyperText Transfer Protocol (HTTP) to request a file from a Web server. The server returns the requested file, encoded in HyperText Markup Language (HTML), which the browser (the client) decodes and displays on the user's computer. All this occurs more or less automatically after you type the address of a server into the client program.

CHAPTER THREE

WHAT YOU NEED TO CONNECT

IN THIS CHAPTER YOU LEARN THESE KEY SKILLS

Y ou don't need the latest and greatest computer to use the Internet, regardless of what the average computer magazine or salesman at your local computer store tells you. If you've inherited a hand-me-down (or hand-me-up) computer because a friend or relative has replaced theirs with something newer, you can probably make a few relatively inexpensive improvements that will get you online in fine form. If you're buying a new computer of your own, you can save several hundred dollars (or more) if you stay away from the top-of-the-line options.

In this chapter, you find descriptions of the basic equipment and services necessary to obtain an Internet connection. If you already have a computer, you may want to skim this chapter anyway; you will probably find some useful suggestions for inexpensive upgrades and improvements.

The Basic Requirements

T o use the Internet, you need a computer and a way to connect that computer to an existing network (you also need an account with an Internet access provider, but you'll have to wait until the next chapter to worry about that). Figure 3-1 shows a very basic connection.

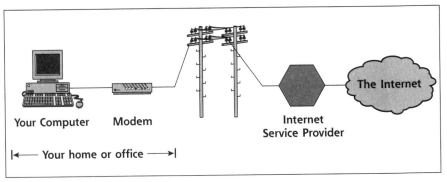

Figure 3-1   You will probably connect your computer to the Internet via a modem.

Buying a new computer is complicated, because it involves a lot of confusing details that all seem to use some kind of strange code: letting your eyes glaze over when the salesman starts talking about RAM, megabytes, CPUs, and all that other technobabble is altogether too easy. The next few sections should help you cut through the jargon.

Macintosh or Windows?

The first thing to choose is the type of computer you want to use. For most new users, there are really only two practical choices — an Apple Macintosh or a computer that uses Microsoft Windows. Because most Windows systems use a central processor made by Intel, they are sometimes called *Wintel* systems, even though they may include a processor from another company. If your computer uses the MS-DOS or PC-DOS operating system, you may be able to upgrade it to Windows.

If you have inherited some other kind of computer, such as an Amiga, an Apple II, or something more obscure like an old Osborne or Commodore, you may want to seriously consider cutting off the top, filling it with potting soil, and planting a nice fern inside. It's possible to set up a simple Internet connection through one of these antiques, but browsing the World Wide Web will be just about impossible without a great deal more expert knowledge than you really want.

You should choose either Windows or a Macintosh; if you already have one or the other, use that one. But if you're buying a new system, here are the advantages of each type, as the following chart shows:

NOTE   The great secret about the Mac versus Windows holy war is that both sides are right: it really doesn't matter which type of computer you choose. Once you learn a little about the way your own system organizes things, you can get along quite happily with either one.

Macintosh	Windows
Easier to Learn	Less Expensive
	More programs available
	More accessories and add-in devices
	Easier to upgrade

This section describes the equipment you need to use the Internet and World Wide Web on a Windows system, because that type is more common. If you have a Macintosh, the specific information won't apply to you, but you will want to consider similar elements for your own computer.

Buying a New Computer

Trying to get the newest and best possible personal computer is a losing battle. New and improved models are constantly appearing, so whatever you buy will be out-of-date by the time you get it home. Although you almost certainly don't need most of the features in these super, jet-hot wonders, you can probably take advantage of the way the market operates: every time a new model comes out, the prices drop on older versions. You should be able to find an entirely acceptable computer for much less than the price of the latest and greatest model.

TIP **In other words, the price of a top-of-the-line computer has remained more or less constant, but performance has improved. If you don't need top-of-the-line performance, you can save money by buying last year's technology. Or the year before that.**

The following sections examine a practical minimum configuration for browsing the World Wide Web on a Windows computer.

486 OR PENTIUM PROCESSOR

The central processor is the internal "brain" that controls your computer. The *486* indicates that the computer contains an Intel type 80486 processor or a similar processor made by some other company. If you can find a 486 with a speed of at least 75 MHz, it will do an adequate job as a Web-browsing machine. However, 486 processors have reached the end of their commercial life; most of the low-end systems you'll see in stores will be Pentiums.

Pentium processors are available with operating speeds ranging from 75 MHz to 200 MHz or more. For Web browsing and most other things you want to do, a 75 MHz or 100 MHz processor can generally do the job; faster CPUs work better for graphics-intensive work. The difference in price between the slower processors and the fastest models available can be as much as $700 or more.

SIXTEEN MEGABYTES OF RAM

Random access memory (RAM) is the memory that your computer uses to hold programs and data while it's working with them. If you don't have enough memory to hold the work, the processor transfers data to and from the hard disk as it needs it, which takes a great deal longer. As a practical minimum, you can get by on Windows 3.1 with 8MB, but you'll be a great deal happier if you install at least 16MB of memory, especially if you plan to use Windows 95.

HARD DRIVE WITH AT LEAST 1,000 MEGABYTES CAPACITY

When you run a program, the processor copies it from the hard drive to RAM. When you save a document that you created with a word processor or spread-sheet, or a Web page that you loaded from the Internet, the processor normally stores a copy on the hard drive. Hard drive prices have dropped even faster than other computer components, and programs have grown larger, so you should get one that's big enough to hold what seems to be a huge amount of data. No matter how large it seems, you will fill it sooner than you expect.

CD-ROM DRIVE

CD-ROMs are compact discs similar to the ones that have replaced phonograph records, but they contain computer data instead of (or in addition to) music. CD-ROM actually stands for *compact disc read-only memory*. Because one CD-ROM can contain as much data as 50 or more floppy disks, a CD is a much more efficient and economical way to distribute software. If you get a computer without a CD-ROM player, you will probably want to add one within a few months. Like other components, you don't need the fastest and most expensive versions; a 4X or 6X drive will do everything you want.

OTHER FEATURES AND FUNCTIONS

Any computer you buy will also include a floppy disk drive, a keyboard, a mouse, serial and parallel input/output ports, and other standard bells and whistles. If your dealer offers a choice, you may want to try different brands and models of keyboards and mice and choose the ones that seem to best fit your own hand.

You will also want a monitor — the video display in a box that looks like a television set without a channel selector. A monitor is one place where you should not cut corners. You will spend a great deal of time staring at that screen, so you should get one that looks good. Because so much of the World Wide Web contains graphic images, you should get a monitor with either a 15- or 17-inch screen and a dot pitch of .28 mm or less (*dot pitch* specifies the size of the individual dots of color that make up the picture on your screen). The best way to choose a monitor is to go to a store that sells several brands and compare their appearance, but try fiddling with the brightness and contrast controls before you make your choice.

TIP   **Some computer dealers may include an inexpensive monitor with low-price systems. Spending an extra hundred dollars or more for a good one is worthwhile; repair shops that specialize in fixing monitors spend most of the time working on "bargain" devices. You probably don't need the most expensive monitor in the store, but you should go with a good, middle-range brand.**

You should be able to find a new computer for less than $1,500 that has all the features you need for Web browsing and most other functions you're likely to want. It won't be the fastest machine on the block, and it won't have this week's newest and hottest processor, but it should do the job quite well.

Finding a place to buy a computer can be difficult simply because of the number of choices you have. One good source of pointers to inexpensive systems is the list of the "Top 20 Budget Desktops" that appears in *PC World* magazine every month. It defines "budget" as costing less than $2,500, but the list usually includes a handful of even less expensive options. In general, the companies (many of them mail-order) whose systems appear on the list offer good equipment at competitive prices, and they're generally able to provide better customer support than your local appliance store.

Using an Older Computer

The trouble with personal computers is that the technology has been advancing too fast. Millions of older computers are out there that work as well as they did when they were new (less than ten years ago, for heavens sake!), but their original owners have replaced them with newer and more powerful systems because they don't work with this year's software.

Many cast-off computers are ending up in spare bedrooms and kitchens of unsuspecting family members who want to "learn something about computers," or "find out about this Internet stuff I keep hearing about." Unfortunately, the current versions of most programs that a home user may want are no less demanding of computer power than the ones that inspired the original owner to get rid of the old computer in the first place. If you have inherited somebody's old personal computer, you have a couple of options: you can use it with older software versions that were designed for your computer or you can try to improve your computer's performance.

Unfortunately, using older software is not always an option, especially when you're trying to use the computer as a Web browser. A few older browser client programs are out there, such as Cello and Lynx, but they don't recognize all the codes and formats used by Web page designers today. If you compare a Web page displayed in those programs with one displayed in Navigator, it's pretty clear that Lynx and Cello don't come close to showing you the image that the page designer had in mind.

To be blunt, it's probably not worth the trouble to try browsing through most of the Web without the most recent generation of browsers, let alone a computer that doesn't work with Windows (or some other modern operating system, such as UNIX or Macintosh). The Web has evolved and grown so quickly that a two-year-old browser program will make applesauce out of a huge number of Web pages. If you don't use a relatively new browser such as Netscape Navigator or Microsoft Internet Explorer, you will miss much of the content and most of the fun of the World Wide Web.

That doesn't mean your new/old computer is useless if it's more than five or six years old. You can still use it for word processing and even connect it to the Internet to send and receive e-mail and use other Internet services that don't require a graphic interface (such as Telnet). You'll find more information about using the Internet without Windows later in this chapter. But if you want to use the Web, you should either upgrade the computer or replace it.

UPGRADING AN OLD COMPUTER

You can replace the processor and other internal pieces of almost any personal computer with newer and more powerful components, but the cost and aggravation may be greater than the possible benefit. It's like trying to fix up an old car: you could spend several thousand dollars to replace the engine in your 1963 Ford and fix the brakes, the transmission, and the carburetor; after you're finished, it may run better than it did 30 years ago, but it will still be a 1963 Ford. If you have to spend more than about $500 or $600 to upgrade your computer, you will be much better off buying a new one.

To install any of these upgrades, you either have to open your computer and swap out some parts or pay somebody else to do it for you. In most cases, you can do the job with nothing more complicated than a screwdriver, but if you're not comfortable doing the work yourself, you can probably pay the place that sells you the parts to take care of it for you. After you have installed the new parts, you may have to run some configuration software, but that's not a big deal, either.

There are several things you can do to improve the performance of an old computer, as the following sections describe.

REPLACING THE PROCESSOR

As a general rule, the current generation of browser programs require either a 486 or Pentium central processor. If your computer has an 8088 or 8086 central processor, there's not much you can do with it. Your only choice is to replace the main circuit board that holds the processor and all the other circuitry. For all practical purposes, you're installing a completely new computer in the old cabinet. By the time you upgrade everything connected to the main board, you will probably spend almost as much as you'd pay for a new computer.

If your computer has a 286 or 386 processor, however, you can install a relatively inexpensive *upgrade chip* that brings performance up to 486 levels. The new processor works with the same main board and external components as the one it replaced, but it operates faster and more efficiently. This book was written on a computer that was converted from a 386 to a 486 with an upgrade chip, and it (the computer, not the book) has worked reliably for more than two years.

ADDING MORE MEMORY

Your old computer almost certainly has less memory than it needs for today's programs. Windows 3.1 can operate on 8MB or less, but it crawls. Windows 95 is a lost cause with less than 16MB. Installing enough memory is the single, least expensive, most effective thing you can do to improve a computer's performance.

TIP **Almost all personal computers have space for additional memory, so installing more is easy; just slip a small circuit board into a socket on the main board. However, many older computers use non-standard proprietary memory modules, and others may not have any empty memory sockets. Still others may not work unless you use an even number of modules.**

Therefore, reading the information about adding memory in your computer's manual before you start is extremely important. If you don't have the manual, or if you have the manual but it's written in advanced technojargon (or badly translated from Japanese or Korean), you're going to need help. Either take the computer to a local dealer or service shop and let their staff do the job for you or talk to one of the mail-order places that specializes in memory upgrades. I've had good luck with H Co. Computer Products (800-347-1182) and L.A. Trade (800-433-3726).

INSTALLING A BIGGER HARD DRIVE

Your old machine probably has a drive with a capacity of less than 100MB, which seemed like a huge amount when it was installed. As the price of storage space of hard drives has dropped, the size of programs has increased. In other words, you won't have any more free space on an enormous hard drive today than you would have had on a much smaller disk a few years ago.

It won't cost very much to add a new drive ten times the size of your old one. Buy a new drive in the $150–$200 range. If there's physical space inside your computer, add it to the existing drive; if not, take out the old one and install a new drive. If you remove the old drive, you'll have to re-install all the programs that were stored on it before you can use the computer again.

INSTALLING A 3.5-INCH DISKETTE DRIVE

Until about 1990, almost all personal computers used 5.25-inch floppy disks, but those drives have been almost completely replaced by the 3.5-inch diskettes that can hold more data in less space. If your computer does not have a diskette drive that accepts 3.5-inch floppies, you will want to add one.

A FEW FINAL WORDS ABOUT UPGRADING

Getting carried away with upgrades is easy to do. You could start with a vintage 1988 286 system and replace everything except the power supply and the cabinet to turn it into a super-duper, high-speed Pentium that does everything a brand new machine can do, but it would cost more than buying a new computer. Before you do anything, make a list of the changes you want to make and the price of each one. Remember the famous law of diminishing returns: you will spend almost as much money for the last 10 percent of improvements as you did for the first 50 percent.

When your total upgrade budget approaches the $500–$600 range with no end in sight, stop. If you have to spend that much money to bring the computer up to snuff, you might as well buy a new one. It will almost certainly cost less and run better than anything you're likely to assemble from parts, even if you put the parts in an existing cabinet.

USING THE INTERNET WITHOUT WINDOWS

If you have an older personal computer that won't work with Microsoft Windows, you can still connect it to the Internet. You won't see pictures and fancy effects on the World Wide Web, but plenty of other Internet services are available, including electronic mail, online conferences such as The Well, and access to text files on computers around the world. You have to learn and use a bunch of somewhat obscure commands instead of pointing and clicking with a mouse, but you'll be able to make the connection with an old, slow computer.

Quite honestly, this is not the best way to use the Internet. Over the last two or three years, most of the Internet's best content is on the Web. But if upgrading or replacing your computer to a system that can use Windows is unfeasible, it's better than nothing.

There are two ways to make a connection through a DOS-only system:

* You can use a DOS-based communications program such as ProComm or Crosstalk to call your Internet access provider through something called a *shell account*. When you buy a new modem, you usually get both DOS and Windows communications programs in the same package.

* You can also use IBM's TCP/IP for DOS to run Internet client programs on your own computer. You can order IBM TCP/IP for DOS by telephone from IBM Direct, at 800-426-2255 (800-IBM-CALL). In the summer of 1996, the cost of single copies was $120.

If you can find a local service provider who offers a shell account, that's probably a better choice than the IBM package, because you won't have to mess with a somewhat complicated setup routine. A shell account may cost less than the TCP/IP access required for the IBM package. It might even be possible to find a local school or library that offers free or very low-cost shell access to the Internet.

Some DOS-based Internet services provide menus. To select an item from a menu, you type the letter or number assigned to that item. The main menu at Northwest Nexus, a Seattle access provider, offers several options to its shell account holders. Among other things, this menu includes access to news, mail, and Gopher, along with Lynx, the character-based Web browser. Different service providers offer different lists of options.

If no menu exists, or if you're using the IBM TCP/IP program to run Internet clients on your own computer, you have to enter individual commands at the C:> prompt. The most common services are as follows:

* **Finger.** Finger is a request for information about a user currently active on a distant host computer.

* **File Transfer Protocol (FTP).** FTP is a request to connect to a distant file server and transfer copies of one or more files back to your own computer.

* **Gopher.** Gopher organizes resources on the Internet into menus that contain pointers to programs, text and data files, and other menus.

* **Lynx.** Lynx is a Web browser for computer users who do not have access to graphical platforms such as Windows or Macintosh.

* **Mail.** Mail exchanges messages between your computer and a mail server that sends and receives electronic mail to and from the rest of the Internet.

* **News.** News sets up a connection to a news server to read news articles and submit your own articles to newsgroups.

* **Telnet.** Telnet is an instruction to set up a remote terminal connection with a distant computer such as a bulletin board or a library catalog.

If your computer limits you to DOS programs, you're going to need another book with detailed information about Internet access through a shell account. One of the best is Ed Krol's *The Whole Internet*, by O'Reilly and Associates.

Connecting to the Internet

Whether you buy a new computer or make due with an old one, you're going to need one more piece of equipment: a device that will move data between your computer and the rest of the world. For most individual users, that device is a modem. If you're connecting to the Internet through a high-speed network such as an office LAN (local area network) or through some other less common type of circuit (maybe your TV cable or a wireless link), you can expect to obtain the interface box from the service provider or network administrator, but most people reading this book will use a modem to connect from a home computer.

A modem (short for **mod**ulator-**dem**odulator) converts the digital signals that the computer uses to sounds that can travel through a telephone line and also converts sounds back to digital signals.

When you look for a modem, you should consider three things: data speed, form, and compatibility with standards.

Speed

The speed of a modem is the rate at which it transfers data across the telephone line. When you use a faster modem, you will not wait as long for a file to move from the distant system to your own computer. Ten years ago, the fastest modems for personal computers operated at 1,200 bits per second (bps). Today, there is no reason to buy anything slower than 28,800 bps.

Don't even think about trying to use a modem slower than 14,400 bits per second (14.4 Kbps) for browsing the World Wide Web. If you try to use, say, a 2,400 bps modem, it will take more than ten times as long for a page to appear on your screen as it would with a 28,800 bps modem. If somebody gives you an old 1,200, 2,400 or 9,600 bps modem, thank them politely, accept it, and hide it someplace where you won't ever see it again.

Form

Modems come in three forms: internal modems that fit inside your computer, external modems in separate boxes that connect through a cable to the communications input/output connector on the back of the computer, and credit-card-size PCMCIA cards that plug into portable computers.

If you have a desktop computer, you should choose either an internal or external modem.

Internal and external modems each have advantages and disadvantages. Internal modems cost less than external ones because they don't need as many parts, but an external unit is easier to install because you don't have to take apart the computer and you don't have to worry about possible conflicts with other devices inside the computer. External modems have status lights that can tell you if data is moving through them. If your computer is more than two or three years old, an internal modem is the better choice because it will avoid a data transmission bottleneck between the central processor and the communications connector.

Standards

When you use a modem, it must use the same kind of signals and timing as the modem at the other end of the connection. In other words, both modems must speak and understand the same digital language. This problem is not a serious one, because almost every modem in the world uses standards established by a branch of the International Telecommunications Union (ITU). If your modem follows the international standard, you can expect it to work with any other modem you're likely to call.

The most important standards are V.32bis for 14,400 bps modems and V.34 for 28,800 bps and 33,600 bps modems (*bis* means that it's the second standard in a series — because the ITU is based in Geneva, the standards are published in French). If you can't find one or both of these numbers marked on the modem package, look for another modem.

You shouldn't have any trouble finding a new 28,800-bps or 33,600-bps modem that meets the V.34 standard; all the modem manufacturers follow it. But if somebody offers you an older one, examine it closely before you try to install it. There are other standards for private data circuits and other specialized uses that won't work with a dial-up telephone line.

You should also watch out for modems that use V.FAST or V.FC. Before the V.34 specification was published, several manufacturers released 28,800 bps modems that followed their own "standards" in the hope that the rest of the world would follow their lead. Unfortunately for those companies, the rest of the world went its own way. Because V.FAST and V.FC are not entirely compatible with V.34, those modems sometimes show up at very low prices, but they're no bargain.

The same kind of problem is appearing again with 56 Kbps modems. Several manufacturers have introduced their own, non-standard modems that may not work with other modems, even though both claim to work at 56 Kbps. It's probably a good idea to avoid early 56 Kbps modems until a standard is adopted.

Most of the current generation of modems also include fax capability. In other words, you can use the same modem to send and receive data to another computer and to exchange faxes with a fax machine. The maximum speed for a fax modem (or a fax machine) is 14,400 bps, even if the same modem can handle higher speeds for data.

In practice, finding a modem is not as complicated as it might sound. As long as you get one that runs at 28,800 bps or faster and complies with the V.34 standard, it's pretty difficult to make a wrong choice.

BONUS

Navigating the Retail Computer Jungle

Whether you buy a new computer or try to upgrade an old one, you're going to have to deal with the people who sell computers and computer parts. Many of these people are honest, ethical, and truly committed to helping their customers find exactly the right computer to meet their needs — and at a fair price. But too many others are not as upstanding. Sometimes it seems like the average computer salesperson was trained at Crazy Charlie's Used Car Lot and Credit Appliance Emporium. Fortunately, there are a lot of places you can go to buy a computer; if you aren't getting the service you want at the first place you try, you can take your business someplace else.

Most computer retailers fit into one of these categories:

* Local computer store
* Computer superstore
* Discount store
* Mail-order business

Each type has its advantages and disadvantages.

Local Computer Stores

A small or medium-size computer store can be either the best or the worst possible place to buy a computer. A good one may sell brand-name systems from top-line manufacturers, such as IBM, Compaq, and Hewlett-Packard, or assemble its own computers made to order from quality parts. Either way, reputable vendors try to match each customer with the right computer and stand behind their products with careful, competent service. The shadier stores might cut corners on internal components, use high-pressure sales techniques, and try to sell everybody the same kind of system, regardless of individual requirements.

Separating the good dealers from the bad ones is a subjective process. Recommendations from friends and colleagues can be helpful, but the best guide is probably your own experience: does the salesperson answer your questions? Can you understand those answers? Does the store have its own service department, or will it send you to a third-party service place out in the industrial district? Many computer failures happen within the first 24 hours of use; does the store perform a "burn-in" test on every system before selling it? Will the staff send you home with a set of sealed boxes and a hearty handshake, or will they assemble and test the system for you?

Computer Superstores

Most computer "superstores" are part of a national chain, such as Computer City or CompUSA, but a few may be local or regional businesses. Either way, superstores are large stores with extensive inventories of computers, software, and accessories. Because these places are able to buy in volume, they can offer wide selections and discount prices that the "mom and pop" retailer may not be able to match.

Superstores are great places to go when you know exactly what you want. It's extremely convenient to walk in and select the cable adapter or software package you need without waiting for someone to order it from a distributor. When a hot, new word processor or a brand-name monitor is on sale, you may be able to save some serious money. And if you discover that the product doesn't work the way you expected, superstores are very good about accepting returns.

On the other hand, the average salesperson on the floor of a superstore is probably not the best source of advice about selecting a new computer system. In most cases, the store is set up to move merchandise in volume rather than to assemble things to order. If the computer you want is exactly the same type as one of the popular configurations on the floor, you may find a good deal, but if not, the sales folks will probably try to convince you to move up to a more expensive system with added features that you really don't need. The store's house brand may have an attractive price, but it probably doesn't perform as well as a comparable brand-name system.

Discount Stores

Discount stores come in several forms: the big electronics stores that sell everything from portable radios and fax machines to big-screen television sets and, oh yes, computers; appliance stores that display the computers over behind the dishwashers; office supply places; and warehouse clubs where you can buy potato chips in ten-pound cartons, tires (which you install), and bath towels, along with a limited selection of computers, all at very low prices.

The prices may be low, but after you read the first three chapters of this book, you probably know more about computers than the salespeople. Most discount places don't even try to provide repairs; the good ones will take a defective unit back and give you a new one, but you won't find anything that resembles on-site service.

Like the superstores, discount stores offer very low prices, but the selection is much more limited and the sales staff is minimal. You might find a good computer for a good price at a discount store, but if you don't know exactly what you're buying, you're better off at a place that specializes in computers.

Mail-Order Suppliers

In addition to the storefront retailers that ship a few computers to customers who order by mail or telephone, there are two other types of mail-order computer suppliers: the catalog places that have hardware and software at discount prices and the manufacturers that bypass the distribution channels and sell their computers directly to consumers.

Catalogs are like the superstores; the good ones offer brand-name products and decent service, but their salespeople are really just order-takers. In most cases, you can expect to receive anything you order from a catalog merchant within two or three days, but you'll probably pay a few extra dollars for shipping. However, when you order a computer from a merchant in another state, you might save $100 or more in sales tax (legally, your state expects you to pay a "use tax" on purchases from out of state, but that's between you and the tax collector).

The other mail-order option is to buy a computer directly from the manufacturer. Several major manufacturers — including Dell, Gateway 2000, and Micron — all offer high-quality systems at very attractive prices. Their telephone salespeople generally know their own product lines well, so they'll usually give you better answers than the sales folks of the neighborhood appliance store. These companies assemble each system to order, and they will send a repair person to your location when your computer needs service. The good ones also have technical support centers with toll-free telephone lines that are open 24 hours a day, but some are notorious for endless busy signals.

Direct purchase from a manufacturer does have a few drawbacks. The prices may be somewhat higher than the cost of similar equipment from a local discounter, and you won't get the same kind of personal service you can expect from a good local store. When you order from a manufacturer, you may have to wait several weeks to receive your computer.

So, where is the best place to buy a new computer? There's no easy answer to that question. You'll probably find the lowest prices on brand-name systems at a discount warehouse or a superstore during a sale, but if you don't know exactly what you want, you'll get more advice and hand-holding buying from a small retail store or directly from a manufacturer.

Summary

Buying or upgrading your computer is as much of a nuisance as buying a new refrigerator or television set (actually it's worse; you don't have to worry about finding butter and ice cream compatible with the refrigerator's Dairy Products Protocol). But once you've got the computer up and running, you can forget about most of the technical details and concentrate on using it. All those technical details are important, but they're not the real point of the exercise. All those bits, bytes, memory, and floppy disks are much less important than the things you'll do with the computer. Just as your kitchen stove is less important than the things you can cook on it, your computer is just a way to connect to the Internet (and maybe to use as a writing or calculating tool). The next chapter explains how to set up that connection.

FINDING AN INTERNET SERVICE PROVIDER

4

IN THIS CHAPTER YOU LEARN THESE KEY SKILLS

So, you have a computer and a modem. Now it's time to connect them to the rest of the world. This chapter describes several alternative methods for adding your own computer to the millions already on the Internet.

As you will remember from Chapter 2, everything on the Internet connects to everything else. Therefore, when you connect to any Internet access provider, you can generally find a way to reach any server that you want to use.

Four major types of Internet service providers exist:

* National services with access points in many locations
* Local and regional service providers that have just a few connection points
* Corporate and campus networks that connect users within a local area network
* Online information services that offer their own proprietary services along with access to the Internet

National Service Providers

About a dozen companies, including AT&T, MCI, Sprint, and IBM, offer nationwide Internet access in the United States and Canada, with local, dial-in connection points in most major cities and toll-free 800 numbers (at a slight additional charge) that subscribers can use when they're away from home. Most national service providers also supply their own access software that makes it easy to set up a new account.

The most important benefit that large national service providers offer is that you can reach them from more than one location. If you live in Chicago, you can make a local call to collect your e-mail when you travel to New York, San Francisco, or Scottsbluff, Nebraska, just as easily as you could reach the provider from home. The downside of using a national service provider may be support; if you have to make a long-distance telephone call to request assistance, the cost may be prohibitive.

The following access providers will send you an information kit containing startup software and detailed information about their rates and the special services that set them apart from their competitors:

AT&T WorldNet	800-WORLDNET (800-967-5363)
internetMCI	800-550-0927
Sprint Internet Passport	800-359-3900
GTE Internet Solutions	800-363-8483
BellSouth.net	888-4DOTNET (888-436-8638)
Pacific Bell	800-708-4638
IBM Global Network	800-455-5056
PSInet	800-774-0852
Netcom	800-353-6600
SPRYnet	800-SPRYNET (800-777-9638)
Earthlink TotalAccess	800-395-8425
InfiNet	800-849-7214

The cost of unlimited Internet service from most national providers is about $20 a month. Many services also offer other, lower rates for a limited number of hours. If you use their long-distance service, AT&T, MCI, or Sprint may give you an even lower price for Internet access. The access business is extremely competitive, so comparison shopping can often be worth the time and trouble.

Local and Regional Service Providers

Big corporations are not the only ones in the Internet access business. Across the United States, thousands of smaller businesses provide Internet connections to one or more metropolitan areas or rural districts. A good, local Internet service provider (ISP) can give you service as good as or better than a national service, at a comparable price.

You should be able to find local ISPs by looking for advertisements in your local newspaper or in the local computer user magazine that you can probably find at a computer superstore. If friends and family members have accounts with local providers, they can also be good sources for recommendations.

You will usually have fewer options in rural or extremely isolated locations. If one of the national access providers cannot give you a local telephone number to reach its system, ask your local library for suggestions.

You cannot automatically assume that a local business will supply good service. Some providers have thrown their systems together on the cheap, without adequate equipment to handle the demand for service or enough qualified staff to respond to customer requests for assistance. The least expensive account is not always the best deal. If a provider offers a free trial period (usually a couple of weeks), use that time to make sure you don't get frequent busy signals when you try to connect; confirm that its access programs, news, and mail servers are easy to use; and verify that its technical support people are truly helpful. If you do not get the quality of service you expect, cancel the account and take your business somewhere else.

Online Information Services

The least painful way to reach the World Wide Web and other Internet services may be through a gateway from an online information service. America Online (AOL), CompuServe, and Prodigy all provide access to the Web along with a great deal of additional content available only to their own subscribers. The Microsoft Network (MSN) is more closely integrated with the Web; you can reach many of MSN's content areas with a Web browser even if you don't have an MSN account. Figure 4-1 shows the content available from America Online.

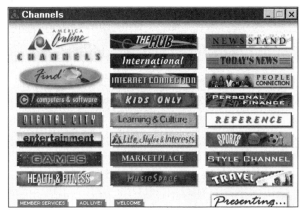

Figure 4-1 The America Online Channels screen represents a variety of services available to subscribers.

The online services are easier to set up and use than many Internet-only access providers, and their in-house content areas are very popular. But if you don't care about the chat rooms and other unique services, an Internet-only ISP may be a better choice.

Each service tries very hard to offer added value that you can't find anywhere else. Mostly, that seems to consist of lots of live chats with actors and rock stars and a few moderated conferences. CompuServe in particular still provides a home for hundreds of hardware and software companies' online technical support, but most of those companies also have their own Web pages, so that feature is not as important as it may have been two or three years ago.

In general, you can find Web sites that contain almost everything that an online service offers, but the information on AOL, CompuServe, or Prodigy may be easier to find and use. Conferences and forums on the online services are all moderated, so you can avoid the extreme *flames* that sometimes turn Internet newsgroups into schoolyard brawls. In the end, the decision is a matter of personal preference. If you feel that you want a lot of hand-holding while you explore the Web, an online service might be for you. If you prefer to go out on your own, you can probably find everything you want through an ISP at the same or a slightly lower cost without all the cheerful pointers and sales gimmicks.

NOTE *Flaming,* in cyber jargon, is the act of chewing someone out online. It can be mild or quite abusive — an occurrence that most of us would avoid in face-to-face communication.

However, millions of people have found their online homes on these services. AOL and the other services can be much more civilized places than the "wild west" feeling of many places on the Internet. If you find one or two conferences, chat rooms, or forums where the community feels right to you, you can be as comfortable and find the experience as rewarding as anything you might find somewhere else on the Internet.

Until recently, AOL, CompuServe, and Prodigy used their own Web browsers, which were slower and less flexible than Microsoft Internet Explorer or Netscape Navigator. Displaying a Web page through Prodigy or AOL rather than through a stand-alone browser could take up to two or three times longer. This is changing, however, as a side effect of the battle between Netscape and Microsoft for market share. All three services have agreed to integrate Netscape Navigator, Microsoft Internet Explorer, or both with their next software releases, so you can expect the same Web-browsing speed and performance from an online service that you can get from any other ISP.

 One word of warning: If you join an online service, you may not be able to use it to reach all the Internet services that you want. For example, as this is written, the current version of Prodigy did not include access to FTP or Telnet. That may have changed by the time you read this.

All the services will happily send you disks with access software and a free trial account. You might want to try all of them, along with one or more of the other ISPs, and see which has the specific content and services that come closest to your own interests and needs. To request a free trial, call the online services at these numbers:

America Online	800-827-6364
CompuServe	800-769-6747
Prodigy	800-PRODIGY (800-776-3449)

Microsoft includes the programs you need to connect to MSN as part of Windows 95.

High-Speed Network Connections

Most people who connect to the Internet from home or a small business probably use a dial-out telephone line and a modem. But that may change in the near future. If you're willing to spend a little more money for your Internet access, you can expect to obtain a faster connection that may use a telephone line, a TV cable, or a radio link some time in the next few years.

Why would you want a faster connection? It might be helpful to think about the Internet as a plumbing system. A two-foot pipe can deliver a great deal of water very quickly. But if you try to pass the same amount of water through a half-inch pipe, it takes a lot longer to fill the bathtub. The Internet moves bits through a wire rather than water through a pipe, but the effect is the same. For example, it may take a minute or two to download and display a Web page that contains a couple of embedded pictures through a 28.8 Kbps modem; with a high-speed data link, you might accomplish the same task in ten seconds or less. When you want to transfer larger files, such as CD-quality music files, the benefits of a bigger data pipe are even greater.

High-speed access to the Internet is available today, but it's too expensive to be practical for most casual users. Using an existing telephone line, it's not difficult to find Internet service for less than $20 a month. Depending on the speed, a high-speed connection can cost up to several thousand dollars.

Fortunately, prices are changing rapidly. As new technology appears, you can expect to see your telephone company and your cable TV service offer high-speed connections at affordable prices.

Corporate and Campus Networks

If your computer is already connected to a local area network (LAN), there's an excellent chance that you already have access to the Internet through that network. The people who maintain your network can tell you exactly what you need to use a Web browser and other Internet tools through the system. You're probably not the first person to ask about an Internet connection, so the network administrator or help desk will have immediate answers to your questions.

There are at least two good reasons to use a LAN instead of a modem if you have the choice:

* You won't tie up a telephone line that somebody else in the organization might need for other business.
* Your link to the backbone will probably be faster and more efficient.

BONUS

Using a Web Browser with an Online Service

If you already have an account with America Online, CompuServe, Prodigy, or The Microsoft Network, you can browse the World Wide Web. Each of these services includes a browser as part of the software you use to reach its own content areas, but you can also use either Netscape Navigator or Microsoft Internet Explorer. To make things even easier, AOL, Prodigy, and the others include separate browsers on the CD-ROMs that they use to distribute their own software.

The most recent software packages from all four services include an integrated Web browser. So, when you follow the link from within AOL, for example, it automatically opens an integrated version of Microsoft Internet Explorer, as shown in Figure 4-2. CompuServe and MSN also use Internet Explorer; Prodigy uses Netscape Navigator.

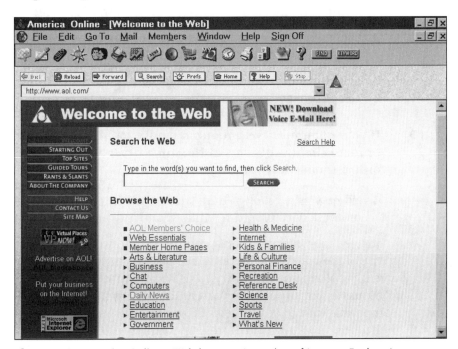

Figure 4-2   America Online's Web browser (a version of Internet Explorer).

Things can get confusing because an experienced user of an online service expects everything to work together — once you've connected to the online service, you can move to a different content area without starting a new program. But when you're using separate Internet programs (say, an external version of Internet Explorer or a Telnet client), you'll have to go back to the Windows desktop and open each program outside the shell that connects you to the online service. In other words, you can do just about anything through an online service that you can do through any other ISP — even if it's not part of the online service's program.

Why is it important to talk about this? Because a huge number of subscribers to the online services assume that they can use an external browser to move out to the World Wide Web or link to a Telnet host exactly the same way they enter an AOL chat room or join a CompuServe forum. The hosts of the Internet Support centers on each of the online services spend most of their time explaining this distinction.

The two important exceptions are mail and news. The online services don't use the same kind of news and mail servers as other ISPs, so external news readers and mail client programs won't always work. Therefore, you must use the software provided by AOL, Prodigy, CompuServe, and MSN to send and receive e-mail and participate in newsgroups.

To use an external Web browser or other Internet client program with an online service account, follow these steps:

1. Connect to the online service just as you would normally.

2. When you are ready to open the external browser, minimize the program window. Do not log off, and do not shut down the program.

3. Start the other Internet client program. For example, if you want to use Netscape Navigator, click the appropriate icon or menu item.

NOTE **If your computer has enough memory to handle them, you can run two or more client programs at the same time, or run a client and the online service software together.**

4. When you're ready to quit, shut down the client program, enlarge the online service program window, and log out.

Ideally, any Internet client program should work with the software supplied by any of these services. If you're using a Macintosh or Windows 3.1, you won't have a problem, unless you try to use a program designed for Windows 95. But if you use a version of America Online or CompuServe software advertised as "compatible with both Windows 3.1 and Windows 95," it won't work with 32-bit application programs. If you're using Windows 95, you should either call your online service and ask them to send you their 32-bit software or download the software from an online file library.

Summary

Before you can browse the World Wide Web, you must set up an account with a service that can connect your computer to the Internet. Depending on your specific requirements, this service might be a large national or international business such as AT&T, IBM, or Microsoft; a smaller local or regional access provider; or an online information service such as America Online, CompuServe, or Prodigy. If you're associated with a business, school, or other institution that operates a LAN, you may be able to connect to the Internet through that network.

Regardless of the type of service you choose, the cost will be about the same. But each of these methods has its own advantages. The large services offer dial-in access from hundreds of locations; the smaller local access providers may give you more personal service and support; and the online services add their own proprietary content areas to the information you can get through the Web.

The best thing about choosing an ISP and configuring an Internet connection is that you only have to do it once — unless, of course, you change providers. When you have the software up and running properly, you should be able to connect automatically whenever you start your Web browser or other Internet client program.

In the next two chapters, you can find detailed descriptions of the most popular browser programs.

NAVIGATING THE WORLD WIDE WEB

THIS PART CONTAINS THE FOLLOWING CHAPTERS

The Web is designed for easy use, as long as you have a few basic skills to find your way around. This section explains the tools you need to move through the Web, including Web browsers, search tools, and directories, and techniques for using them.

It was very exciting. We had just come from our first open house — on a whim, we had stopped after passing a sign. We had been talking about buying our first home, but we kept putting it off, not knowing where to begin. So, every Sunday, we read the real estate ads in the *Globe* and dreamed about what the homes looked like, how perfect they were, and how the treasures we had collected over the years would fit so nicely in them. But we never got beyond reading those ads. The next Sunday would come, bringing with it a new set of ads and a new set of fantasies.

But this day was different. We were *actively looking*. The house we viewed wasn't the home we dreamed about, but it didn't matter — we had taken the first step. Now we wanted to see everything that was available. Suddenly, those Sunday real estate ads just weren't enough. We devoured home-buying information. We scrambled to every supermarket in town, gathered up bunches of real estate magazines, raced home, and dreamed some more. But it just wasn't enough. Then it hit us — the Web!

We hooked up with Sally King, FWP, a real estate agent in Plymouth, Massachusetts, through her agency's Web site. From the moment we connected and searched for "*Massachusetts Real Estate,*" we knew we were seriously on our way. The best sites requested a specific profile of our dream home — how many bedrooms, how much land, price range, square footage, right down to such specs as garage, basement, and fireplaces. Just enter the profile and click the button. Within seconds, glorious, full-color GIFs graced our screen with photos of prospective dream homes. Inside. Outside. And a complete description of the home and property. Some sites even offered community profiles and let you calculate the estimated mortgage costs on the home. It was like magic.

"I have more and more folks just like you contacting me because of profiles they saw on the Web," Sally says. "It's really changing the way people are shopping for homes because it cuts through a lot of the up-front legwork and gets right to the specifics of what people are looking for." Sally's agency is just one of dozens in eastern Massachusetts that utilizes the powers of the Web to connect home buyers with properties. But the pickins' can be frustratingly slim. "People still aren't realizing the full potential of the Web," Sally adds. "Not just agencies but shoppers as well."

Of course, nothing can replace the good, old-fashioned walk-through. But for busy folks, cutting through the mystery of what the home will look like beforehand is a blessing that saves valuable time. We're gearing up to close on our new home in the next few months. Now we have to turn our attention to interior design and gardening. I wonder if there's a Web site that can help.

BROWSERS: REACHING THE WORLD WIDE WEB

IN THIS CHAPTER YOU LEARN THESE KEY SKILLS

5

Finding a Web Browser

Along with a computer and a connection to the Internet, the third essential item you need to explore the World Wide Web is a client program that receives documents encoded in *HyperText Markup Language* (HTML) and related files through the Internet and displays them on your computer — a browser. At least three dozen browser programs are available from almost as many software developers, but if you have the computing power to support them, you should choose one of the two browsers that dominate the market: Netscape Navigator and Microsoft Internet Explorer.

Between them, the Netscape and Microsoft browsers account for more than 90 percent of all *hits* on most Web sites that keep track of such things. As a result, most Web page designers optimize their designs to look best on Navigator, Internet Explorer, or both. Although HTML is supposed to be a standard, each browser displays documents differently. Many pages look better and are easier to use if you stick with one of the market leaders.

NOTE A *hit* is an access to a Web page by a browser. If a page has embedded images or other files in addition to the HTML document, the "hit count" will include one for each file — so accessing a single page with a bunch of images can produce lots of hits. Webmasters tend to tally up hits as an indication of interest in their Web site.

Microsoft has tried very hard to integrate Internet Explorer into Windows 95 and with the software provided by many major online services and ISPs, so you may have some version of the program already. But installing Netscape Navigator is a simple matter if that's your preference. After installation, it's equally easy to use either browser.

Which is better? It's a matter of taste. The two programs are so similar that it's difficult to find any important reason to choose one of them. When a new feature appears in a new release of either program, you can be sure that the other company will match it within two or three months. If you prefer the way one organizes commands into menus and toolbars, choose that one. Otherwise, you will probably be equally happy with either program. Because you can obtain Netscape Navigator and Internet Explorer at little or no cost, your best bet is to install both programs and decide for yourself which browser you prefer. It's hard to go wrong with either one.

Obtaining Netscape Navigator

Netscape distributes Navigator in several forms, through many channels:

* **Through retail software dealers.** Netscape Navigator Personal Edition and Netscape Communicator both include all the software you need to set up an account with your choice of leading ISPs, to browse the World Wide Web, and to use other Internet services such as e-mail and news. Communicator also includes tools you can use to create your own HTML documents and exchange information with other users and a "shared whiteboard" that allows multiple users to jointly mark up a shared document.

   Netscape Navigator is also bundled with other commercial software products including Corel's Office Suite, WordPerfect 8, and Hilgraeve's HyperAccess communications application software.

* **Through ISPs and online services.** Many service providers supply Navigator to new customers as part of their startup packages. Others will give you a copy on request, even if their default browser is Microsoft Internet Explorer.

* **Through the Internet.** The latest version of Navigator is always available for free download directly from Netscape. If you are a student, teacher, or staff member of a school, college, other educational

institution, a public library, or a charitable nonprofit organization, you can use the program for free — the rest of us are expected to pay after a 90-day evaluation period (but in practice, there will probably be a newer version to evaluate before the 90 days expire).

If you already have a Web browser, you can find instructions for downloading the latest version of Navigator at `http://home.netscape.com/`. If you have an FTP client, try one of Netscape's servers at `ftp2.netscape.com`, `ftp3.netscape.com`, and so on up to `ftp9.netscape.com`.

A couple thousand other people are probably trying to download software from Netscape at any time, so it's not unusual to see one or more servers refuse to accept new connections, especially during the week or two after it releases a new update. If you do connect, a download may take three or four times as long when many other people are receiving files at the same time. As a general rule, you'll have better luck late at night rather than during business hours or early in the evening.

Netscape has separate versions of Navigator available for Windows 3.1, Windows 95, Macintosh, and other operating systems. Whether you get the software from an ISP, buy it from a retailer, or download it directly from Netscape, remember to specify the right version for your own computer.

Newer and better versions of Navigator seem to appear on Netscape's Web site every month, so it's a good idea to check for the latest update even if you got a copy of the program from some other source. Netscape doesn't charge for updates, so you might as well make sure you're using the most recent release.

SIDE TRIP

HOW TO JUMP ONTO THE TREADMILL

Downloading a Web browser is one of those chicken-and-egg problems: to download a browser through the Web, you must already have a browser on your computer. Unless you're there already, you can't get there from here.

If you don't have a browser or an FTP program, don't give up hope. There are some other possibilities:

- Ask your ISP for advice. The ISP may be able to give you a diskette with the software you need or tell you how to use a *shell account* to download the software without a browser in place.

- Call one of the ISPs or online services listed in Chapter 4 and ask it to send you software for a free trial account. During the trial period, use the Web browser in their package to download Navigator.

- Use your modem communications software to download a copy of Microsoft Internet Explorer from the Microsoft Download Service, as described later in this chapter.

Obtaining Microsoft Internet Explorer

Microsoft's Internet Explorer Web browser has a smaller share of the Web browser market, but it's gaining rapidly. Microsoft distributes the program with Windows 95 and as part of the Microsoft Network and Internet Starter Kit software. Microsoft also has distribution deals with other major online services, including America Online and CompuServe, and with several of the largest Internet service providers. Internet Explorer is also available for download through the Internet. Microsoft is so anxious to cut into Netscape's control of the marketplace that it gives away Internet Explorer. That's free — no charge.

Microsoft distributes Internet Explorer through several channels:

* With Windows 95 and the Microsoft Plus add-on package
* As part of the Microsoft Internet Starter Kit or the Internet Explorer Starter Kit
* Through online information services, such as America Online and CompuServe
* Through major Internet service providers
* Via free download from Microsoft. If you already have some other Web browser, you can obtain Internet Explorer from http://www.microsoft. com/ie/ie.htm. It's also available via FTP from ftp.microsoft.com/ msdownload/ieinstall (for Windows) or ftp.microsoft.com/ msdownload/iemac (for Macintosh). This directory contains subdirectories with versions of Internet Explorer in many languages. The index.txt file in each directory contains a description of all the files in that directory.

  If you don't have access to the Internet yet, you can use a communications program such as CrossTalk or HyperTerminal to get a copy of the American English version of Internet Explorer from the Microsoft Download Service, which you can reach by using your modem to call 206-936-6735. Unless you're in the metropolitan Seattle area, this is a long-distance call, so you may want to wait until late at night when the rates are low. The Internet Explorer software is hidden under the Miscellaneous Files library in the Microsoft Windows/Windows 95 Menu. Look for a file called MSIE*XXX*.EXE, with the current version number in place of the *XXX*.

Installing Your Browser

You have Navigator or Internet Explorer (or both) and you're ready to install it. Now what? If you have the browser software on a CD-ROM, look for a program called Setup.exe in the CD's root directory or folder. Run that program and the browser will install itself on your hard drive.

If you have the software on diskette or if you downloaded it, you probably have an .EXE file with a bunch of letters and numbers in the name that contains the browser files in compressed form.

Follow these steps to open the compressed file and install the program:

1. Create a temporary folder or directory and copy the compressed file to it.

2. Run the program. Several new programs will appear in the same folder or directory.

3. Run the Setup.exe program from the temporary file. The browser's installation routine creates a new directory or folder to contain the program files, copies the necessary files to that folder, and then starts installing your browser.

Configuring Netscape Navigator

It's entirely possible to use Netscape Navigator just as it installs itself, but there are a few things you can do that make it easier to work with the program. Among other things, you can change the size and typeface that Navigator uses to display text with larger, easier-to-read options, and you can change the background color. To change the configuration, open the Options menu and click General Preferences.

Color

Figure 5-1 shows the dialog box that appears when you click the Colors tab. As a general rule, the best color choices give you as much contrast as possible between the text and the background. For most people, dark text on a light background is easier to read than light-on-dark. Therefore, you may want to use black text on a white or off-white background.

To change a color, follow these steps:

1. Select the element whose color you want to change and click the Choose Color button on the same line.

2. When the Color dialog box appears, click the color that you want to use.

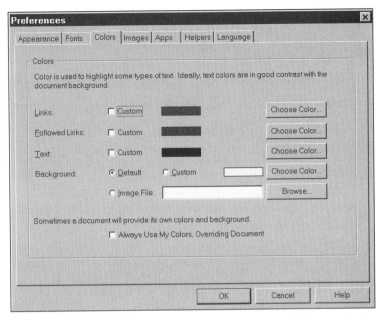

Figure 5-1 Use the Colors dialog box to set text and background colors.

Type

Web pages use two kinds of text: *proportional fonts* and *fixed fonts*. In a proportional font, different letters have different widths. For example, compare the width of the letters *i* and *m* in this sentence. Most headlines and body text in Web pages appear in a proportional font. Fixed fonts display all letters and other characters with the same width. You will see fixed fonts on Web pages in tables and columns of numbers.

Serifs are the little marks at the top and bottom of letters in many type fonts. They are supposed to lead the reader's eye from one letter to the next, which makes a block of text on a printed page easier to read. However, typefaces on a computer screen without serifs are easier to read than serif faces. In particular, Arial is a good choice for a proportional font, and Lucida Console is a good fixed font.

To change fonts, follow these steps:

1. Click the Fonts tab to display the dialog box in Figure 5-2.

2. Click one of the Choose Font buttons to see a list of available fonts for each type of text display.

3. Use the scroll bar in the Font list to find the typeface you want to use and then highlight the name of that font. An example of the currently selected font appears in the Sample box.

4. Select a type size from the Size list.

5. Click OK to save your choice and close the Choose Font dialog box.

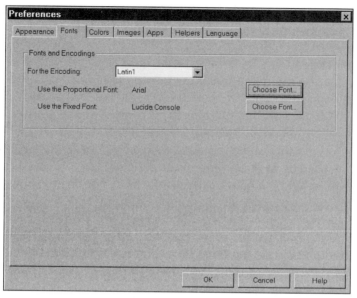

Figure 5-2 The Netscape Fonts dialog box.

Several other tabs appear in the Preferences window, but you probably won't want to make any changes to those options right now. To save your configuration, click OK.

Configuring Internet Explorer

The first time you run Internet Explorer in Windows 95, an Internet Connection Wizard may ask if you want to establish a new connection to the Internet or use one that already exists. If you have set up Dial-Up Networking to use an account with an ISP, select that option. Otherwise, choose the option that sets up access to either Microsoft Network or another ISP of your choice.

After you've specified a connection, Internet Explorer automatically connects you to an online setup site, where you can register the program and download some add-on programs that will enhance Internet Explorer's operation. Microsoft has also arranged for free access to some Web sites that charge for access with other browsers (part of the ongoing battle with Netscape for market share). Registering is generally a good idea, because that gives the software developer a way to tell you when new versions of the program (or fixes to the existing version) become available.

Changing Your Start Page

After you work through the Welcome to Internet Explorer pages, you end up at a list of links to other Microsoft Web sites. One of these sites is the default Internet Explorer Start Page at home.microsoft.com, which automatically opens when you start the program unless you choose to change it. If you obtained your copy of Internet Explorer from an ISP or online service, you might have a different default start page.

You can use the default as your start page if you want, but that page is not your only option. If you prefer, you can let Microsoft create a customized home page for you, you can create one of your own, or you can use any other Web page as your start page. The best choice depends on the way you expect to use the Web; if you start all your online sessions by checking the same site, you can save some time by making that your start page. But if you go somewhere different every time you log on, the choice of a start page is less important.

To specify a different Web page as your start page in Internet Explorer, follow these steps:

1. Use the Internet Explorer Address field or a link to open the Web page that you want to use as your start page.

2. Select ☐ **View** → ☐ **Options** .

3. Click the Navigation tab to display the dialog box in Figure 5-3.

4. In the Customize box at the top of the dialog box, use the drop-down menu in the Page field to select Start Page.

5. Click Use Current.

Figure 5-3 The Internet Explorer Navigation Properties dialog box.

Changing the Appearance of Internet Explorer

If you don't like the way Internet Explorer looks when you install it, you can change the text and background colors, change standard typefaces, and hide portions of the toolbar that you don't expect to use. In general, the default settings are more-or-less acceptable, but you might want to do some minor tweaking to make Web pages easier to read.

To change the appearance of the Internet Explorer screen, either right-click the Internet icon on your desktop or select View → Options . Click the General tab to display the dialog box shown in Figure 5-4.

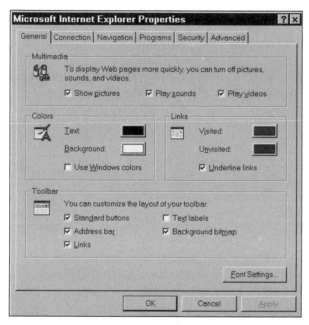

Figure 5-4   The Internet Explorer General Properties tab.

The options that appear in the General Properties tab are described in the following sections.

MULTIMEDIA

Many Web sites include pictures, audio recordings, and animated images along with text. These multimedia elements may make pages more interesting, but they also increase the amount of time needed to transfer a page to your computer. If you turn off one or more of these embedded file types, the Web pages will load and display a lot more quickly — even if you miss part of the page designer's original intention.

If you don't have a sound card in your computer, sounds in Web pages won't do you any good even if you do download them. Therefore, you should turn off the Play sounds option to speed up download time.

When you have Show pictures or Play videos turned off, Internet Explorer displays a frame with the name of the image in place of the picture or video. If you want to see the image, click inside the frame.

COLORS

If the designer of a Web page did not specify text and background colors, Internet Explorer uses the colors specified in the Colors box. If the Use Windows colors option is active, Internet Explorer uses the colors that Windows uses for other programs. If Use Windows colors is not active, you can specify text and background colors by clicking the buttons that show the current color selections.

As a general rule, the best combination is dark text on a light background.

LINKS

Internet Explorer displays links to other Web sites in contrasting colors so that they are easy to identify. Text links appear in a different color from surrounding text, whereas image links have a colored border. After you visit a site, the link color changes. The Visited and Unvisited buttons specify the colors used for links.

If contrasting colors are not enough to let you spot links easily within a block of text, you can also underline them.

TOOLBAR

The Internet Explorer toolbar is the block of controls located at the top of the screen. Some controls are more useful than others, and most are also accessible from a menu. If you don't ever use part of the toolbar, you can remove it by removing the check mark next to the name of that element.

FONT SETTINGS

HTML code does not always specify the typeface in which text appears on your screen. When no other information is provided, Internet Explorer uses the fonts specified in the dialog box that appears when you click the Font Settings button.

The typeface specified in the Proportional Font field is used for body and headline text; it's called *proportional* because different characters have different widths. As the name suggests, the Fixed-width font is used in places where every character must have the same width, such as tables and columns of numbers.

The fonts you use in Internet Explorer should be easy to read on your screen. The default typefaces, Times Roman and Courier, are okay, but some better choices are available. Arial is a good alternative proportional font, and Lucida Console is a similar fixed-width font.

BONUS

Keeping Up with New Releases

It's important to remember that a Web browser is a tool; you should be much more interested in using it to find content on the World Wide Web than in mastering every obscure command and function of Netscape Navigator or Internet Explorer. Many of those features are no more essential to navigating the Web than the cup holders in your car are essential to driving. And like those cup holders, the browsers' features will change in the next model.

Remember that both companies are trying to make their money by selling Web servers rather than browsers. Therefore, when they release a server with new features, they are anxious to get browsers that recognize those features onto as many users' computers as possible. That's why these companies give away browser software — it's not quite as bad as the America Online diskettes that used to come with the peanuts on airplanes, but it comes close.

Both Netscape and Microsoft are scurrying to create new versions of their Web browsers. These programs have been under constant revision since they were introduced. Every new release supports a new set of server features and looks somewhat different from the one it replaced. Therefore, don't be surprised to discover that the pictures of Navigator or Internet Explorer screens in this book don't look exactly like the ones you see on your own screen.

Where to Find New Software

Before you update your current software, you should find out which version you're currently using. Open the About Internet Explorer window (Figure 5-5) or the About Netscape window (Figure 5-6) from the Help menu to see the version number.

Figure 5-5 The About Internet Explorer window, including the current version number.

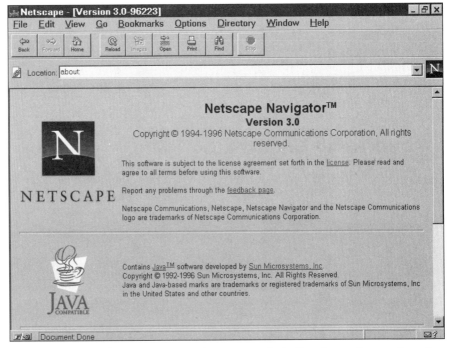

Figure 5-6 The About Netscape Navigator page, including the version number of the software.

To update Microsoft Internet Explorer to the latest release, follow these steps:

1. Jump to the Microsoft Internet Explorer Web site at `http://www.microsoft.com/ie/default.asp`. The Internet Explorer page shown in Figure 5-7 appears.

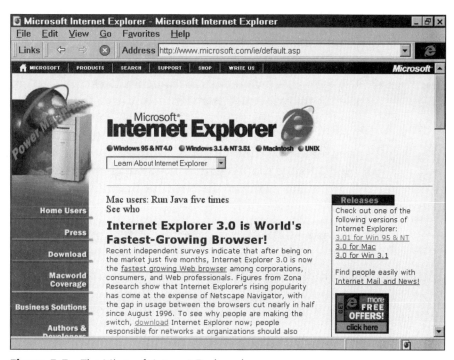

Figure 5-7   The Microsoft Internet Explorer home page.

2. Find the list of Releases and confirm that there is a version for your operating system with a higher release number than the one you're currently using.

3. If a newer version does exist, click the link to jump to the Download Area.

4. Use the drop-down menus to select the version and language you want to use and the source from which you want to download the software. These are big files, so they take a while to download — possibly an hour or more, depending on your modem speed.

TIP **To reduce the download time, select one of the Typical or Minimum install options. You can download the additional features separately later.**

5. When the computer asks if you want to open the program or save it to disk, choose Save it to Disk and store the file in a new temporary directory.

6. Close your browser and disconnect from the Internet.

7. Open the temporary directory where you stored the new software and run the program. The setup program will uncompress the files, load them over your existing files, and install the new version of Internet Explorer.

To update Netscape Navigator to the most recent release, follow these steps:

1. Jump to the Netscape download page at `http://home.netscape.com/comprod/mirror/client_download.html`.

2. Use the drop-down menus in Figure 5-8 to choose the version, operating system, and language you want to use, and the region from which you are requesting the software. For the Web browser only, choose the highest version number of Netscape Navigator — Standard. For additional browser features and functions, choose the "plus components" version. For a package that includes a newsreader and mail client along with the browser, choose one of the Netscape Communicator options.

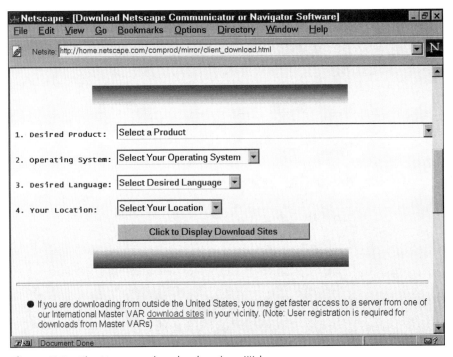

Figure 5-8 The Netscape download options Web page.

3. Click the link to Download sites to see a list of servers from which you can download the version you specified.

4. Choose one of the download links. If that server refuses the connection, try other links until you are able to get through to a server.

5. Transfer the Netscape file to a temporary folder on your hard disk.

6. When the download is complete, run the self-extracting file to install the program.

Preliminary versus Final Versions

During the development cycle, both Netscape and Microsoft make preliminary *beta* versions of new releases available for users to test and evaluate. In traditional software development, the earliest (or *alpha*) versions are tested within the company that created the software. During the beta test stage, the developers allow outside users to work with the program and identify bugs and potential problems in "real world" settings while the developers have time to fix them.

Before the Internet, beta testing was limited to carefully selected users who agreed to send back periodic test reports, because of the high cost of duplicating and distributing the software. Today, many companies, including Netscape and Microsoft, make some beta software available to anybody who wants to download it through the Internet. The software usually has a cut-off date built in to the program that disables it at or before the anticipated release date of the final product. If you're a Web page designer or a developer of servers or plug-in client programs who wants to make sure your work will be compatible with the browsers that your users will be using six months from now, you need to keep up with the beta versions of both browsers.

Most people reading this book are probably not in any of those categories. Assuming that you're a consumer rather than a creator of Web sites, you can generally get along just fine with the current release. If you want a preview of coming attractions, or if you like to be among the very first on your block to see new products, you may want to consider playing with beta software. But if you do, don't be surprised when it doesn't work properly — or even when it crashes your computer. That's why the developers are still testing it. If you do have a problem, please take the time to tell the developer what you've discovered so the final release includes a fix.

Summary

This chapter explained how and where to obtain and install the two most popular Web browsers: Netscape Navigator and Microsoft Internet Explorer. Both programs are widely available and about equal in features and ease of use.

Now it's time to start exploring the World Wide Web. In the next chapter, you find information about using search engines, directories, online Internet guides, and other tools for locating specific information.

6

Using URLs

Every Web page and every other file on all the servers connected to the Internet have a unique identity that your Web browser can use to find that file. The World Wide Web uses a standard format for filenames and addresses called a *Uniform Resource Locator*, almost always abbreviated as *URL*.

You will use URLs to instruct your Web browser to take you to a new site and to tell somebody where to find a particular item on the Web. For example, the pointers to Web sites that you see in magazines, on television, and on the sides of buses are URLs. You'll also find URLs throughout this book. For example, in

85

Chapter 5, when I pointed to the Netscape site where you can download the latest version of Navigator, I used the URL `http://home.netscape.com`.

URLs look like this:

type://address/path/file.name

A URL includes the following information:

* The type of server on which the file is located. The most common types include http (**h**ypertext **t**ransfer **p**rotocol) for Web pages and other HTML documents, ftp (**f**ile **t**ransfer **p**rotocol) for files available for download from ftp servers, and gopher for Gopher menus. You may see other type designators in URLs, but these are the most common.

* The most common URL type designation is http. If you enter a URL without a type, both Netscape Navigator and Microsoft Internet Explorer automatically add the http designation.

* A colon and two forward slashes (://). This combination of symbols identifies the string of characters that includes it as a URL.

* The address of the server. Many sites identify their Web servers by adding a subdomain onto the Domain Name Service (DNS) address they use for e-mail and other Internet services. So, a company whose DNS address is widgets.com might use www.widgets.com for its Web site and ftp.widgets.com for its FTP archive.

* The location of the HTML document or file within the server's file structure. As you know, DOS and Windows systems use a backslash (\) to separate directories and subdirectories in a path. Other operating systems, including UNIX (which is used on many Internet file servers), use a forward slash (/). You may see either forward- or backslashes in a URL, but almost never both types in a single URL.

* The full name of the document or file.

Some URLs are carefully constructed to be easy to remember; they look like plain language, more or less. The site called home.microsoft.com is pretty clearly a Microsoft home page. But others seem to have been designed by computer programmers for their own convenience, such as `ftp://sunsite.unc.edu/pub/micro/pc-stuff/eisa-configs/ACB-2322.tgz`. Either way, typing the URL into your browser exactly as it was provided to you is essential; if you get even a single character wrong, you won't be able to reach the site that it identifies.

Using the Address Field

Now you know what a URL looks like. How do you turn a URL into a Web page on your screen? Both Navigator and Internet Explorer have boxes in their toolbars where you can enter a new URL. Microsoft and

Netscape use different names for this field, but the procedure for typing in a URL is about the same in both programs.

Follow these steps to enter a new URL in Netscape Navigator:

1. Type the URL into the Location field in the toolbar, as shown in Figure 6-1.

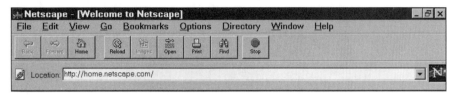

Figure 6-1 The Location field within the Netscape Navigator toolbar.

2. Press Enter. The Web page or other file you requested appears in the main section of the Netscape window.

Follow these steps to enter a new URL in Internet Explorer:

1. Type the URL into the Address field in the toolbar, as shown in Figure 6-2.

Figure 6-2 The Address field within the Microsoft Internet Explorer toolbar.

2. Press Enter.

Using Hot Links

The entire World Wide Web is based on *hot links* from one Web site to another. A hot link in a Web page is a pointer to another Web page or to some other kind of file. You can jump from the current page to the new one by clicking the link.

A link can be a picture, a graphic image (such as a company's logo), or a word or phrase in a headline or within a block of text. Text links usually appear on your screen in a different color from other text; some (but not all) graphic links may have a border around them in the same color as a text link.

When your cursor is over a link, your browser may display the URL of the destination in the status bar at the bottom of the window. While a copy of the new page is loading, information about the progress of the transfer appears in the status bar. For example, take a look at a Web site in Singapore that has lots of links to other sites in that country:

1. In the Address or Location field, type **http://www.sintercom.org/ makan/award/sin.html** and press Enter. You will see the Best of Singapore page shown in Figure 6-3.

Figure 6-3 The Best of Singapore home page.

2. Move your mouse over the Food/entertainment link. Notice that the arrow changes to a pointing finger. This shape identifies this word or phrase as a link, even if it's not underlined.

3. Click the Food/entertainment link. You will jump to a list of specific links, as shown in Figure 6-4.

4. Click the first entry, Makan Time in Singapore. You will jump to a site called the Singapore Unofficial Food Page, with links to information about places to eat in that country and places to find Singaporean food in other parts of the world (including some recipes for those who want to prepare it in their own kitchens).

NOTE Many links appear in text as underlined words in a contrasting color. But others are hidden within pictures and graphic images such as maps and symbols. When you move your mouse around the screen, if you see the cursor change to a pointing finger, you're over a link. Click the mouse to jump to a new site or to a different location within the page.

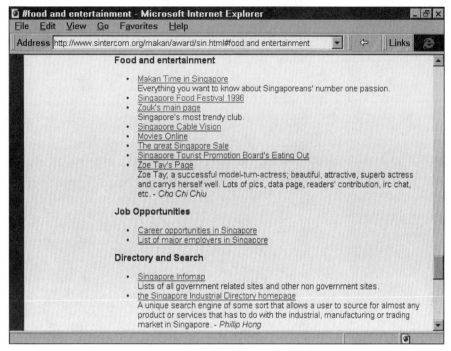

Figure 6-4 Food and entertainment on the Best of Singapore page.

For example, in the Singapore Food page shown in Figure 6-5, you'll see an image link in the upper-left corner, called Dining Guide. Click the image to jump to a directory of eating places.

Note that a link doesn't always take you to a new page. Sometimes links at the top of a page contain a sort of table of contents for that page; when you click a link, you jump down to another section of the same page. Many pages also have Return to the Top links that take you back to the beginning of the page without using the scrollbars.

Once you've found a list of interesting links, you can easily jump from one page to another by following the links on each page to yet another page. In fact, it's almost too easy. If you're not careful, you can find yourself spending hours jumping to "just one more page" that sounds like it might be interesting. You have been warned.

One final warning about following links: they don't always work. The Internet is full of pages that somebody has placed on a server and then ignored. In the meantime, the destinations of the links on some of those pages have either changed or disappeared. When you click one of these out-of-date links, you will see a message like the one in Figure 6-6. The text may be slightly different, but the message is the same — you can't get there from here. The only thing you can do when you see one of these "Not Found" messages is to return to the page from which you tried to jump and try some other link.

Figure 6-5   Click Dining Guide to see a directory of eating places.

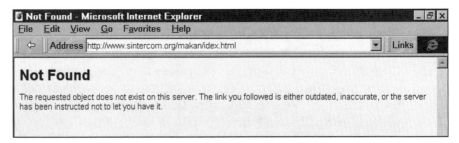

Figure 6-6   The result of an attempt to jump to a non-existent Web page.

Retracing Your Steps

Eventually, you will want to return to a page you've already seen, either because you've come to a dead-end site with no more links to follow, you want to try another path from one of the sites you've seen, or you want to refresh your memory about some of the information on a page. If you've been keeping careful notes, you could retype the original URL, but the reality is that you haven't kept that kind of record – nobody does. The easier method is to use the forward and backward arrows in your browser's toolbar. Figure 6-7 shows the Microsoft Internet Explorer and Netscape Navigator toolbars.

Figure 6-7   The Microsoft (top) and Netscape (bottom) toolbars.

Follow these steps to return to a site:

1. Click a link in the current page of your browser. You will jump to a new site.

2. Click another link in the new page to jump to a third page.

3. Now click the "back" arrow (pointing to the left) in the toolbar. You're now back at the second page.

4. Click the back arrow again to return to the original page.

5. This time, click the "forward" arrow (pointing to the right). This repeats the last link you used from this page, so you're now at page 2.

Using Bookmarks and Favorites Lists

L iterally millions of pages are on the World Wide Web; keeping track of pages you want to re-visit can be a major nuisance. Arrow buttons give you an easy way to move back and forth between Web sites during a single browsing session, but they don't do you much good when you want to return to a site you visited last month.

The solution to this problem is to create and use a list of links to sites that you expect to use again. Netscape calls the items on this list *bookmarks*, whereas Microsoft does exactly the same thing with *favorites*.

Internet Explorer

Follow these steps to add a site to your Favorites list in Internet Explorer:

1. Open the page you want to save by using a link from another site or by typing the URL in the Address box.

2. Select   Favorites → Add to Favorites . If you prefer, you can use the Favorites button in the toolbar instead of the menu.

The next time you open the Favorites menu, you will see the title of that page on the list. To jump to a site in your Favorites list, double-click the site's name.

Netscape Navigator

The process is almost exactly the same in Netscape Navigator. Here's the procedure:

1. Open the page you want to save by using a link from some other page or by typing the URL into the Location field.

2. Select Bookmarks → Add Bookmarks .

The name of the current site appears in the Bookmarks list the next time you open it, as shown in Figure 6-8. To jump to that site, click the name.

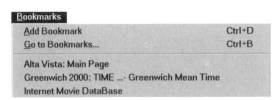

Figure 6-8 The Netscape Bookmarks list.

Organizing Your List

Bookmarks and favorites are a convenient way to store links to interesting sites, but when you have more than about 20 links, the list begins to get out of control. Even if you arrange everything in alphabetical order, it's no longer easy to find a link when you want it. There's an easy solution to this problem: create a batch of folders within your list for different categories.

Once again, the procedure is almost exactly the same for both browsers. Follow these steps in Netscape Navigator:

1. Select Bookmarks → Go to Bookmarks to open the window in Figure 6-9.

2. To create a new folder, select Item → Insert Folder .

3. Type the name you want to assign to this folder.

4. Drag and drop the name of the new folder to the position where you want it to appear within the list of bookmarks.

5. Drag and drop the name of the bookmarks you want to place in the new folder to the folder where you want it to appear.

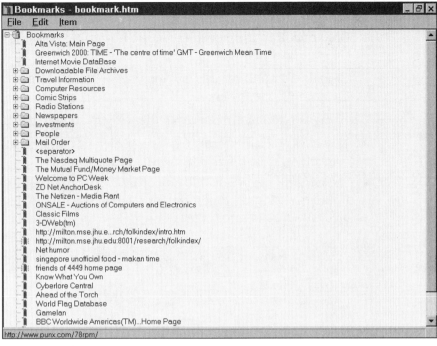

Figure 6-9 The Netscape Bookmarks window.

Follow these steps in Microsoft Internet Explorer:

1. Select **Favorites** → **Organize Favorites** .

2. When the Organize Favorites window shown in Figure 6-10 appears, click the button with the file folder on it. An entry called New Folder will appear at the end of the list of links.

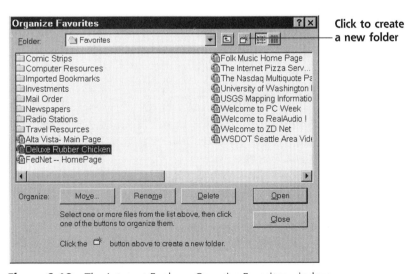

Click to create a new folder

Figure 6-10 The Internet Explorer Organize Favorites window.

3. Type the name you want to assign to this folder over "New Folder."

4. Drag and drop the new folder to the beginning of the Favorites list, or click the Move button.

5. Drag and drop the names of items you want to place in the new folder to the name of the folder.

There are two major differences in the way the browsers handle their lists:

✳ The list of sites in Internet Explorer is always in alphabetical order, but you can arrange them in any order in Netscape.

✳ Netscape allows you to add one or more separator lines like the ones in Figure 6-11. The separator makes a long list easier to read, because it breaks it up into smaller pieces.

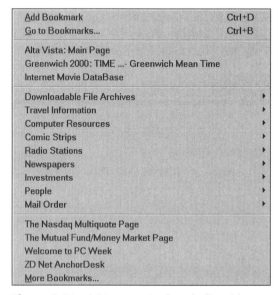

Figure 6-11 A Netscape Bookmarks list with separator lines.

Using Permanent Links

In addition to the Favorites list, Internet Explorer's toolbar contains a Links panel with five buttons that take you directly to specific Web sites of your choice. Netscape gives you a set of Directory buttons that have a similar function, but you can't change the destination of the Netscape links.

When you install Internet Explorer, all five Links point to Microsoft sites, but changing them to the sites you visit most often is an easy enough task. For example, if you use the Web to read a couple of out-of-town newspapers every day, or if you want to check the current value of your investments, you can assign those sites to Links buttons.

How are Links different from the Favorites list? They really aren't, except that they require fewer mouse clicks. Microsoft has created a hierarchy of permanent Links that looks like this:

* **Start Page.** Loads automatically every time you open Internet Explorer (no mouse clicks)
* **Links.** Loads when you click a button in the toolbar (one mouse click)
* **Favorites.** Loads when you open the `Favorites` menu and click a name (two or three mouse clicks)

To change one of the Links, follow these steps:

1. Use the Address toolbar or a link from another site to open the page you want to assign to a Links button.

2. Select `View` → `Options`.

3. Click the Navigation tab to display the dialog box shown in Figure 6-12.

Figure 6-12 The Internet Explorer Navigation options tab.

4. In the Customize box, click the arrow button at the right side of the Page field to open the drop-down menu.

5. Double-click the Quick Link number of the button you want to use.

6. Click the Use Current button. The URL of the current page will appear in the Address field.

7. Type a very brief description of the site in the Name field. The toolbar only has space for about 14 letters, so you may not have room for the whole title; for example, you'll only see "The Washin..." instead of "The Washington Post."

8. Click OK at the bottom of the window to save this choice and close the dialog box.

If the added convenience of avoiding one whole mouse click every time you want to jump to your favorite site doesn't appeal to you, you can hide the Links panel and forget about the whole idea.

To hide the Links toolbar, follow these steps:

1. Select View → Options .

2. If it's not already visible, click the General tab. You see the dialog box shown in Figure 6-13.

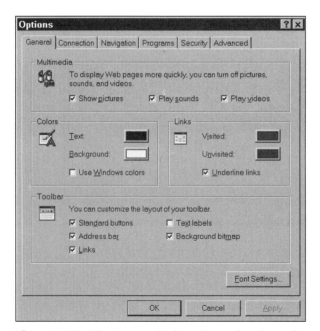

Figure 6-13 The Internet Explorer General options tab.

3. In the Toolbar box at the bottom of the window, click Links to remove the check mark.

4. Click OK to close the dialog box.

BONUS

Using Other Application Programs within Your Browser

A s the two major Web browsers continue to add features, the line between your own computer and the rest of the Internet will grow even more vague than it is today. In future versions of Internet Explorer, you will see Web-browsing features built into the Windows desktop and into local application programs such as Microsoft Word and Excel. It's inevitable that Netscape will offer similar features in Navigator.

The current versions of both Netscape Navigator and Internet Explorer are not as tightly integrated into the operating system as they will be a year from now, but they do include a few features that enable a user to hide some of the boundaries. In this section, you can find information about using other Microsoft programs from inside Internet Explorer and creating direct shortcuts to Web sites from the Windows desktop.

Opening Local Files within Internet Explorer

Today, both Navigator and Internet Explorer come as separate applications rather than as part of the operating system. However, you can open some other Microsoft application programs from within Internet Explorer, using Microsoft's ActiveX technology. If this is important to you, it could be a reason to choose Internet Explorer rather than Netscape Navigator as your Web browser.

This feature has several uses:

* You can download files and documents from Web sites with all the original formatting intact.
* You can import text, data files, and graphic images from a Web page directly into your own document, spreadsheet, or presentation page.
* You can move between Web pages and local documents or files without opening two separate application programs.

When you load a Word, Excel, or Access file into Internet Explorer, the browser automatically incorporates the menus and toolbars for the appropriate application into the Internet Explorer window. For example, Figure 6-14 shows a Word document within Internet Explorer. Note that the menu bar includes both

Word menus and Internet Explorer menus, and that the Word toolbars are visible under the Internet Explorer toolbars. For all practical purposes, you can use both sets of commands, just as you would use them when running each program separately. The only Word commands that are not accessible from within Internet Explorer are the ones in the Window menu; if you want to open a second Word document, select File → New Window .

Figure 6-14 A Microsoft Word document within Internet Explorer.

Figure 6-15 shows an Excel spreadsheet inside Internet Explorer. Once again, notice that the menus and toolbars from both programs are visible within the Internet Explorer window.

When you access Word, Excel, or some other program within Internet Explorer, keep in mind that you're opening a link between the browser and the other application. If you don't have a copy of the second application, you won't be able to use this feature.

Follow these steps to load a local document or file into Internet Explorer:

1. Select File → Open or press Ctrl+O. The Open dialog box in Figure 6-16 appears.

2. Type the full path of the file you want to open or click the Browse button to open a file directory.

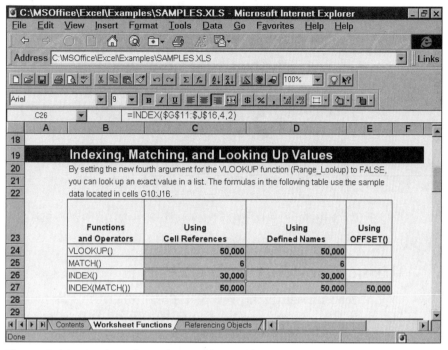

Figure 6-15 A Microsoft Excel spreadsheet within Internet Explorer.

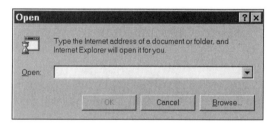

Figure 6-16 The Internet Explorer Open dialog box.

3. Click OK in the Open dialog box to open the file. The dialog box in Figure 6-17 may appear.

4. Select Open It and click OK. The file you requested will open within the Internet Explorer window.

If you prefer, you can type the full path of the file you want to open in Internet Explorer's Address toolbar instead of using the Open command.

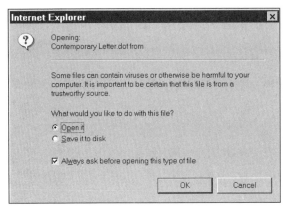

Figure 6-17 The Internet Explorer "opening file" dialog box.

Using Shortcuts to Web Pages

Your Web browser treats Web pages and other URLs as files that it downloads through the Internet to your computer. As far as the operating system is concerned, a URL is a file type that is associated with your browser, just as a data file might be associated with a spreadsheet application. Therefore, Windows can treat shortcuts to Web pages just as it handles shortcuts to data files located on your own system. In other words, when you select a shortcut, Windows automatically starts the correct application, which loads the file that is the shortcut's target. Thus, you can place shortcuts to Web sites on your desktop or in the Windows 95 Start menu.

You can think of this feature as a sort of super-level Favorites or Bookmarks list. Just as those lists eliminate the need for re-typing a full URL every time you visit a Web site, a desktop shortcut eliminates the need to open the browser before you jump to a site that you visit frequently.

For example, if you use one of the stock market Web sites several times a day to check the current value of your investments, you could create a shortcut that takes you directly to that site. To visit the site, just click the shortcut icon.

Follow these steps to create a shortcut in Netscape Navigator:

1. Start Navigator and jump to the site for which you want to create a shortcut.

2. Move your cursor to a location on the page where it is *not* over a link.

3. Click the right mouse button. A menu appears that includes the options shown in Figure 6-18. The menu may also include some other options, but you will always see these four.

Figure 6-18   The Netscape Navigator right-click menu.

4. Click Internet Shortcut. The Create Internet Shortcut dialog box shown in Figure 6-19 appears.

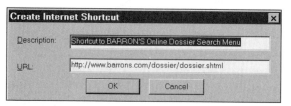

Figure 6-19   The Create Internet Shortcut dialog box.

5. The text in the Description field will be the title that appears under the shortcut icon on your desktop. If you want to change the title, edit the Description field text. For example, in this sample, you may want to change it to "Barron's Dossier" or even "Stock Quotes."

6. Click OK to create the shortcut.

7. Close the browser. You will see the shortcut you just created on your desktop. The shortcut uses the Netscape icon. You can change this to another icon just as you would change any other icon.

Follow these steps to create a shortcut in Internet Explorer:

1. Start Internet Explorer and jump to the site for which you want to create a shortcut.

2. Select | Menu | → | Create Shortcut |. The information window shown in Figure 6-20 appears.

Figure 6-20   The Internet Explorer Create Shortcut information window.

3. Click OK.

4. Close Internet Explorer. You will see the new shortcut on your desktop.

5. To change the title of the shortcut, right-click the icon and use the | Rename | command.

If you don't want to clutter your desktop with shortcuts to Web sites, you can move them to your Start menu by dragging each icon to the Start button and dropping it.

Summary

The information in this chapter is enough to get you started exploring the World Wide Web without getting hopelessly lost. If you haven't already done so, you may want to spend a few hours exploring Web sites and following links, just to see where they take you.

But wandering around the Web without a trained, native guide is not the most effective or efficient way to find anything. You'll probably discover half a dozen other fascinating sites, but when you're facing a deadline, or when you just *know* that a particular tidbit of information is out there somewhere, you probably need help.

It's helpful to think about the World Wide Web as a gigantic version of the public library. Just as the library might have millions of books on the shelves, millions of sites are on the Web (including a great many library catalogs). And like the library, you can use catalogs and other search tools to find the things you want. In the next chapter, you learn about some of the best online search tools and guides and how to use them.

CHAPTER SEVEN

FINDING THINGS ON THE WEB

Search Tools

Search tools (also called *search engines*) are interactive sites on the World Wide Web that contain databases with lists of other Web sites, organized by name, subject, or other category. When you type a keyword into a search field, the search tool gives you a set of links to Web sites that contain information related to that keyword. Depending on the keyword, you might get as many as several thousand matching *hits*.

When you choose the keywords for a search, you should type them in a form that allows the search engine to limit the search. You'll get better at this with practice, but don't be surprised when you enter the keywords *apple cider*, and AltaVista returns 50 or 60 items about fermented fruit juice and 40,000 links to sites related to Apple computers.

Each search tool uses a different list of sites and a different set of rules for matching sites to keywords, so you may get somewhat different lists with each tool. Therefore, knowing how to run the same search through more than one search engine can be helpful.

All the Web search tools have their own Web sites, with text fields where you can enter keywords, and links to topic directories or other Web pages offered by the company that maintains the service. Because most of these pages offer detailed instructions for using their particular search engine, it's a good idea to take a look at them at least once or twice. Another possibility is to submit a request directly to a search engine from other Web sites. You will see links to one or more of the major search engines from many other Web sites.

When you enter more than one keyword, most search engines return items that include one or more of those words. It may list the pages first that have all the words you requested, but (as in the apple cider example) you will also get pointers to many pages that contain only one keyword. There are several ways to limit your search:

* To treat two or more words as a phrase rather than unrelated words, place quotation marks around them. An AltaVista search for **"apple cider"** (with quotation marks) found about 2,000 matching documents.

* To limit the search to pages that include more than one keyword (even if they're not a single phrase), place a plus sign (+) between the words. As you would expect, a **keyword1+keyword2** (no quotation marks) search will find all the pages that a **"keyword1 keyword2"** search finds, plus others where the two words appear separately.

* To restrict a search to pages that include one or more keywords but do *not* include some other keyword, use a minus sign (-). Make sure you place a space before the minus sign, or the search engine will treat it as a hyphen. For example, to look for pages about apple cider that don't talk about vinegar, search for **apple+cider -vinegar.**

* To search for more than one form of a keyword, use an asterisk (*) as a wildcard in place of one or more letters. For example, a search for **apple*** would produce links to *applesauce, applewood* and *Appleton* as well as *apple* and *apples.*

Searching with Yahoo!

Yahoo! (`http://www.yahoo.com`) organizes Web sites into categories, which makes it a good place to start when you want to find many sites related to a general topic. But it usually doesn't find as many direct hits as some other search engines.

One of Yahoo!'s strengths is its capability to let you drill down from a broad general category to more specific subtopics. At each level, Yahoo! tells you the number of links to sites related to each subtopic. Under the list of subtopics, each page shows links to related sites.

Follow these steps to perform a search through Yahoo!:

1. Type one or more keywords into the search field. For example, "apple cider." The quotation marks tell the search engine to read the two words as a single phrase.

2. Click the Search button. Yahoo! returns a page that contains a list of all matches. In this case, Yahoo found only seven matches, of which four are duplicated listings. But if you want to know about sources for other beverages, you can click on the Business and Economy:Companies: Drinks topic heading and find links to several hundred other sites.

Searching with Excite

Excite (`http://www.excite.com`) uses something called a *concept search*, which means that it will give you links to sites related to your keywords, even if the words themselves don't appear there. Each link includes a number expressed in percent, which shows Excite's level of confidence that this link matches the topic you want. Excite also offers subjective reviews of Web sites, which can be useful when you want to see a description of a site before you visit it.

Even more than some of its competitors, Excite works best when you use a very specific set of keywords. For example, a search on *apple cider* found 6,171 documents. Among the first 20 items were recipes for cider vinegar and hot spiced cider and a home page for an antique shop called The Cider Mill. When you search on *"making apple cider"* (with quotation marks around the words), you get 1,898 documents, all more-or-less related to pressing and producing the stuff rather than using it after it's already been made. If you leave out the quotation marks, however, you get more than 2 million hits, because Excite includes every single page with any of those three words.

To run an Excite search, follow these steps:

1. Go to the Excite home page at `http://www.excite.com/`.

2. Type the keywords for your search in the What field.

3. In the Where field, select World Wide Web from the drop-down menu.

4. Click the Search button.

To obtain Excite's review of sites that match your keywords, use the drop-down menu to select Excite Web Site Reviews.

Searching with AltaVista

AltaVista (`www.altavista.digital.com`) was the first full-text Web index. When you submit a keyword, AltaVista searches its index of more than 30 million Web pages on about 275,000 servers and returns a list of links to every site that contains the keyword. It's also one of the fastest of the major Internet search engines. Several other Internet search tools, including Yahoo!, use the software originally developed for AltaVista.

NOTE AltaVista is the only search engine that has its own blimp, which appeared over Yankee Stadium during the 1996 World Series.

As you might expect, many AltaVista searches produce a *huge* number of hits. It assigns a score to each hit and lists pages with the highest scores first. AltaVista assigns a higher score to pages where the keywords appear in the first few words of the document, pages in which the keywords appear closer to one another within the document, and where pages the keywords appear more than once. Like other search engines, it lists what it thinks are the best matches at the top of the list.

With quotation marks around the words "apple cider," AltaVista returned about 2,000 matching documents. Without the quotation marks, the search engine found five times as many hits. *Making apple cider* (no quotes) produced about 30,000 matches, but most of them contained only one or two of the three words.

AltaVista is an excellent tool when you know what you want to find before you start looking. For example, follow these steps to find historical information about the famous Johnstown Flood, which destroyed much of that Pennsylvania city in 1889:

1. Type **"Johnstown flood"** in AltaVista's search field and click the Submit button.

2. Within a few seconds, you will receive a list of matching sites, Click the first entry in the list to jump to a page about the flood prepared by the Johnstown Redevelopment Authority.

Searching with Lycos

Lycos (`http://www.lycos.com`) gives you several different kinds of searches. In addition to the now-familiar keyword search of the whole Internet, the Lycos site also includes a sites-by-subject list that organizes pages by topic and its list of the Top 5 percent of all sites. You can use Lycos to run separate searches for text, topics, sounds, and pictures. On a keyword search, Lycos shows an excerpt from each page that includes the subject of the search.

Lycos does an okay job of finding the most prominent sites, and its list of the Top 5 Percent Sites is a good way to let somebody else filter out the heavy-duty junk, but the Lycos search tool is not always as precise as some of the others. A Lycos search on *Apple Cider* produced 30,000 hits including pages related to *applelink, appletalk,* and *applets,* as well as orchard fruit. When you click on Related Sites, you get a list of about a hundred sites, but most are about Apple computers.

Other Search Tools

Yahoo!, Lycos, and AltaVista are not the only search engines out there. Several other general purpose sites, including WebCrawler (www.webcrawler.com), Magellan (www.mckinley.com), HotBot (www.hotbot.com), and Infoseek (guide.infoseek.com), offer similar services. It's probably worth the time to take a look at several to see which feels best to you.

If you include specialized search services such as the ones devoted to a specific topic and those that work in a single language, there are probably hundreds of Web sites that will help you find other Web sites. For example, Figure 7-1 shows Channel Hong Kong (www.chkg.com), which limits searches to sites in or related to Hong Kong. Other sites offer searches in Estonian, Korean, Italian, Dutch, and other languages. You can find links to many of these services by running a Yahoo! search on *"Search Engines"* and then jumping to one of the items in the Yahoo! Categories list.

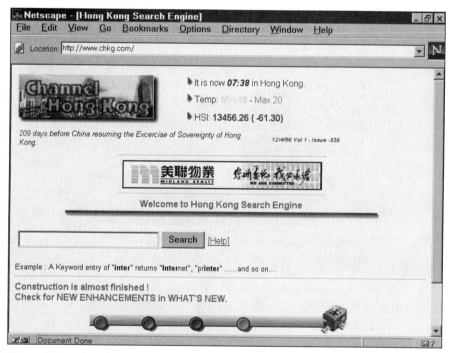

Figure 7-1 The Channel Hong Kong search page.

Another good place to look for links to other directories and search tools is Search.com (www.search.com), which provides descriptions of several hundred general and specialized sites.

Using Your Browser's Direct Links to Search Tools

Both Netscape Navigator and Microsoft Internet Explorer have permanent links to a search page. In Internet Explorer, you can set the link to open your favorite search engine, but the Netscape link jumps to a page maintained by Netscape.

To jump to the Netscape Net Search page shown in Figure 7-2, select `Directory` → `Internet Search`. You can choose a different search engine by clicking the name of the engine you want to use near the top of the page. The Net Search page also has links to many other search services farther down the same page.

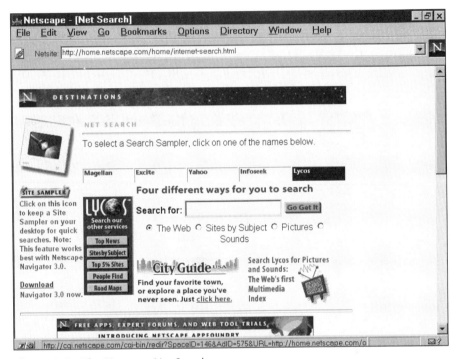

Figure 7-2 The Netscape Net Search page.

In Internet Explorer, you can open the search page by clicking the Search icon in the toolbar or selecting `Go` → `Search the Web`.

Microsoft's Find it Fast! page is the default search page. It contains a pretty good set of links to search engines and other information sources, but if there's another Web page that you would prefer to use as your starting point for searches, you can replace the default with a link to that page.

To change the Internet Explorer search page, follow these steps:

1. Jump to the page you want to use as your search page, using the Address toolbar or a link from another page.

2. Select `View` → `Options`.

3. Click the Navigation tab to open the dialog box shown in Figure 7-3.

Figure 7-3 The Internet Explorer Navigation tab.

4. Click the arrow at the right of the Page field to open the drop-down menu.

5. Select Search Page.

6. Click the Use Current button. The address of the current Web page will appear in the Address field.

7. Click OK to close the Options window and save your new search page.

Performing Multiple Searches

As you may have noticed in the results of the searches for *apple cider,* each search engine came up with at least a few sites that the others missed. If you want to make sure that you didn't miss a single site related to a topic, you should try the same search on more than one engine. The easiest way to accomplish this is to use a Web page that automatically submits the same keywords to several search engines and compiles the results into a single list.

One of the best of the multiple-search tools is MetaCrawler (http://www.metacrawler.com), shown in Figure 7-4. MetaCrawler simultaneously searches for the same keywords using Yahoo!, AltaVista, Lycos, and several other search engines. It automatically eliminates duplicate listings, so it can be an excellent starting place for your searches.

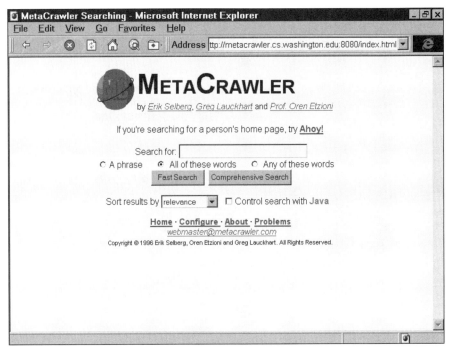

Figure 7-4 The MetaCrawler search engine.

Follow these steps to perform a search through MetaCrawler:

1. Point your browser to `http://www.metacrawler.com`.

2. Type the keywords that describe the topic you want to find in the Search for field.

3. Click the Fast Search button or the Comprehensive Search button to send the keywords to MetaCrawler. When the search is complete, you will see a list of hits with a link to each one.

Using Web Guides as Starting Points

Search tools are great when you know what you want to find, but sometimes you will want to do some less specific browsing by following links that look interesting, just to see where they take you. In this section, you find pointers to some Web sites that contain lists of other interesting sites. Some of these Web guide sites are maintained by commercial concerns who want you to pay attention to the advertisements that surround the links, whereas others were created by Internet service providers, primarily for the use of their own subscribers. Either way, these sites are accessible to anybody who wants to use them, so you don't have to worry about poking your browser where it's not welcome.

As you explore the World Wide Web on your own, you will probably find still other Internet guides that you like as well or better than the ones listed here. New guide sites pop up all the time, so it's likely that someone somewhere out there has created one that matches your interests and needs.

Both Microsoft and Netscape maintain their own Internet guide sites, which they use as the default starting pages for their browsers. Both sites are somewhat more blatantly hard-sell commercial than some of the other Internet guides, but they do provide reasonable starting places for exploring the Web.

The Netscape home page (`http://home.netscape.com/`) is primarily a vehicle for news and promotion of Netscape's own activities, but if you scroll down about a third of the way, you will find the Netscape Destinations section shown in Figure 7-5. If you want to let Netscape provide your home page, a better choice would be the Destinations page at `http://home.netscape.com/escapes/index.html`, which has links to subject-based pages that point you to many of the best news, entertainment, and directory sites. The What's New? and What's Cool? lists are frequently updated guides to new and unusual sites.

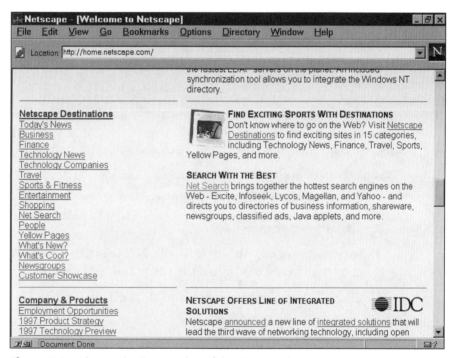

Figure 7-5 The Destinations section of the Netscape home page.

Microsoft has a similar set of guide pages for Internet Explorer users. The Internet Explorer start page shown in Figure 7-6 has a tab that can take you to a Best of the Web page, along with several other tabs with information about various Microsoft products and services. Within Best of the Web, separate pages are devoted to various subject areas.

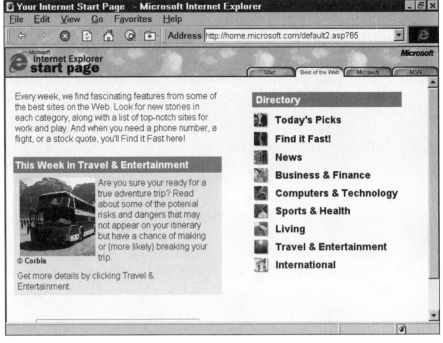

Figure 7-6 The Microsoft Best of the Web page.

After you decide that a particular guide site (or any other Internet page, for that matter) is a page that you want to visit regularly, you may want to consider instructing your browser to load that page every time you start the program. Netscape calls this your *home page*; Microsoft calls it a *start page*.

Follow these steps to change your Netscape home page:

1. Select Options → General Preferences .

2. Click the Appearance tab.

3. In the Startup box shown in Figure 7-7, select the Home Page Location option and type the URL of the site you want to use in the location field.

4. Click OK to save your choice and close the dialog box.

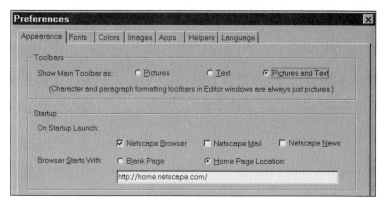

Figure 7-7   The Netscape home page locator.

Follow these steps to set a new Internet Explorer start page:

1. Jump to the page you want to use as your start page.

2. Select **View** → **Options** .

3. Click the Navigation tab.

4. In the Customize box shown in Figure 7-8, open the drop-down menu in the Page field and select the Start Page option.

5. Click the Use Current button.

6. Click OK at the bottom of the window to save your choice and close the dialog box.

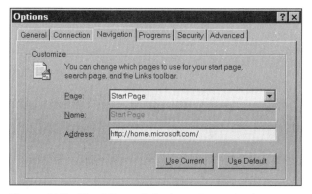

Figure 7-8   The Microsoft Explorer Customize box.

Many of the search tools you read about in the last section can also act as Internet guides. Yahoo!, Excite, WebCrawler, and Lycos all offer lists of other sites, organized by category, with reviews or descriptions of each site. These companies have staffs who spend all their time searching for new and otherwise interesting Web sites and adding them to their lists.

EINet Galaxy

EINet Galaxy (`http://galaxy.einet.net`) is yet another subject guide to the World Wide Web, but it's one of the best because it includes a very wide range of topic headings. The heart of Galaxy's top-level directory is nothing more than a list of links. Each link takes you to a more detailed list of topics, which, in turn, contains a list of related sites.

LookSmart

LookSmart (`http://www.looksmart.com`) specializes in non-technical topics for "average" Internet users who are more interested in home and family, travel, and hobbies than in hard-core computer topics. It's designed specifically for first-time users who want to find things on the Web without sifting through a lot of irrelevant material. Based in Australia but targeted at users in North America, LookSmart is supported by *Reader's Digest*.

Unfortunately, when you use LookSmart to jump to a recommended site, it places the new Web page in a frame surrounded by advertisements, so less actual content fits into your screen. This is, quite frankly, an irritating way to operate a directory; to get around this problem, you can select **Edit** → **Copy** to store a site's URL, close the LookSmart window, and paste the URL in your browser's Address field.

The Huge List

The Huge List (`http://www.thehugelist.com/`) is yet another place to look for links to other Web sites. As the name suggests, The Huge List offers a very large number of links, organized into about three dozen main topics.

NetGuide

NetGuide (`http://www.netguide.com`) was created by the magazine of the same name. In addition to the by-now familiar search engine and list of categories, NetGuide also includes links to live, online events such as concerts, sports events, and celebrity chats; a Net Digest with pointers to somebody's choice of the Web's top sites; and various, other helpful information about moving around the Web.

The Scout Report

The Scout Report (`http://rs.internic.net/scout/report`) comes from the University of Wisconsin. It's a list of new and newly discovered sites, updated weekly. The Scout Report is probably not the best choice as a home page, but if you want to try to keep up with new sites and services, it could be a good one to add to your list of bookmarks or favorites.

Eye on the Web

The biggest difference between Eye on the Web (http://www.eyeontheweb.com) and the other Web guide sites is that it encourages users to create a personalized version with the specific set of links that they actually use. Along with the usual lists of categories, you can configure the page to include links to news from your choice of providers, local weather, sports, and even a comic strip or two.

Maple Square

Maple Square (http://maplesquare.sympatico.ca/) bills itself as "Canada's Internet Directory." One of the Internet's strengths is its capability to jump across national borders in seconds, so limiting yourself to sites from a single country seems a little strange. But if you're in Canada or interested in Canadian affairs, Maple Square looks like a good place to look for Canadian news, government information, and heritage and cultural resources.

Using Databases to Find Online Information

The guide sites described in the preceding section contain pointers to a wide variety of Internet resources. Databases, on the other hand, are more tightly focused lists and search engines that allow you to find specific information about a single topic. For example, you can find databases that contain archives of historic photographs, answers to questions about pet care, collections of recipes, movie reviews, and a guide to summer camps for children.

In fact, hundreds of specialized databases exist all over the Web. One of the best places to find the ones that interest you is C|net's Search.com site (http://www.search.com), shown in Figure 7-9.

To find information through Search.com, follow these steps:

1. Jump to http://www.search.com. You will see the Search.com home page.

2. Look at the list of Search Subjects on the left side of the screen as you scroll down the page. When you find a general category that applies to the subject you're looking for, click that link. For example, if you're looking for information about golf course, click Sports.

3. When the table of contents for the topic area appears, scroll down the list until you find an item that meets your specific interest. In this example, you might choose the golfcourse.com Course Locator.

4. You will jump to a search field for the specific database you requested, such as the one shown in Figure 7-10. If you prefer to see more information about the database before running a search, click the link.

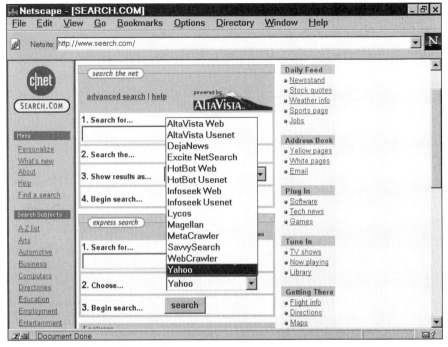

Figure 7-9 The Search.com home page.

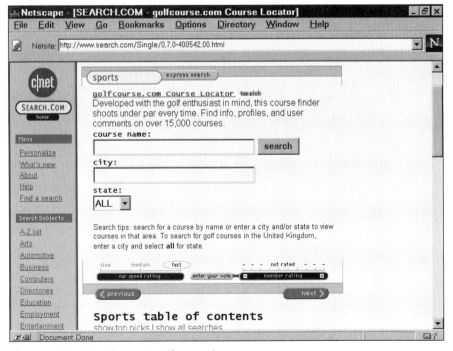

Figure 7-10 Search.com's golf course locator page.

Type the information requested by the search field or fields and click the Search button to send your request to the database. After a few seconds, the database should automatically take you to a Web page that contains the information you requested.

Using Gopher Menus

The Internet Gopher is a system that organizes pointers to files and other Internet resources into menus. A Gopher menu may include items within a specific geographical area or organization, or it might be a list of entries related to a particular topic. Gopher menus can contain just about any kind of Internet file or service, including files, database searches, and other Gopher menus. Searching through a series of Gopher menus can be a fast way to start with an approximate location or subject area and move directly to related information.

Gopher was introduced a few years before the World Wide Web, when almost all Internet users had text-only access to the Internet. It was created at the University of Minnesota, whose mascot is a Golden Gopher. In the last few years, the World Wide Web has become much more popular than Gopher as a way to organize online information, but several thousand Gopher menus still remain on servers around the world.

Unlike the Web, where the author of every page can control the appearance of the material he or she distributes through the Internet, Gopher menus are nothing more than structured text, as shown in Figure 7-11. Your Web browser can recognize and display Gopher menus along with HTML documents, so you don't need a separate tool to use them.

Moving Around Gopherspace

Because most Gopher menus include pointers to other menus, you can start at any menu and reach almost any other menu very quickly. For example, start with a menu at the University of Illinois and move to a picture of a Kentucky quilt at the Smithsonian Institution in Washington:

1. Type this URL in your browser's Address field or Location field and then press the Enter key: **gopher://gopher.uiuc.edu**. The top-level Gopher menu from the University of Illinois will appear, as shown in Figure 7-12.

2. Click the Other Gopher and Information Servers link. You will see a list of servers.

3. Scroll down to the USA link about halfway down the list and click it. A list of states will appear in a new menu.

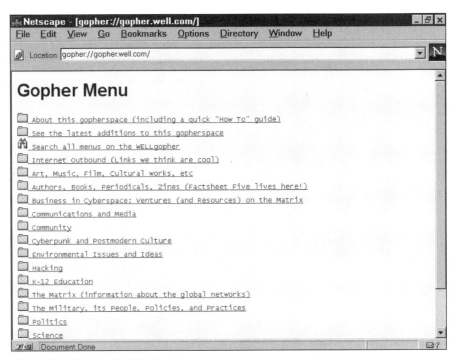

Figure 7-11 A typical Gopher menu.

4. Click the Washington DC link close to the end of the list. A menu of servers located in Washington will appear.

5. Scroll down the list of servers until you find the one for the Smithsonian Institution's National Museum of American Art. Click that link.

6. Choose the link to Art & Exhibitions.

7. Click Artists P–R.

8. Scroll down to the entries for Residents of Bourbon County, KY. Click Fan Quilt (.GIF). A picture of the quilt will appear.

SIDE TRIP

SOME PLACES TO START EXPLORING GOPHERSPACE

When you want to use Gopher to find items of interest without a specific goal in mind, you may want to start with one of these menus:

```
gopher://gopher.mountain.net
gopher://cwis.usc.edu:70/11/Other_Gophers_and_Information_Resources/
    Gopher-Jewels
gopher://gopher.well.sf.ca.us
```

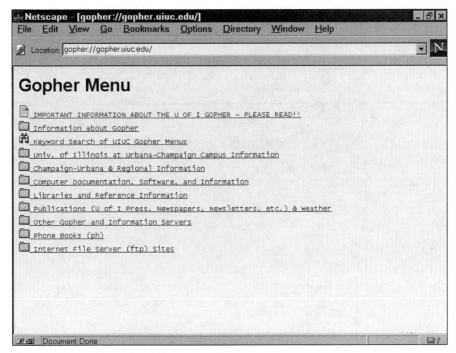

Figure 7-12 The top-level Illinois Gopher menu.

Searching for a File

You can spend a great deal of entertaining time wandering around in Gopher menus, but that's not always the best way to locate a specific item of information out of more than 15 million separate entries. Fortunately, a special search tool for Gopher menus called *Veronica* (Very Easy Rodent-Oriented-Net-wide Index to Computerized Archives) is available. Many large Gopher servers offer access to Veronica searches.

Follow these steps to conduct a Veronica search:

1. Point your browser to gopher://gopher.uiuc.edu. You will jump to the top-level Gopher menu at the University of Illinois.

2. Select the Other Gopher and Information Servers item from the menu.

3. Scroll about halfway down the page to the Search Titles in Gopherspace Using Veronica menu item and click it. The list of Veronica servers in Figure 7-13 will appear.

4. Click the simplified veronica: find ALL gopher types option. The Gopher Search screen in Figure 7-14 will appear.

5. Type one or more keywords that describe the topic you want to find in the text field and press Enter. After a few seconds, you will see a list of

links to menus and files that contain your keywords. Click an item from the list to jump to that menu or file.

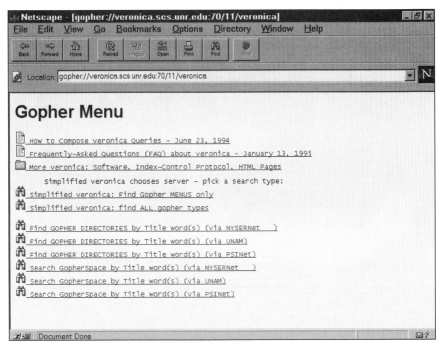

Figure 7-13 The Veronica Gopher menu at the University of Illinois.

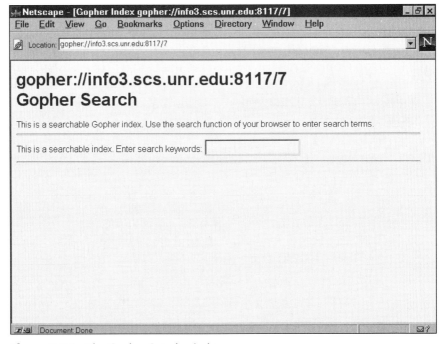

Figure 7-14 The Gopher Search window.

Finding People (Even if They're Not Online)

You can find a lot of stuff on the World Wide Web, but an even bigger world is just outside your window. In spite of everything you may have heard about the Internet, most people are still not connected. But that doesn't mean you can't use the Web to find them. This section tells you where to look for addresses and telephone numbers of people who may not own computers, let alone Internet connections.

Online telephone directories are just what you'd expect them to be: type in a name and get back the matching address and telephone number. Of course, if you're looking for "George Johnson" or "Susan Anderson," you're going to have to choose among several thousand people with that name. But if you know any additional details, such as a partial address or even a middle initial, you've got a pretty good chance of finding the one you want.

Beyond the most obvious uses for a nationwide directory, such as finding a telephone number for your cousin in the suburbs of Chicago, you can also use it to search for old friends, distant relatives, or college classmates. In addition, directories can also be a great tool for genealogical research. When you run a search on you own family name, you may discover connections with people you never knew about before.

Most directory Web sites are limited to a single country, which is not usually a problem, because you probably know before you start that the person you want to find is in the United States, or Denmark, or wherever. Like most other things related to the Internet, there seem to be more American directories than for any other country, but at the end of this section, there are pointers to a couple of Web sites with links to similar telephone directories around the world. If you don't find the person you want in the first directory you try, looking at one or two others is a good idea; each uses a slightly different search technique, so you may have better luck in the second place you look.

As you run a search in any of these directories, remember that the result will be no better than the database it consults. If the person you want to find is not in the database, you won't find that person. Because many people have asked to have their names removed from various databases, and others are missed for other reasons, you won't always find every name you look for.

7

CLIMBING YOUR FAMILY TREE

AltaVista is also a good place to search for family names. When I ran a search on my grandmother's maiden name, I found an entire set of distant relatives in eastern Europe who were completely unknown to my immediate family. As Fats Waller once said in an entirely different context, "One never knows, do one?"

Switchboard

Switchboard (http://www.switchboard.com) usually responds to requests for telephone numbers and addresses in less than a second. To enter a Switchboard search, follow these steps:

1. Jump to http://www.switchboard.com.

2. Click Find People. You will see a screen similar to the one in Figure 7-15.

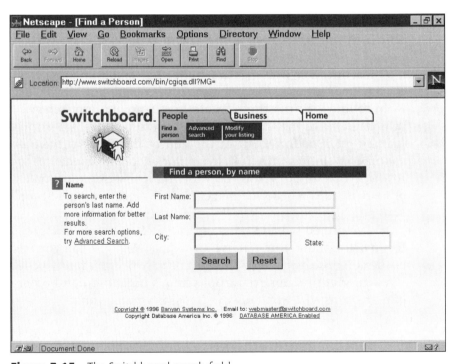

Figure 7-15 The Switchboard search field.

Type the name of the person you want to find in the First Name and Last Name fields. If you know where they live, type this information in the City and State fields. Click the Search button. Switchboard will return a list of all matching names from its database, with addresses and telephone numbers. You may have to step through two or more screens to see all the names and numbers that fit your request.

InfoSpace People Search

The InfoSpace People Search (`http://infospace.com/`) is similar to Switchboard, but it can also provide some useful additional information, including a map that shows the location of an address and sometimes an e-mail address. InfoSpace offers a similar service for Canada at `http://206.129.166.151/canada.html`. Like Switchboard, you begin an InfoSpace search by typing a name. Figure 7-16 shows the InfoSpace search page.

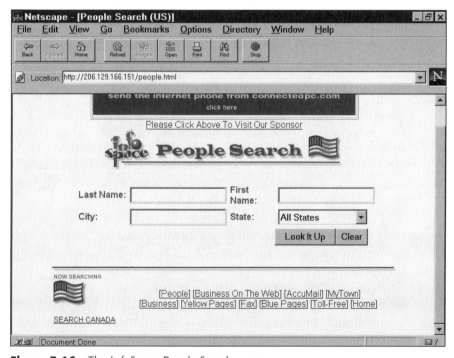

Figure 7-16 The InfoSpace People Search page.

Four11

Four11 (`http:///www.four11.com`) calls itself "the Internet white pages." It offers an e-mail directory with more than 10 million unique listings, a telephone directory that includes more than 100 million names, an e-mail directory for members of the U.S. Senate and House of Representatives, and a separate Celebrity Directory with e-mail and street addresses for hundreds of famous actors, authors, models, sports stars, and other prominent people. Four11's directory databases are also used by Yahoo!, Infoseek, and several regional telephone companies.

Finding people in other countries

Similar telephone directory services are available for many countries. You can find lists of these sites at the following two URLs: `http://www.contractjobs.com/tel` and `http://www.infobel.be/infobel/infobelworld.html`.

BONUS

Cutting Through the AltaVista Underbrush

An AltaVista search that gives you a list of 40,000 pages containing a specified keyword is not particularly useful, especially if you can't find what you want within the first ten or twenty listings. To make the search engine more useful, Digital has added a tool to AltaVista called *LiveTopics* that can refine the results of a search. LiveTopics automates the process of adding and excluding additional keywords in a search, so you can reduce the number of matching sites to a manageable number.

LiveTopics uses the documents that it finds in response to your search request and identifies *topics* that appear frequently in matching Web pages. The topics are "live" because they are taken from the Web pages that match your original keywords rather than from some standard list. When you select a topic, LiveTopics adds or excludes it from your keyword query, so the second search is almost always more tightly targeted to the pages you really want to see.

LiveTopics offers information in two different formats: lists of topic words and (if your browser supports Java) Topic Relationship maps. The topics most relevant to your keywords appear first, with the words under each topic in order of frequent appearance. To select a word, click the box in the column with a check mark at the top; to exclude a word, click the box in the X column. When you add or exclude a word, note that it appears in the query box at the top of the window. When you're ready to run a second search, click the Submit button.

The Java version uses an interactive program that downloads along with the data. As you move your mouse around the list, a box appears around the word currently under the cursor. Click once to select the current word, or click twice to exclude it. Click one more time to ignore a previously selected word.

When two topics in the map have a line between them in a Topic Relationships map, those topics usually appear in the same context. So, there's a clear connection between *apple* and *Powerbook,* but little or none between *Ethernet* and *cider.* When you move your cursor over a topic, a drop-down list of words related to that topic appears. Click once to select a word or twice to exclude it.

The number of yellow bars next to each topic indicates LiveTopics' estimate of the relevance of that word. In this case, no yellow bars appear next to *cider,* which suggests that the program is assuming that you're interested in computers rather than fruit. In fact, LiveTopics doesn't know the difference between an Apple Macintosh and a Macintosh apple. It's really just showing you how often words appear in the same Web page. Therefore, you will get a much more useful result if you make your initial search more specific.

The real value of LiveTopics is that you can use it to eliminate irrelevant topics and to add related words to a keyword search. In the cider example, if you want to find Web pages related to apple cider for drinking but not for cooking, you can exclude the *vinegar, jellies,* and *syrup* topics. If you still get a list of matching pages that is too big to be useful, look at a LiveTopics analysis of the revised search and try refining the search again.

As you use LiveTopics, don't forget that you're looking for Web pages rather than topic lists and maps. It can be fascinating to discover unexpected relationships that emerge out of a search, but they're more likely to be a distraction than a pointer to the information you really want.

Summary

This chapter told you where to find a variety of World Wide Web search tools and directories and explained how to use them to move quickly to Web sites that contain exactly the items you want.

It should not be surprising that search tools such as Yahoo!, AltaVista, and Excite are among the most frequently used sites on the entire Web. Using a good search engine can make the difference between the Web seeming to be an overwhelming mass of confusing information and a tightly focused source of specific items. If knowing how to use your browser is the first step toward mastering the Web, then finding and using search tools is a close second.

Gopher is an older but still useful system that organizes Internet resources into menus. You can use Gopher to start with a general topic area and move quickly to files and services.

Hundreds of directories and databases are available on the Web. If you know where to look, you can find everything from your cousin's telephone number to a hotel in Bermuda with just a few keystrokes.

WORLD WIDE WEB DESTINATIONS

THIS PART CONTAINS THE FOLLOWING CHAPTERS

Millions of Web pages are waiting for you to visit. Where do you begin? This section contains descriptions of many of the most useful, informative, entertaining, and otherwise intriguing sites on the Web.

MUSIC TO MY PC

To Welton Barker, music is more than just an entertainment medium. A classical pianist since an early age, Welton says, "It's definitely the one vocation that I derive the most satisfaction from in my life." And the World Wide Web has changed the way Welton embraces his vocation.

Welton's love of music has been augmented by the resources now at his disposal thanks to the Internet and the Web. "There's a newsgroup dedicated to practicing techniques," he said. "I grit my teeth when I'm practicing; there was a whole discussion on just that subject one night, real lengthy; and, of course, I never realized it was so common."

Although newsgroups open the door to such online communities, the Web itself offers resources that music lovers of all kinds can take advantage of. "I haven't bought a CD from anywhere but the Internet in more than a year," continues Barker. "I used to be a member of those record clubs, where transactions were done through the mail. Now those clubs are online, along with dozens of other CD retail sites. I'm no longer restricted to the selections in the catalog because their entire library is available online. And shopping around for the best price is a snap." But the best thing about shopping for CDs on the Web? "Sound files. I can listen before I buy. You still can't even do that in most stores."

Most sound files available on the Web are one of three basic file types: WAV files, Musical Instrument Digital Interface (MIDI) files, or RealAudio. RealAudio produces a variation of a WAV file, but it doesn't require the user to download the file before listening — which makes it an ideal format for sample CD sound files. "With RealAudio, the source streams the file to your desktop, so you get an actual recording that starts right away," Welton says. And what about hardware? "Beyond your average computer system with a sound card and the RealAudio plug-in, there's nothing special that you need to listen."

But what about the legality of distributing copyrighted work/music over the Web? Welton has a couple of insights on why that issue hasn't been a big problem yet. "First of all, CD quality is 44.1 KHz, and RealAudio tends to be, at best, half that, so quality suffers. Also, it's a very inconvenient way to listen casually to music," he says. "Listening to music over the Web isn't going to replace making a purchase. If it gets to the point where (Web listening) is more attractive than buying, which seems unlikely, these sites can start charging for the service. But right now, it's simply an excellent marketing tool. It's like letting the whole world into your record store to listen to tunes. What better way to sell your product?"

CHAPTER EIGHT

ONLINE NEWS SOURCES

IN THIS CHAPTER YOU LEARN THESE KEY SKILLS

You have a computer connected to the Internet. You have a browser and you know how to use search engines and directories to find things on the World Wide Web. In this chapter, you begin to explore some of the specific kinds of content on the Web. Specifically, you look at sources of news, including newspapers, newswire services, broadcast news, and information providers that tell you about weather and sports.

Newspapers on the Web

Hundreds of newspapers in all parts of the world have created Web sites that contain all or part of the news that appears in their paper editions. Some newspaper sites also include articles from back issues and material that does not appear in the ink-on-paper version of the paper along with current stories. In addition, many newspaper sites also provide links to reports from one or more of the major national and international news agencies, such as the Associated Press and Reuters.

Newspaper Web sites are among the most useful categories of Internet resources. Although most of us would prefer to read the news from a physical newspaper rather than from a computer screen, getting instant access to news stories from around the world is very convenient, even if the stories in online newspapers may be a few hours old. When a news story makes the national media, more detailed coverage usually appears in the newspapers close to the scene. When your brother-in-law runs for city council in another state, you won't find any news about his campaign in your local paper. And if you're a sports fan, you may enjoy reading news and columns about visiting teams before they arrive to play your hometown favorites.

Like the newspapers themselves, the quality of newspaper Web sites ranges from excellent to awful. Although many papers provide a substantial amount of news on their Web sites, others use them as little more than a place to sell subscriptions. And just as you would expect to get different new coverage from a major metropolitan newspaper such as the *Washington Post* or the *New York Times* from what you'd see in a small-town weekly such as the Eureka, Montana *Tobacco Valley News*, you will find very different news stories on their Web sites.

Unfortunately, a handful of newspapers are experimenting with Web sites available only to subscribers who pay a monthly or annual fee. If these first efforts are successful (and it's too soon to tell if they will succeed), you can expect many more to convert their existing, free sites to pay-as-you-go services.

As you might expect, several Web sites offer directories of online access to newspapers. One of the best places to start is the *American Journalism Review*'s NewsLink (`http://www.newslink.org/news.html`), which provides links to individual newspapers sorted by location or type of newspaper. It also separates promotional and limited sites from the ones that actually contain news, so that you can avoid dead-end searches for news from a newspaper that gives you nothing but classified ads.

For examples, take a look at a couple of major newspaper sites and one from a small-town weekly.

The Washington Post

The *Washington Post* is the hometown newspaper of America's capital city. The *Post*'s Web site, washingtonpost.com (`http://www.washingtonpost.com`), gets updated several times a day. It includes everything in the print edition, plus extra material for online readers and links to the Associated Press (AP) for even more information. The *Post* keeps a two-week online archive of its own stories and those from the AP.

From washingtonpost.com's home page, you can jump to most of the other major sections of the Web site, including the national, business, and local news sections and pages devoted to sports, entertainment, and what the *Post* calls Style. Links to The Print Edition take you to the stories that appear in today's newspaper, but if you want even more up-to-date stories, you click a link to Today's Top News.

A tremendous amount of additional material is available on washingtonpost.com. For a full description, jump to the site index.

The Electronic Telegraph

For a variety of historical and economic reasons, "serious" British newspapers provide a quite different (and in many cases, more detailed) view of the world from those published in the United States. The Electronic Telegraph (`http://www.telegraph.co.uk`) contains all the news and feature reports that appear in the daily and Sunday *Telegraph*.

The *Telegraph* is not the only British national newspaper on the Web. You can also find online versions of the *Times* and the *Sunday Times* (`http://www.the-times.co.uk/`), the *Guardian* (`http://www.guardian.co.uk/`), and the *Observer* (`http://www.observer.co.uk/`).

Like the newspaper that sponsors it, the Electronic Telegraph is divided into sections devoted to British news, international news, sports, and so forth. A set of links exists to each section near the top of every page. The front page and each section page provide headlines and one- or two-sentence summaries of each story in that section. To jump to the full story, click the headline.

A Small-Town Weekly: The Wallowa County Chieftain

Wallowa County, in the northeastern corner of Oregon, ranks among the most isolated places in the United States. But the county's weekly newspaper is as easy to reach on the World Wide Web as the *Washington Post* or the *Los Angeles Times*. As Figure 8-1 shows, the *Wallowa County Chieftain* has its own Web site (`http://www.aracnet.com/~chieftan`) with all of this week's important news. The electronic version of the *Chieftain*'s front page includes headlines that also serve as links to individual news stories.

Internet News Sites

Newspapers are not the only organizations that provide news on the Web; several independent Web sites also provide round-the-clock news updates. Some of these sites are maintained by news media outlets such as CNN or NBC, but others are operated by Internet service providers or online information services as a *value-added service* for their subscribers.

8

Figure 8-1 The *Wallowa County Chieftain* home page.

Many American sites use the same sources for their news — the Associated Press or Reuters. Each site has a different layout and presentation style, but you'll find the same stories in many places. Most newspapers have their own reporters who write local stories, so a local newspaper is a good place to look for information that the AP may have ignored. And, of course, major national news providers such as NBC and Time Daily use material from their own reporters along with the material they get from the agencies.

MSNBC

MSNBC is a joint venture of Microsoft and NBC News. It includes an all-news cable TV channel and a Web site (`http://www.msnbc.com`). Other sites do a better job with fast-breaking news, but MSNBC offers some useful perspectives along with its coverage of the day's news. MSNBC takes advantage of its close relationship with NBC's broadcast news operations to include links to audio and video clips along with text.

MSNBC also provides links to other Internet sites with additional information related to each story. For example, when it reported on a summit meeting between the Presidents of the United States and China, the page that contained the article also had links to a U.S. Department of State site, with the full text of policy speeches on China, a background paper on China from the Brookings Institution, and the directory of China-related Web sites from *China News Digest*.

CNN Interactive

CNN Interactive (http://www.cnn.com) is the Web site for the Cable News Network. It's well-organized and updated throughout the day. CNN combines its own staff reports with information from the Associated Press and other sources. The site's front page shows headlines in several categories, with direct links to more detailed reports. At the end of most articles, links to related stories provide additional background information.

Time Daily

Time is a weekly, but its Web site (http://www.pathfinder.com/time) includes an area called Time Daily, which contains a handful of articles from *Time* reporters. Like the magazine's print version, its online news coverage is somewhat less terse and more colorful than the typical wire service stories that appear on many other sites. You won't want to use Time Daily as your main source of news, but it's a good supplementary site.

Nando.net

Nando.net (http://www.nando.net) originates at *The News and Observer* in Raleigh, North Carolina, but unlike most newspaper sites, it's a 24-hour service designed for the Web, with updates every two to six minutes rather than just a reworking of articles from the printed newspaper. One of Nando.nets's best features is that it shows the exact time of the most recent update for each story; when you're trying to keep up with new developments, this can save you a great deal of time (see Figure 8-2).

New Jersey Online

You don't have to live in New Jersey to take advantage of the news reports on the New Jersey Online Web site (http://www.nj.com), shown in Figure 8-3. It includes a NewsFlash page with the latest national and international news feeds from the Associated Press, updated every minute. Each headline is a link to the full AP story. Separate pages contain news in specific categories (including national, international, and New Jersey regional news) and an assortment of features targeted to residents of the Garden State. Besides the AP reports, NJO gets news from the *Newark Star-Ledger*, the *Jersey Journal*, and the *Trenton Times*.

Figure 8-2 News from Nando.net.

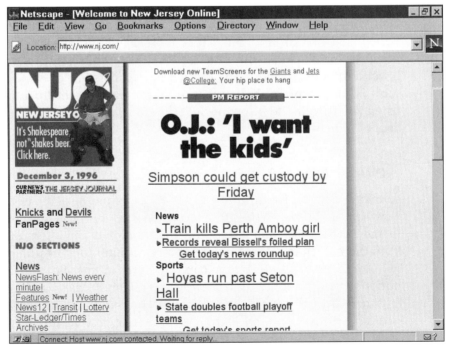

Figure 8-3 The New Jersey Online home page.

Wire Services

Most newspapers and almost all radio and television newscasts get their news from one or more of the major national and international news services: the Associated Press (AP), United Press International (UPI), Reuters, and Agence France-Presse (AFP) are among the largest and best known services. These organizations are known as *wire services*, because they originally used telegraph circuits to distribute news to their subscribers. News reports from wire services are all over the Web. Each wire service has reporters and bureaus in most major cities around the world and arrangements with many of their subscribing newspapers to distribute local stories to other subscribers.

You can find AP and Reuters reports on many Web sites maintained by newspapers, broadcasters, and online services, but it's also possible to go directly to sites maintained by the wire services themselves.

The Associated Press

The Associated Press is the largest and oldest American news wire service. AP offers its Web site, The Wire, as a supplement to the Web services provided by its subscribers. You cannot jump directly to The Wire unless you start at another news site such as New Jersey Online.

To open The Wire, follow these steps:

1. Jump to `http://www.nj.com/news/` to open the New Jersey Online News page.

2. Click the link on the left side of the window to The Wire: AP. You will see The Wire home page.

The frame at the top of The Wire contains drop-down menus with links to other sections of The Wire and to other services on the host service (in this case, New Jersey Online). Directly under the two drop-down menus is a headline display that changes after about ten seconds. You can return to The Wire's home page at any time by clicking the logo at the left side of the frame. To return to New Jersey Online, click its logo at the right side of the frame.

United Press International

United Press International (UPI) is the other major American wire service. UPI has fallen upon hard times in the last few years, but it still provides a useful alternative to the dominant AP service.

UPI's news reports are distributed through the Internet by an organization called *Clari.net*, which posts individual UPI articles to special newsgroups. However, you won't be able to access these newsgroups unless your Internet service provider buys the news feed from Clari.net.

The easiest way to find out whether you have access to Clari.net newsgroups is to ask your service provider or network administrator. Most ISPs that offer the service promote it as a valuable part of their packages, so it shouldn't be too hard to find somebody who can tell you whether or not it's available. If all else fails, you can jump to Clari.net's Web site (`http://www.clari.net/iap`), where you will find a list of subscribers.

Assuming that you do have access, you also need a newsreader integrated with your Web browser program. Both Netscape Navigator and Microsoft Internet Explorer include newsreaders as options, so this should not be a problem for you. If you're using a browser version that does not have a newsreader, you should download a newer version from Microsoft or Netscape.

Follow these steps to read UPI news reports through Clari.net:

1. Point your Web browser to `http://www.clari.net/newstree.html`.

2. Choose the Clari.net edition that your ISP provides. If you're not sure which one to use, look in `http://www.clari.net/iap`.

3. Click the name of a subject area. Your browser will open the news reader program and display a list of articles.

4. Double-click the article you want to read. It will appear in the bottom half of the newsreader window.

Reuters

Reuters is based in England, but it provides service to customers in more than 150 countries. The company has been in business since 1851, when Paul Julius Reuter used carrier pigeons to deliver stock prices to places where telegraph cables were not yet available. Today, Reuters offers news services in 24 languages from editorial bureaus around the world.

In general, Reuters' online news articles seems to be a bit longer and more detailed than the ones from the AP, but they also offer a one- or two-paragraph summary of each story. Reuters' News Room Web site (`http://www.reuters.com/reutersnews`), shown in Figure 8-4, has separate sections for international news, U.S. news and politics, business, and sports. You can also watch the latest headlines scroll across the top of the main News Room page.

OTHER CONNECTIONS TO THE WIRE

Many other AP members have added The Wire to their Web sites. You can find links to The Wire from any of the following:

Access Atlanta	Cox Interactive Media	www.accessatlanta.com/
Albuquerque Journal Online		www.abqjournal.com
@marillo Globe-News	*Amarillo Globe-News* (Tex.)	www.amarillonet.com/
Arizona Central	The *Arizona Republic* (Phoenix, Az.)	www.azcentral.com
APP.com	*Asbury Park Press*	www.app.com
@ugusta	The *Augusta Chronicle* (Ga.)	www.augustachronicle.com/wire/
charlotte.com	The *Charlotte Observer*	www.charlotte.com/
The Commercial Appeal	*Memphis Commercial Appeal*	www.gomemphis.com
Connect Oklahoma	The *Oklahoman* (Oklahoma City)	www.oklahoman.net
The courant	The *Hartford Courant*	http://www.courant.com/page1.stm
Denver Post Online	*The Denver Post*	www.denverpost.com
@dallasnews.com	*The Dallas Morning News*	www.dallasnews.com/
Deseret News Web edition (Salt Lake City, Utah)	*The Deseret News*	www.desnews.com
Evansville Online (Evansville, Ind.)		www.evansville.net
The Freep	The *Detroit Free Press*	www.freep.com/the_wire/
FYIowa	The *Cedar Rapids Gazette* (Iowa)	www.fyiowa.com/gazette
Greene County Online	The *Greeneville Sun* (Tenn.)	greene.xtn.net/wire
newsday.com	*Newsday* (Long Island, N.Y.)	www.newsday.com/
PIX Page	KPIX-TV/FM (San Francisco, Calif.)	www.kpix.com
PioneerPlanet	*St. Paul Pioneer-Press* (Minn.)	www.pioneerplanet.com
Reporter Online	*Abilene Reporter-News* (Tex.)	www.texnews.com
Rocky Mountain News online	The *Rocky Mountain News* (Denver, Colo.)	www.denver-rmn.com

(continued)

SJ-R.COM	The *State Journal-Register* (Springfield, Ill.)	`www.sj-r.com`
Schuylkill online	*Pottsville Republican & Evening Herald* (Penn.)	`www.pottsville.com`
The Seattle Times Extra	*Seattle Times*	`www.seattletimes.com`
StarText.Net	The *Star-Telegram* (Fort Worth, Tex.)	`www.startext.net` `Sun One`
	The *Gainesville Sun* (Fla.)	`www.sunone.com/ap`
SunSpot	The *Baltimore Sun*	`www.sunspot.net`
Texas Online	The *Plainview Herald* (Tex.)	`www.texasonline.net/` `pageone`

Reuters also supplies news to Yahoo! (`http://www.yahoo.com/headlines`), Time-Warner's Pathfinder (`http://pathfinder.com/news/latest`), CNNfn (`http://cnnfn.com/`), IBM infoMarket (`http://www.infomarket.ibm.com`), and other Web sites, as well as to America Online, The Microsoft Network, and CompuServe. Not all of these services provide the same amount of detail as the Reuters site, but you may discover that you like their presentations better.

Agence France-Press

Agence France-Press (AFP) is the third of the "big three" international news agencies, along with Reuters and the AP. AFP operates from four regional centers in Paris, Washington, Hong Kong, and Cyprus, with correspondents in 165 countries. AFP provides news to clients around the world in French, English, German, Spanish, Portuguese, and Arabic. AFP is an important alternative to the other major services because they often have reporters in places where other services do not.

EYEWITNESS TO HISTORY

Reuters reporters have been witnesses to most of the great historical events of the last 140 years. In Tales From the Archives, (`http://www.reuters.com/thisis/archives/archives.html`), you can find accounts of Reuters' coverage of the assassinations of Abraham Lincoln and Mahatma Ghandi, the discovery of Tutankhamen's tomb, the rise and fall of the Berlin Wall, and other major stories and personalities.

Figure 8-4 Reuters' News Room Web site.

When this book was written, AFP's online service was not as extensive as the ones from the AP and Reuters, but it's planning a "broad new range of commercial AFP online products" that should be comparable to AP's The Wire and Reuters' News Room. AFP does offer a World News Roundup updated four times a day, in English, at `http://www.afp.com/monbref/monbrefva.html` and a very extensive World Sports Report (`http://www.afp.com/sportsreport/`) that provides full coverage of everything from American football to international badminton. AFP also offers news summaries in French and Spanish.

ITAR-TASS

ITAR-TASS, the Information-Telegraph Agency of Russia, is not as big as the AP, Reuters, or AFP, but it is big enough to be among the top five news services in the world. Based in Moscow, ITAR-TASS has 74 bureaus in the former Soviet Union and 62 more in 59 other countries. ITAR-TASS is the successor to the old TASS (the Telegraphic Agency of the Soviet Union) but, unlike its predecessor, it's no longer a propaganda arm of the government. You won't find a complete world news report on ITAR-TASS, but it's unmatched for detailed coverage of Russia and the other CIS nations.

ITAR-TASS places its daily, English-language service on its Web site (`http://www.itar-tass.com/news.htm`). The service includes both full-text reports from Russia and the other CIS nations and a PhotoInformation page (Figure 8-5) with apparently endless pictures of visiting dignitaries, winners of competitions, and openings of exhibits. To read more than the headlines, you must send a request to the e-mail link on the English Service Web page.

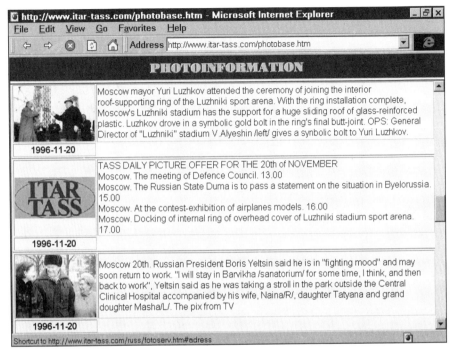

Figure 8-5 The ITAR-TASS PhotoInformation page.

Canadian Press

The Canadian Press (CP) is the Canadian national news agency, owned cooperatively by Canada's daily newspapers. CP has bureaus across Canada and in Washington and London, as well as exchange arrangements with AP, Reuters, and AFP. Broadcast News (BN) is a subsidiary of CP that supplies news to Canadian radio and television stations. CP's home page (http://www.canpress.ca/canpress) offers a daily picture service and a page of links to member newspapers' Web sites.

PA NewsCentre

The Press Association (PA) provides about 1,500 British and Irish news stories per day to print, broadcast, and electronic media in both countries. The PA NewsCentre Web site contains news from Britain and Ireland in several forms: news headlines updated every hour, a continuous videoprint news feed, full text of selected stories, brief summaries of the lead stories in the British national newspapers, separate sections for sports, weather, television, and radio listings, and a photo archive. The NewsCentre Home Page can be found at `http://www.pa.press.net`.

Kyodo News

Kyodo News is the leading independent Japanese news agency. Its members and subscribers include almost every newspaper and radio-TV network in Japan. Kyodo News specializes in news from Japan and the Asia-Pacific region. It offers news in English on its Web site (`http://www.kyodo.co.jp/`).

From the index page, you can jump to news summaries, headlines, and two-paragraph stories from the Asia-Pacific region, edited for overseas (that is, non-Japanese) media. Kyodo News transmits about 300 headlines every day. The Japan Weekly pages feature full text of top news stories posted every Monday morning. If the Kyodo News site doesn't provide enough details for you, it also includes links to more than 30 member newspapers that maintain their own Web sites in both Japanese and English.

Mercopress

Mercopress is a news agency based in Montevideo, Uruguay that focuses on the Mercosur (*Mercado Commun del Sur*, or Common Market of the South) countries of South America. Mercopress posts a weekly Mercosur News bulletin, and a separate bulletin of news from and about the Falkland Islands. The Mercopress home page is at `http://www.falkland-malvinas.com`.

News Highlights

With so many online news sources on the World Wide Web, the most difficult part of keeping up with the news is deciding where to look for today's headlines. Of course, that's what the editors of traditional newspapers have to do every day: they receive information from many sources and select the most important items.

Several Web sites do something similar; they gather news articles from many wire services, newspapers, and other publications and combine them into daily or hourly bulletins. You can use links on both of the following sites, Top News and New Century Network, to jump directly to the full text of stories from many newspapers and other information providers.

Top News

Top News (`http://topnews.com`) is run by Lycos, one of the search engines you read about in Chapter 6. The editors at Top News gather news stories from news media around the world and place links to individual stories on their own Web pages. Top News uses local and regional news reports along with the major international services, so you might see a link to the *Toronto Globe and Mail* for a story about Canada or to the *Jerusalem Post* for one about Israel. But if the *Times* of London or the *Christian Science Monitor* has a better story, Top News will take you there instead. The Top News Web site is a sort of one-stop center for news from around the world.

Top News has separate pages that contain links to the latest world news, business, sports, and weather information, and other pages devoted to news about the Internet and people. Each section provides a list of linked headlines and a very brief description of each story. For more information about a story, you can easily jump to the full text at the originator's Web site.

New Century Network

The New Century Network (NCN) is a consortium of the nine major media companies that publish more than half the newspapers in the United States. The NCN Web site (`http://www.newcentury.net`) compiles news, sports, and features from their members and provides links to them from a central location. It's an excellent way to keep up with dozens of newspapers without taking the time to visit a separate Web site for each one.

NCN's home page includes links to the Story of the Day in one of its affiliated newspapers and to major headlines and features from many others. Along the side of the window, you can find links to other sections devoted to news, entertainment, science, and other topics.

Another particularly nice feature of NCN is the Archives page, which contains links to searchable back issues of several newspapers. You can search these archives to find stories that go back as far as ten years.

Most stories on NCN are taken from the printed versions of its member newspapers, so they may not be quite as timely as the information you can find from other online news services. But NCN does include a link to the news summaries at *The Washington Post* that are updated several times an hour.

NCN's news coverage is not as extensive as Top News because it's limited to news and features from affiliated newspapers. But that list of affiliates includes many of the best American papers, so that may not be a serious problem. In general, NCN feels more like reading a newspaper through your computer, because it includes many more features and specialties along with the "hard news" that's available on so many other Web sites.

Radio and Television Networks and Stations

If you prefer to obtain the latest news by listening rather than reading, the Web has plenty of places where you can download radio newscasts. Many networks and local stations around the world have created direct, live audio links to the Web, and others encourage you to download and listen to newscasts at your own convenience.

To listen to these newscasts, you must have a computer with a sound card, separate speakers (the computer's built-in speaker won't do the job), and special plug-in software for your Web browser. The latest versions of Microsoft Internet Explorer and Netscape Navigator both include audio players, and they're also available as free, separate programs. Almost every Web site that includes an audio feed also provides a direct link to a source of the software required to listen. When you click a link to a newscast, the audio player connects to a host that contains the newscast audio files, downloads the files, and plays them through your speakers.

The most widely-used audio player on the Web is RealAudio, which uses sound files with a .ra or .ram file extension. RealAudio is a *streaming* system, which means that you can start to play back the recording while it is still downloading. You can also listen to live RealAudio feeds of broadcasts and other events as they occur. Chapter 9 contains more detailed information about live broadcasts through the Web.

National Public Radio

National Public Radio (NPR) has more than 300 affiliated, noncommercial stations across the United States. Its daily, long-form news magazine programs *Morning Edition* and *All Things Considered* are among the best on radio. NPR also produces a shorter newscast every hour and many special-feature programs.

News from NPR is available from its Web site (`http://www.npr.org/news`) in RealAudio format. The News Now page includes the most recent hourly newscast and direct links to some of the day's major stories and recent features from *Morning Edition* and *All Things Considered*.

The NPR site also includes a complete archive of *Morning Edition* and *All Things Considered* since 1995 and less extensive archives of a few other NPR programs.

To listen to a story from a past program, follow these steps:

1. From any page in the NPR Web site, click the Programs button at the top of the page. You will see a program list.

2. Click the name of the program whose archive you want to use. If you can't find an archive, don't assume that you've done something wrong — NPR only offers audio from a few shows.

3. Click the link to Archived Programs. You will jump to a calendar for the current year.

4. Click the date when the item you want to hear was broadcast. This moves you to an index of the stories used in that day's program.

5. To listen to the entire program (which could take almost two hours), click the link at the top of the index. Otherwise, scroll down the page until you find a description and link to the story you want to hear.

Pacifica Radio

The Pacifica Foundation owns and operates community-based radio stations in California, New York, Texas, and Washington, D.C., and also distributes a daily, half-hour national newscast to stations across the United States. Depending on your point of view, Pacifica is either a shining example of creative broadcasting and free speech or a predictable voice of the political left wing.

The daily Pacifica Network News program usually covers a few stories in greater detail than NPR or other broadcasters. The newscast combines journalism with commentaries that may be outside the limited spectrum seen and heard on other media. Pacifica Network News is available in RealAudio format from `http://www.webactive.com/webactive/pacifica`.

ABC RadioNet

ABC Radio places a new, three-minute newscast on its Web site (`http://www.abcradionet.com`) every hour at 15 minutes past the hour, along with separate sports reports and news commentaries.

CBC Radio

The Canadian Broadcasting Corporation has jumped into the Web with both feet. In addition to hourly newscasts in RealAudio format and better-sounding but slower-to-download .au file format, the CBC's Web site (`http://radioworks.cbc.ca/`) also offers live, RealAudio connections to its two, national, English-language radio networks and to Radio Canada International. The two domestic program services are CBC Radio, which is mostly news, interviews, and current affairs; and CBC Stereo, which offers classical music through the week, with some jazz and lighter fare on weekends. Radio-Canada, the French CBC service, is also available (`http://www.radio-canada.com/`).

World Radio Network

The World Radio Network (WRN) distributes radio news and feature programs, in English and other languages, from 25 different public and international broadcasters, including Radio Australia, Radio France International, Radio Telefis Eireann (Irish Radio), Channel Africa, Polish Radio, KBS Radio Korea, Vatican Radio, and many others. The WRN Web site includes links to newscasts from all the participating broadcasters.

To listen to a newscast, select a broadcaster from the WRN Audio File Index and then select the program you want. For example, follow these steps to listen to the news from RTE Dublin:

1. Jump to the WRN Audio File Index page (`http://www.wrn.org/audio.html`). You will see the list of stations shown in Figure 8-6.

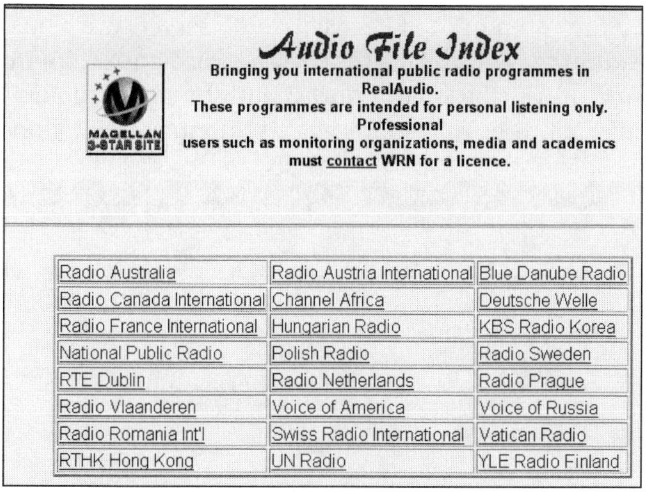

Audio File Index
Bringing you international public radio programmes in RealAudio. These programmes are intended for personal listening only. Professional users such as monitoring organizations, media and academics must contact WRN for a licence.

Radio Australia	Radio Austria International	Blue Danube Radio
Radio Canada International	Channel Africa	Deutsche Welle
Radio France International	Hungarian Radio	KBS Radio Korea
National Public Radio	Polish Radio	Radio Sweden
RTE Dublin	Radio Netherlands	Radio Prague
Radio Vlaanderen	Voice of America	Voice of Russia
Radio Romania Int'l	Swiss Radio International	Vatican Radio
RTHK Hong Kong	UN Radio	YLE Radio Finland

Figure 8-6   The WRN Audio File Index.

2. Click the link to RTE Dublin to jump to the WRN page that contains a menu of news programs from Dublin in English and Irish and a link to RTE's own home page.

3. Select a link to the newscast you want to hear. Your RealAudio player program will open and load the audio file as the computer receives it. After a few seconds, the newscast should automatically begin to play.

Like many other international broadcasters, RTE has its own Web site (`http://www.rte.ie`), where you can find current news, program schedules, and other information. You can also connect to RTE's own RealAudio server to listen to several other daily and weekly radio programs.

Other Broadcasters

Hundreds of other broadcasters are also experimenting with distribution of their programs through the World Wide Web. Many of these stations specialize in music (try `http://www.king.org` for classical music or `http://www.kpig.com` for country music), but others include their newscasts along with other programs.

One of the best places to look for Web sites that include audio services is the list of broadcasters and *bitcasters* maintained by WMBR radio at MIT (http:// www.wmbr.mit.edu/stations). As Figure 8-7 shows, the MIT List is available as sorted by each station's name, location, or broadcast frequency, with separate lists for international broadcasters and networks. Entries for stations whose program service is available through the Internet have a lightning bolt symbol next to the link.

The Real Radio List at http://www.radiotv.com isn't as complete as the MIT List, but it does provide a list of stations sorted by format, so you can limit yourself to stations that carry the type of programming you want to hear.

To find Internet audio sites that are not attached to radio stations, the guides maintained by the companies of licensed audio servers are a good place to start. The Web sites at http://www.timecast.com/ (for RealAudio) and http://www. xingtech.com/content (for StreamWorks) both have links to audio services that carry live events, concerts, and sports events, along with all kinds of talk.

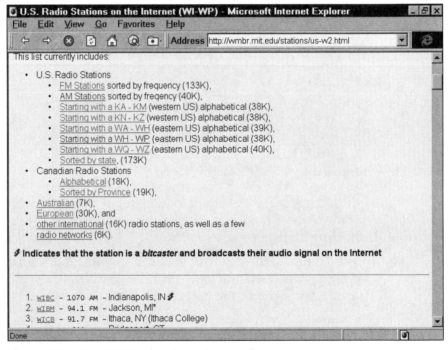

Figure 8-7 The MIT List of Radio Stations on the Internet.

BONUS

Gathering the Whole Story

The number of news media with Web sites offers a serious news junkie an opportunity that wasn't available before the world was connected. When a major news event occurs, you can compare and contrast the coverage of the same story from many sources.

For example, every newspaper in the world reported on the death of Chinese leader Deng Xiaoping on February 19, 1997, but the amount and nature of the coverage was quite different in different places. It's instructive to look at some examples.

The *Christian Science Monitor* is an international daily newspaper based in Boston. Figure 8-8 shows part of the *Christian Science Monitor*'s report (`http://www.csmonitor.com`). The *Monitor*'s page includes both audio clips from Monitor Radio and longer articles from the print version of the newspaper. They also provide links to important stories from earlier editions of the *Monitor* and to reports and background information from other sources around the world.

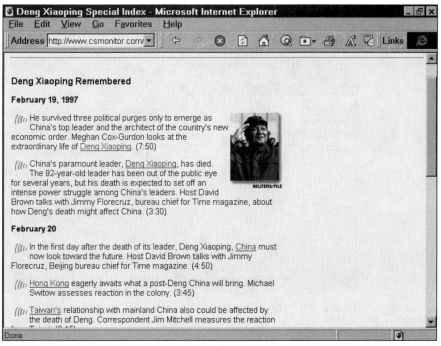

Figure 8-8 The *Christian Science Monitor*'s report on the death of Deng Xiaoping.

The *International Herald Tribune* (`http://www.iht.com/IHT/`), jointly owned by the *New York Times* and the *Washington Post,* is edited in Paris and printed in cities around the world. It has access to all the material published in both of its parent newspapers. The *Herald Tribune* used the *Post*'s report of the Deng story on its front page and its Web site (Figure 8-9).

Several newspapers from the Chinese mainland have Web sites in Chinese and English. The *China News Daily* (`http://www.cnd.org:8021/`) offered a special text-only report with six articles from several domestic and international sources.

Of course, newspapers in Hong Kong and Taiwan devoted the most attention to the story of any media outside China itself. Figure 8-10 shows the special report in Hong Kong's most serious paper, the *South China Morning Post* (`http://www.scmp.com`). Characteristic of Hong Kong's position as a business center, the lead story on the day after Deng died was about the impact on the Hong Kong stock market. Separate stories included an evaluation of the impact on the scheduled handover of Hong Kong to China, analysis of China's future under Deng's successors, reaction from other world leaders, and several pages of photographs. The report also includes audio clips of the announcements from China Central Television in both English and Chinese.

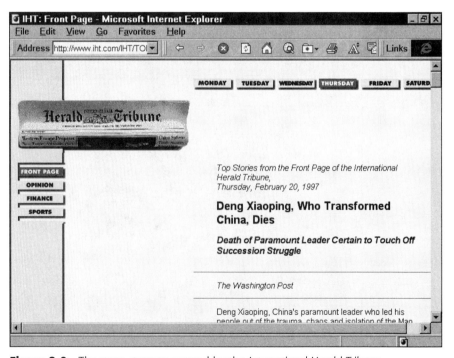

Figure 8-9 The same story as covered by the *International Herald Tribune.*

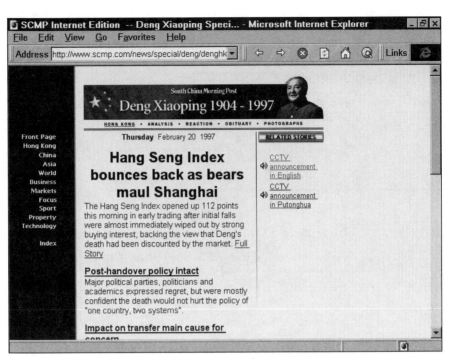

Figure 8-10 The first page of the *South China Morning Post*'s special report.

The *Hong Kong Standard* is a daily, English-language tabloid. The *Standard*'s Tigernet Web site led with a front-page story about how the Chinese Army went on maximum alert after Deng's death. Separate stories covered many other aspects of the story.

In south Asia, Singapore's *Straits Times* (http://straitstimes.asia1.com) produced a special edition for Deng's death with more than a dozen separate stories. The *Straits Times* led with the reaction in Singapore and included the same kind of international stories as other newspapers in the region, but they also included some local features, including one about the impact of Deng's death.

Taiwan's bilingual News Center Web site (http://sinanet.com/bay/news) includes the English language Taiwan Headline News from the Central News Agency. The entire report on February 20 was related to local reaction to Deng's death.

As you move farther away from China, the newspapers devoted less space to the story. Most English language newspapers used reports from Reuters or AFP, but some provided coverage from their own corespondents. In Australia, the *Sydney Morning Herald* offered a reminiscence from a reporter who had been in Peking.

The *Times of London* (http://www.the-times.co.uk/) ran several stories from their own man in Beijing (Figure 8-11) and analysis by an editor based in London. The *Times* treated the story as the major overseas story of the day, but it was overshadowed by several British items.

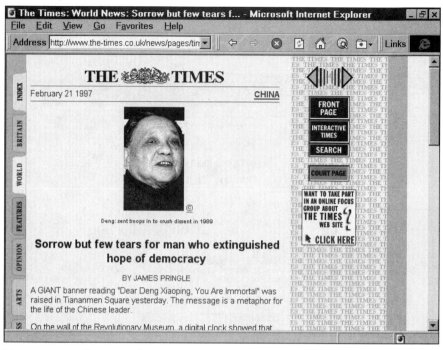

Figure 8-11 The *Times of London*'s report from Beijing.

A handful of newspapers in the United States still pay serious attention to foreign news. The *Baltimore Sun*'s top news stories, located on the SunSpot Web site (`http://www.sunspot.net`), were all devoted to Deng, including reports from their own foreign staff in Beijing and others from the Sun's Washington bureau and from Reuters and Xinhua, the official Chinese news agency.

The *Miami Herald* is the best newspaper in the United States for coverage of Latin America, but they made the Chinese leader's obituary the lead story in HeraldLink (`http://www.herald.com`). Other stories on the Web site's front page were from Mexico, Colombia, Peru, and Haiti.

Finally, New Century Network, the American newspaper consortium, treated Deng's death as the Story of the Day, with links to reports and analysis from the *Washington Post,* the *Detroit Free Press,* and *Newsday*.

Obviously, on a major story like this one, your choices range from a one- or two-sentence summary to as much detail as you could possibly want. Newspapers on the World Wide Web are a great way to gather information quickly from many sources when you want to compare reactions and impact in different parts of the world, or if you're interested in learning how people around the world view a story.

Summary

More than 1,000 newspapers, wire services, and broadcasters have established Web sites that contain current news. Some of these sites are electronic versions of ink-on-paper publications; others contain the latest news, updated throughout the day. Downloading and reading or listening to news from halfway around the world is as easy as reading a web site from a newspaper published in the next town. As a result, the Web is a tremendously powerful tool for following stories that are not adequately reported in your local media, if they're covered at all.

This chapter described examples of large and small newspapers, major national and international news wire services, and broadcasters around the world who distribute news reports through the Internet. It also included information about directories of newspapers, audio services, and Web sites that sift through the huge volume of material available online to provide pointers to reports from many sources.

One person can't possibly keep up with all the news on the Web. There's just too much information available. Even the most dedicated news junkie won't spend every minute of the day reading news online. But when you hear a one-sentence report on local radio or see a four-line story in the newspaper, the Web can give you quick access to more details. And if a region or topic interests you that doesn't get much attention in other media, you can use the Web to go directly to the source.

The next chapter takes a look at some sites that are dedicated to other topics, including sports, weather, and financial information.

WEATHER, SPORTS, AND BUSINESS NEWS ON THE WEB

9

IN THIS CHAPTER YOU LEARN THESE KEY SKILLS

The Internet and the Web are ideal tools for keeping up with events that change frequently — such as the weather, the stock market, and the score of the big game. If you know where to look, you can find plenty of weather, financial, and sports-related Web sites that tell you about the very latest developments around the world.

This chapter contains pointers to weather sites that include detailed forecasts, satellite and surface weather maps, and everything else you might need to decide whether or not to wear your raincoat or your woolies; pointers to online sports pages with news and scores for all kinds of sports; and pointers to business sites that offer stock quotations, corporate news, and other information for investors.

Weather on the Web

The trouble with getting a weather forecast from radio or television is that you have to wait for it to come around; if you miss it by five minutes, you're out of luck until the next broadcast, which may not air for hours. You could pick up a newspaper, but the forecast you would see there is at least a few hours old — when there's a storm on the way, you need to know what's happening right now. And if you're trying to decide what kind of clothes to pack for a trip to a distant city, the local forecast won't do you much good.

Many of the newspaper Web sites discussed in Chapter 8 also contain weather reports. But you can get much more detailed maps, forecasts, and one-stop information about weather around the country or the world from the weather sites described in this section.

Unlike news suppliers on the Web, almost all the weather sites get their information from the same sources: the National Weather Service in the United States, the Met Office in Britain, and similar agencies in other countries. The important differences among sites have more to do with presentation than content. You can get much the same information from any good weather site, but some sites are easier to use than others.

And more so than the rest of the Web, weather sites link to many of the same places. For example, if you go to the National Weather Service site and click a link to Doppler Radar, you'll find yourself looking at an Intellicast map from the MSNBC Web site. You will find other links to the same Intellicast maps from dozens of Web pages operated by other organizations, including universities, television stations, and Web directories.

The Weather Channel

The Weather Channel is an American, 24-hour, cable television service that broadcasts nothing but weather reports and forecasts. Along with current conditions and forecasts, The Weather Channel's Web site (http://www.weather.com) also includes a great deal of information *about* weather, such as a glossary of weather words, highlights of weather history ("On this day in 1889, a railroad bridge in Ashtabula, Ohio, collapsed during a snowstorm"), and special reports about major, recent hurricanes, tornadoes, and blizzards. The Weather Channel also converts statistical information for various cities into easy-to-read graphic pages.

Intellicast

Intellicast is associated with MSNBC, but you will see its maps all over the Web. Besides forecasts for major cities, the Intellicast Web site (http://www.intellicast.com) contains national and regional satellite images of cloud patterns and radar pictures from ground stations. Figure 9-1 shows a typical Intellicast Four Day Forecast.

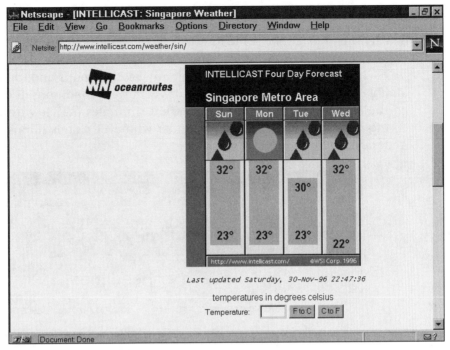

Figure 9-1 An Intellicast Four Day Forecast.

In general, Intellicast provides faster access to forecasts but doesn't give you as much detail as The Weather Channel. If you're looking for a quick answer (Will it rain in Chicago tomorrow?), Intellicast may be the better choice; but if you want more information, you may be happier using The Weather Channel or the information from one of the Chicago newspapers or TV stations.

WeatherNet

The University of Michigan's WeatherNet (`http://cirrus.sprl.umich.edu/wxnet`) doesn't contain much original content, but its home page has links to other sites with local forecasts, live-to-the-Net weather cameras in dozens of cities across the United States, radar and satellite images, and weather-related Web sites at universities, television stations, and government agencies. Unfortunately, almost everything on WeatherNet is focused on weather in the United States and Canada; you'll have to look someplace else for weather information about the rest of the world.

NOTE This site is a great starting point for serious weather crazies, but the rest of you will probably want to use another site to obtain quick information.

EarthWatch

EarthWatch has all the same forecasts as the other weather sites, but its graphic presentation is stronger than most. As Figure 9-2 shows, EarthWatch (`http://www.earthwatch.com`) displays regional weather maps and radar images that double as links to detailed explanations of current conditions. It also has a slick, virtual-reality WeatherFlight feature that simulates the view from an airplane flying across the country over or under whatever clouds happen to be visible that day.

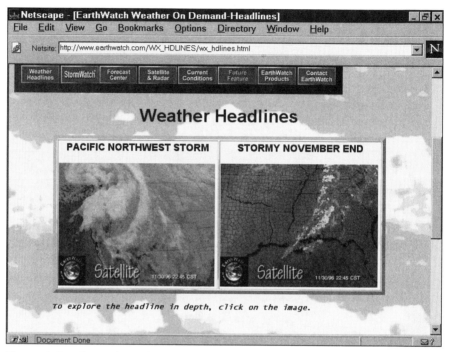

Figure 9-2   The EarthWatch Weather Headlines page.

Weather Sites outside the United States

Some major American weather sites include forecasts for the rest of the world, but other, more detailed local and national weather sites are available in many foreign countries. Table 9-1 lists some good places to look for overseas weather forecasts (assuming that you're reading this in the United States; if you're someplace else, these sites may be more local than the American sites).

TABLE 9-1 Weather Sites for Locations outside the United States

Site Name	Web Address
BBC WEATHER CENTRE (BRITAIN)	http://www.bbc.co.uk/weather
ENVIRONMENT CANADA PUBLIC WEATHER FORECASTS	http://www.on.doe.ca/text/index.html
THE WEATHER NETWORK (CANADA)	http://www.theweathernetwork.com
THE FINNISH METEOROLOGICAL INSTITUTE	http://www.fmi.fi
METEO FRANCE	http://www.meteo.fr
GERMAN CLIMATE RESEARCH CENTER	http://www.dkrz.de
WEATHER UNDERGROUND OF HONG KONG	http://underground.org.hk
JAPAN WEATHER ASSOCIATION	http://www.jwa.go.jp:80
THE WEATHER IN ISRAEL	http://weather.macom.co.il/
ITALIAN WEATHER LINKS	http://www.dsi.unive.it/~amartini
NEW ZEALAND WEATHER PAGE	http://crash.ihug.co.nz/~stormy/forecst.htm
WEATHER OUTLOOK FOR SINGAPORE	http://www.gov.sg/metsin/fort.html
CENTRAL WEATHER BUREAU TAIWAN	http://www.cwb.gov.tw
THAI WEATHER FORECASTS	http://www.nectec.or.th/bureaux/met-dept/

Sports

Millions of people around the world are sports fans, so it should not be a surprise that the Web has lots of sites that contain scores and other information about every major and minor sport and activity. If your local newspaper doesn't tell you anything about the NCAA Division I Field

Hockey Championships, let alone the Australian Rugby League or the Swedish Open table tennis competition, you can probably find details on a Web site.

With a couple of important exceptions, general sports-related Web sites are usually targeted to fans in a particular country or region; for example, American sites don't cover European football leagues, nor do Australian sites pay attention to American baseball. But on the Internet, that's not a big deal, because jumping to a Web page in another country is as easy as jumping to one in your own backyard. If you're looking for more details about a less popular sport, you may find better coverage on a page that specializes in that sport rather than in one of the general-interest sites.

AFP World SportsReport

The Agence France-Press World SportsReport Web site (`http://www.afp.com/sportsreport`) is an important exception to the rule that most sports on the Internet are limited to one country. World SportsReport covers sporting events that take place all over the world.

AFP World SportsReport has a separate page for each sport that it covers. On the left side of the browser window is a list of sports. For other, less popular activities (such as field hockey, rowing, table tennis, or weightlifting), click Other Sports to see another list. When you click the name of a sport, a linked list of current headlines related to that sport appears in a separate frame. You can either jump directly to stories that interest you or scroll down the whole frame to read everything AFP has posted about that sport.

ESPN SportZone

ESPN is the largest American all-sports cable television network. Its Web site (`http://espnet.sportszone.com`) is almost entirely limited to American and Canadian sports, but it offers extensive coverage of sports in those countries. It's a well-organized site that does a fine job of supporting a sports fan's interest — offering predictions before the game, on-the-spot reports of what happens on the field, and even more analysis after the game is over. ESPN says SportsZone has more than 60,000 separate pages, including live audio feeds of selected games, video highlights, and complete statistics.

The ESPN home page contains full text of the day's top story and linked headlines to other important sports news. On the left side of the page is a list of individual sports with a link to a separate home page for each one. If your favorite sport or league isn't on the list, click More Sports for links to such sports as minor league baseball, speed skating, and bowling.

Nando Sports

Nando.net originates at the *Raleigh News & Observer*, but it's a separately edited news service for online readers. The SportsServer pages (`http://www.nando.net/SportServer`) have separate pages for every team in all major professional sports and all the main college conferences. Nando.net also has links to just about every sports story on the Associated Press, Reuters, and AFP wires.

Nando's Hot off the Wires and Hot off the Photo Wires pages contain the most recent sports stories and pictures listed in chronological order. Because these stories are not sorted by the sport that each covers, the Hot off the Wire page frequently contains a great deal of obscure material along with the stories you really want.

Sports Illustrated Online

Like the magazine that produces it, Sports Illustrated Online (`http://pathfinder.com/si/`) combines live scores and up-to-the-minute results with background stories and more reflective features. Like other sports sites, separate sections exist for individual sports.

Canadian Sports: TSN

TSN is the Canadian cable sports channel. Because American television makes its way across the border into Canada, and because many of the U.S. professional leagues have teams in Toronto, Vancouver, and other Canadian cities, TSN's Web site (`http://arena.tsn.ca`) covers American sports along with more distinctively Canadian games, such as hockey and curling.

NOTE For those who did not grow up playing the game, *curling* sounds like something invented by a slightly demented scoutmaster to keep the troops entertained on a winter camp-out. It's a form of shuffleboard on ice, played with great big polished granite rocks with handles. When a player throws the rock down the ice toward a bull's eye at the far end, the other players on the team use brooms to sweep like mad in front of the rock's path, creating a thin layer of water which reduces the amount of friction under the rock. You can find an explanation of how the game is played at `http://www.everynet.se/curling/howtoplay.html`.

Of course, TSN's real emphasis is on Canadian sports, including amateur, college, and professional teams. Figure 9-3 shows a typical TSN story, about football at the University of Saskatchewan.

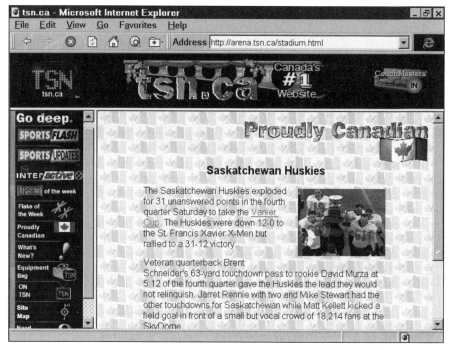

Figure 9-3 Canadian sports from TSN.

Sports from the Rest of the World

AFP, Nando, and other international sports Web sites have extensive information, but they don't cover every sport and every league in the world. But somewhere on the Web, a site can probably give you the information you want. When you're looking for news about an obscure sport or a less prominent team, it's time to start using the search tools you read about in Chapter 7.

For example, news about professional football (soccer) in Singapore doesn't usually make it to the international news media, but several local sites in Singapore report on every game. To find recent scores in the Singapore Professional Football League, follow these steps:

1. Point your browser to Yahoo! (http://www.yahoo.com) or some other search engine.

2. In the Search field, type **Singapore football**. Yahoo! will return a list of Web pages related to football in Singapore.

3. Select the link to S. League Soccer. You will jump to the Singapore League's home page, which includes scores, league tables, and links to individual pages for each team in the league.

Obviously, if you want to know about cricket in the West Indies instead of football in Singapore, you'd instruct the search engine to find different keywords.

The other approach to finding specialized sports stories is to look in newspaper Web sites. This method can be effective when you want to find things like reports about high-school football games.

For example, follow these steps to find out about a game in Tacoma, Washington:

1. Use a Web search tool such as Excite to find the *Tacoma News Tribune* Web site (`http://www.tribnet.com`).

2. Click the link to Sports Sections.

3. Click the link to H. S. Sports. You will see a page with recent articles about local high school sports.

Every newspaper organizes its Web site differently, but finding the Sports section from the paper's home page should not be difficult.

Web Sites Devoted to Individual Sports

At least one official or unofficial Web site is devoted to just about every imaginable sport, from basketball to rodeo and from golf to tug-of-war. You can find newsletters, results of competitions, and fan information by using the name of the sport in a keyword search from Excite, Yahoo!, or some other search engine.

For example, Figure 9-4 shows the home page at golf.com (`http://www.golf.com`), a Web site operated jointly by NBC, *Golf Digest*, and *Golf World*. In addition to news about recent tournaments and professional golfers, it has links to pages that describe many other facets of the game. A Golf Links page also is available, with a list of more than 750 other golf-related Web sites.

Similar pages exist for almost every other sport. Although it's true that golfers are a large and attractive audience for potential advertisers (which is why there are more Web sites about golf than, say, handball or lacrosse), you should be able to find at least a few Web sites related to just about any sport you can think of.

Figure 9-4 The golf.com home page.

Live, Radio-to-the-Web Broadcasts

Many professional and college teams place live broadcasts of their games on Web sites for the benefit of out-of-town fans who can't pick up the stations carrying the games on the radio. If you're a fan of the New York Mets who lives in Arizona, or if your favorite college football or basketball team is five states away, it's worth looking for a *webcast* of their play-by-play.

 NOTE To listen to one of these broadcasts, you need a computer with a sound card and speakers (or headphones). You won't always find every game you want to hear, but check. It might be on the Web.

To find a play-by-play broadcast, follow these steps:

1. Go to the Yahoo! Net Events directory of live sports events on the Web by pointing your browser to `http://events.yahoo.com/Sports/`.

2. Click the link to the type of game you want to find.

3. Follow the links to lists of individual games that are being broadcast on the Net. For example, for a college basketball game, click Basketball and then click College Basketball Live.

4. When the list of events appears, scroll down the list until you find a listing for the game you want to hear and click the Go to Event link.

5. If you can't find a listing for the game on the Yahoo! events list, try the Timecast directory of live, RealAudio events at `http://timecast.com`.

6. If the game is not on one of those lists, you're probably out of luck. As a last resort, use the Yahoo!, Excite, or Lycos search engine to look for the team's home page. If the team broadcasts to the Web, a link to it is probably available there.

Financial News and Investment Information

Stock market reports and other financial news are one more type of information that can be distributed quickly and efficiently through the World Wide Web. Independent business and financial news services such as Bloomberg and CNN have Web sites that report new developments throughout the day, and each of the major stock exchanges has an interactive Web site that reports current prices (usually on a 15-minute delay — up-to-the-minute quotations are available from several sites in exchange for a monthly subscription fee).

CNNfn

CNN's Financial News Web site (`http://cnnfn.com`) is updated throughout the day with business news, stock market reports, and investment-related features. The CNNfn home page provides current headlines in a news ticker; the Dow Jones Average, NASDAQ Composite, and 30-year treasury bond rate, all updated every 3 minutes; and links to other pages containing more detailed information.

Other sections of the CNNfn site include the following:

* **Hot Stories.** The top-level Hot Stories page contains more headlines, each of which links to a full story. Subsections are devoted to deals, individual companies, the economy, and business features.

* **Markets.** The Markets page contains graphs of the Dow Jones, NASDAQ, and Standard & Poor's 500 indexes, updated every 15 minutes, as well as links to data about U.S. stock markets, world markets, currencies, interest rates, and commodities.

* **Your Money.** The Your Money section contains information for individual investors and advice for managing your day-to-day finances.

* **Stock Quotes.** The Stock Quotes page is an interactive link that supplies the prices of stocks and mutual funds, delayed by 15 minutes.

Bloomberg News

Bloomberg Personal Online (http://www.bloomberg.com) is the online version of the Bloomberg Business News service provided to more than 50,000 dedicated information terminals and on Bloomberg News radio stations around the world. Bloomberg offers much of the same information about American and foreign markets and financial news as CNNfn, but with more attention to international events. A live audio link to Bloomberg's all-news radio station in New York City, WBBR, is also available.

Quote.com

Quote.com (http://www.quote.com) specializes in news and financial data for investors. It has several useful features:

* Free quotes on stocks, options, commodity futures, mutual funds, and indexes from U.S. and Canadian markets and exchanges on a 15-minute delay
* Real-time quotes for subscribers who pay a monthly fee
* Charts of daily, weekly, or monthly performance
* Links to earnings forecasts and reports, annual reports, and company profiles

An automated tracking system enables a user to keep the names of several stocks and other securities in a portfolio and obtain the current status of the entire portfolio with a single command.

SIDE TRIP

INFORMATION FROM INDIVIDUAL EXCHANGES

Many major stock and commodity exchanges have interactive Web sites that provide detailed information about the stocks or other securities listed on that exchange. Much of the same information is available from Quote.com and other sources, but if you're interested in a particular exchange, you may want to take a look at its site. If you're investing in securities listed on exchanges outside the United States, one of these sites may be the best way to obtain a quick quote.

For a complete list of exchanges, jump to http://www.yahoo.com/Business_and_Economy/Markets_and_Investments/Stocks.

Industry and Trade Publications

9

You may not ever want to subscribe to magazines such as *American Sweeper* ("the voice of the contract street-sweeping industry") or *Rug News* ("the magazine for professional rug dealers"). But if you're trying to follow developments in a particular industry, understand new technologies (assuming there are any new street-sweeping technologies), or evaluate possible investments, you can find information in Web sites operated by trade magazines, professional journals, and newsletters long before the same information appears in more popular media. Hundreds of these magazines appear on the Web, and more are popping up all the time.

And, of course, Web sites are available that contain directories of online magazines. One of the best sites is the Ecola list, at `http://www.ecola.com/news/magazine`, which organizes its lists by topic, location, and title. If Ecola doesn't list the publication you want, try a keyword search in AltaVista.

BONUS

Special Web Services

After you find out about the essentials in life — if your favorite team won today and whether or not it's likely to rain — you can use the World Wide Web to take advantage of all kinds of other useful and amusing services. This section contains pointers to a handful of Web sites that provide special services that can save you some time and aggravation, and maybe give you a chuckle or two.

Package Tracking

Have you ever sent an overnight package and waited to find out if and when it actually arrived? You could telephone the delivery company and ask them to track the shipment for you, but you'll probably spend half the afternoon listening to horrible, on-hold music before you reach somebody who can help you. Fortunately, you can bypass the overworked person taking telephone calls and go directly to the package-tracking computers through the Internet.

All the major domestic and international package delivery service companies have package-tracking Web sites that can tell you the current location and status of any shipment. If you're waiting for an important package or document to arrive, or if you need to know who signed for it when it was delivered, these services will obtain the information you need in just a few seconds.

FEDEX TRACKING

FedEx's Tracking service uses the tracking number on your airbill to follow a package as it works its way through the FedEx system.

To use FedEx Tracking, follow these steps:

1. Jump to the FedEx Tracking Web page at `http://www.fedex.cm/track_it.html`.

2. Copy the tracking number from the original airbill into the Airbill Tracking Number field.

3. Type the approximate date that the package was shipped into the Ship Date field.

4. Click the Request Tracking Info button. After a few seconds, FedEx returns detailed information about your shipment.

Every time a package moves from a truck to a terminal to an airplane, FedEx notes the current status. You can follow the progress of a shipment in the Tracking report's Scan Activity entries.

If the package in question has been delivered, you will also see the date, time, and location of the delivery, as well as the name of the person who signed for it.

UPS PACKAGE TRACKING

UPS offers a similar service for any shipment with a bar code label.

To track a UPS package, follow these steps:

1. Jump to the UPS Package Tracking Web page at `http://www.ups.com/tracking/tracking.html`.

2. Copy the tracking number from the airbill or other shipping form into the Tracking number field and click the Track this package button. After a few seconds, a UPS Tracking Information pageappears.

Like the FedEx report, UPS Tracking Information includes the date, time, and location where the package was picked up and delivered.

AIRBORNE EXPRESS SHIPMENT TRACKING

To track an Airborne Express shipment, follow these steps:

1. Jump to the Airborne Express Shipment Tracking Web page at `http://www.airborne express.com/trace/trace.htm`.

2. Copy the airbill number to the blank field in the Web page and click the Track Shipment Now button. A Shipment Tracking Report appears.

OTHER DELIVERY COMPANIES

By now, you should have the general idea. Jump to the tracking Web site, type in the number, and click a button. You can also use the Web to track a package through these companies

Express Mail (U.S. Postal Service)   `http://www.usps.gov/cttgate`

DHL Worldwide Express   `http://www.dhl.com/track/track.html`

Burlington Air Express   `http://www.baxworld.com/tracking/track.html`

Converting Your Money

Most of us don't have to calculate the value of foreign money very often. It's always a nuisance to figure out how much those unfamiliar coins and brightly-colored banknotes left over from your last trip are worth. And here's a Web site from Kuala Lumpur that sells a great-sounding Southeast Asian cookbook — they'll take payment with a credit card, but the price is in Malaysian Ringgit. Is it a bargain or not?

Before the Web, you had to find a newspaper that published a list of foreign exchange rates and run the numbers through your calculator to get that answer. As you may have already guessed, however, a couple of Web sites will do the arithmetic for you.

EXPEDIA'S CURRENCY CONVERTER

Microsoft's Expedia Web Site has a currency converter page at `http://www.expedia.com/` that recognizes about 200 different kinds of money, from Albanian Leks and Algerian Dinars to Zambian Kwachas and Zimbabwe Dollars.

To convert between any two currencies on the list, follow these steps:

1. Jump to the Expedia site at `http://www.expedia.com`. The Expedia home page appears.

2. Find the Newspoint table of contents and jump to Currency Converter page.

3. Open the Convert From drop-down menu and select the type of money you want to start with. If you can't find the country whose money you want to convert, click the Expand Currency List to see a much larger list.

4. Type the amount in the original currency in the Units field.

5. If you're converting to a currency other than the default U.S. Dollars, select it in the Convert to list.

6. Click the Convert Now button. The value of the converted currency appears in the Results section at the left side of the window, as shown in Figure 9-5.

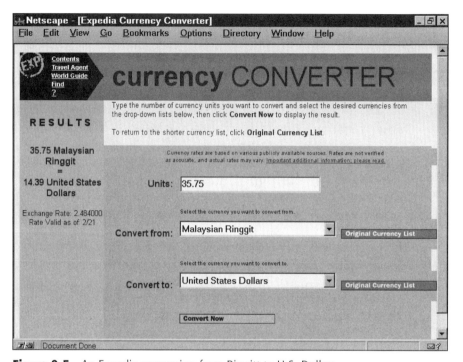

Figure 9-5 An Expedia conversion from Ringitt to U.S. Dollars.

XENON LABORATORIES' UNIVERSAL CURRENCY CONVERTER

Xenon Laboratories' Universal Currency Converter (http://www.xe.net/currency/) provides the same kind of service as the Expedia site, but some users may prefer the simpler page layout, as shown in Figure 9-6.

When you click on the Perform Currency Conversion button, the Converter returns the result you requested in a separate window like the one in Figure 9-7.

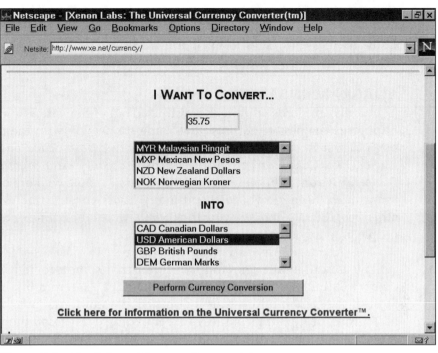

Figure 9-6 The Universal Currency Converter's input screen.

Figure 9-7 The Universal Currency Converter's output window.

Playing with Words

Okay, so these two sites aren't particularly useful. But they're fun, and that ought to be worth something, shouldn't it?

ANAGRAM INSANITY

Anagrams are words or phrases constructed out of the letters in some other word or phrase. The best anagrams have some connection with the meaning of the original words, such as *dormitory* (dirty room), *Nova Scotia and Prince Edward Island* (Two Canadian provinces: lands I dread!), and *Webster's Unabridged Dictionary* (Grand edition used by ABC writers). People who are addicted to such things have been known to spend many hours constructing anagrams (some other people can't imagine why they would waste their time on them, but those people probably have their own strange hobbies).

The Anagram Insanity Web site (`http://Infobahn.com/pages/anagram.html`) is an automatic anagram generator that some people will love but that others will think is just silly. Figure 9-8 shows the Anagram Insanity input page. Most of the combinations that it discovers are nonsense, but every so often, a surprising phrase jumps out at you. For example, *Microsoft* produces two interesting anagrams: *Storm foci* and *comfort is*. *Web sites* produces *We is best*.

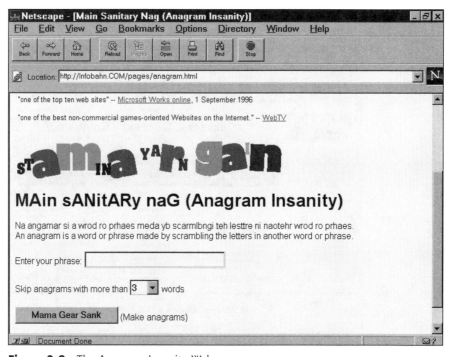

Figure 9-8 The Anagram Insanity Web page.

A ZILLION KAJILLION RHYMES AND CLICHÉS

When you're looking for a rhyme or a cliché, Eccentric Software's Zillion Kajillion Web site (`http://www2.eccentricsoftware.com/eccentric.ZKDemo.html`) is the place to look. It's a combined rhyming dictionary and thesaurus of clichés and related terms.

Summary

Weather, sports, financial news, and trade publications are all well-represented on the World Wide Web. Weather forecasts, the latest scores, and stock quotations all appear on the Web as soon as they become available at their respective sources. Live-audio play-by-play, satellite images, and business news are all as close as your keyboard.

This chapter provided pointers to general-interest Web sites and others that are more tightly focused on a single geographic area, a single sport or team, or a specific type of investment. In all three cases, hundreds of other related sites are available that you may want to visit. To find these additional Web sites, either follow the links on the pages described in this chapter or use one of the search engines.

The next chapter looks at some sources of other kinds of specialized information, including libraries and other reference sources, government agencies and elected officials, and health-related Web sites.

CHAPTER TEN

SPECIALIZED INFORMATION ON THE WEB

10

IN THIS CHAPTER YOU LEARN THESE KEY SKILLS

T he World Wide Web is much more than just a newspaper with new editions every few minutes. Literally millions of Web sites and other files contain just about every imaginable kind of information — library catalogs,
documents from every level of government, health and science data, and information about all kinds of hobbies. In this chapter, you learn about some specific
sources of information in all these categories, as well as how and where to look
for other information that meets your specific needs and interests.

Libraries

T he World Wide Web contains a lot of information, but even more is located
between the covers of books and other documents. In spite of what you
may see or hear from people devoted to the Web, good, old ink-on-paper
has not yet been completely replaced by electrons. In this section, you learn how

to use the Web to locate information in libraries, bookstores, and similar sources of printed material.

Libraries, especially the ones at colleges and universities, were among the earliest organizations to share resources through the Internet. Almost every large library and many smaller libraries have replaced their old card catalogs with computer databases. Connecting the libraries' catalog computers to the Internet was an obvious next step. Today, hundreds of public and university library catalogs are online.

What good does a catalog do, you may wonder. If the book you want is in a library thousands of miles away, what does it accomplish to find it listed in a catalog? It depends on the specific services that each library offers, but there are several possibilities.

First, you can use an online catalog to find out if a book is available at your local library. When you find something you want, you may be able to place it on reserve. For example, Figure 10-1 shows part of the catalog at the Seattle Public Library (telnet://spl.ib.wa.us) that shows which branches have copies of a book about train wrecks. The system shows which copies are currently on the shelf and enables a user to instruct the library to hold it for pick-up.

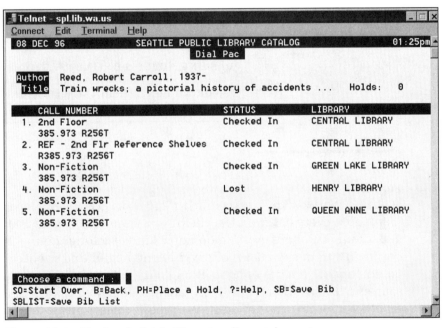

Figure 10-1 The Seattle Public Library's online catalog system.

If your local library doesn't have the book you want, or if you want to find additional material on a specific topic, you can run a search in the catalog of a major research library. For example, the New York Public Library for the Performing Arts is one of the world's most extensive collections of books, recordings, and other material related to the Broadway theatre. It's an excellent place to search for information about obscure musical comedies, such as *The Golden Apple*, which ran for a few months in 1954.

To search for The Golden Apple *in the New York Public Library's collection, follow these steps:*

1. Jump to the library's home page at http://www.nypl.org.

2. Click the link to Catalogs & Indexes.

3. Select the Connect to CATNYP option to jump to the library's catalog of research collections.

4. Click the link to WORDS in Title, Organization Name, or Subject to jump to a search page.

5. Type **"The Golden Apple"** in the search field and press Enter. CATNYP will return a list of items that match those keywords.

6. At least one of the items in this list refers to *Musical comedies. The golden apple.* Click the link to that item to jump to a description.

7. Follow the links to find other items related to *The Golden Apple,* including reviews and other clippings, photographs, and even a short film of a partial performance.

Of course, all this material is in a library in New York City. If you're in Denver, how do you take advantage of it? You have a couple of options. First, a telephone call, letter, or e-mail to the library might convince somebody to send you copies of the material you want; an address and telephone number appear on its home page. Librarians are, generally, extremely helpful people who will sometimes go out of their way to assist a researcher.

The second possibility is a little-known service called *inter-library loan.* If you request a book at your local library that doesn't have it in its own collection, the library may be able to borrow it from some other library and loan it to you just like the books on its own shelves. You may have to wait a month or more for your request to make its way through the system, but eventually, you'll probably get the book you want. Some libraries charge for this service, but many others will obtain books for you at no charge.

When you request a book through inter-library loan from your library, you can make the librarian's job much easier if you provide as much information as possible: the title, author, date of publication, and everything else you find in the distant library's catalog.

TIP If you can include an actual printout of the catalog listing with your request, that's even better. Don't forget to identify the name of the library in whose catalog you found the listing.

Under the agreements that make inter-library loans possible, the library that requests a book must go to similar libraries first; so, a public library won't try to get a book from a university library unless it can't find one in another public library. In fact, some universities don't lend books to public libraries as a matter of policy. Therefore, if you find a book in a university library's catalog, you may want to go to the library at a nearby college or university and ask for help, even if you're not a student or faculty member.

Finding a Library

There are several good Web sites that contain extensive directories of online libraries. Libweb (`http://sunsite.berkeley.edu/Libweb/`), based at the University of California, contains links to separate lists of academic libraries, public libraries, state libraries, special collections, and other categories. Within each list, individual libraries are listed by name in alphabetical order. LIBCAT: A Guide to Library Resources on the Internet (`http://www.metronet.lib.mn.us/lc/lc1.html`) includes another very extensive list of links to catalogs and other library services.

Some online library catalogs are interactive Web sites, but many others use Telnet connections to the Internet. Either way, your browser will make the correct type of connection when you select a link from one of the catalog directories. Be sure to notice if the directory listing includes a password or other login instructions. If it does, you'll need that information to start using the catalog computer.

Libraries of Online Books

Library catalogs can tell you where to find a book, but in almost all cases, you'll have to get the book itself from a library, bookstore, or other source. However, a growing number of Internet archives contain full or partial texts of books that you can download directly to your computer.

Because modern books are protected by copyright, the vast majority of the books in these archives are classics, in editions that are more than 70 years old. A few exceptions do exist, but you're more likely to find a copy of *Moby Dick* or *Gulliver's Travels* in an online archive than a modern bestseller.

Quite honestly, reading text off a computer screen is a pain. It can be convenient to have the entire text in a form that you can search for specific words or phrases, and access to an online edition can be a lifesaver when you've left a reading assignment to the very last minute — but trying to read a whole book on a computer monitor is an easy road to eyestrain. Of course, you could try printing the text file, but the costs of paper and printer supplies can cost more than an inexpensive paperback edition of the same book (300 pages × .03 per page equals $9.00, versus maybe $4.50 for a published book).

Three good places to look for online texts are as follows:

* The Internet Public Library (`http://www.ipl.org/reading/books`), which contains lists arranged by author, title, and Dewey Decimal classification

* The On-line Books Page (`http://www.cs.cmu.edu/books.html`), with an index of more than 2,500 English works and links to many other collections

* Alex: A Catalogue of Electronic Texts on the Internet (`gopher://rsl.ox.ac.uk:70/11/lib-corn/hunter`) at Oxford University in England

Government and Politics

Many government agencies at all levels have started to use the Internet as an efficient and inexpensive way to distribute information. If you know where to look, you can use your Web browser to find meeting agendas, public documents, reports, and blank forms from city, county, state, and federal governments.

Just because you don't live within a certain city, county, or state doesn't mean you can't still take advantage of their Web sites. Many county extension services, local consumer affairs agencies, and other groups have information that can be just as useful to people outside of their own districts.

In this section, you can find pointers to some typical government Web sites and instructions for finding similar information from other agencies.

U.S. Federal Government Agencies

Just about every U.S. government department and agency has some kind of presence on the World Wide Web, from the Coast Guard and the National Agricultural Statistics Service to Uniformed Services University of the Health Sciences and the Mount Rushmore National Monument.

Fortunately, several good online directories of government Web sites are available. The Government Information Xchange (`http://www.info.gov`), or GIX, shown in Figure 10-2, is the government's own, top-level source for access to just about everything it has online, with separate links to state and local governments, foreign governments, and international organizations such as the United Nations and the European Space Agency.

The GIX Federal Directory is organized as a top-down listing; therefore, you'll find it the most useful if you already understand the structure of the government and where the agency you want fits into that structure. To find a specific agency's site, you must start by choosing the branch of government and then work your way down to the individual department and agency.

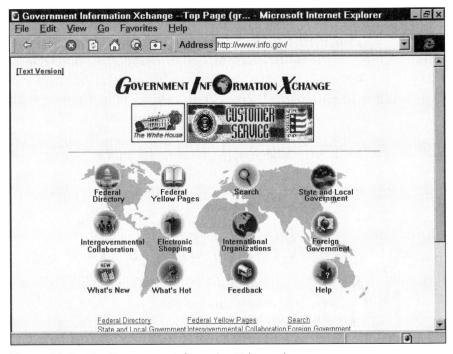

Figure 10-2 The Government Information Xchange home page.

For example, follow these steps to find information about the U.S. Mint's proof sets and other special coins:

1. Start at http://www.info.gov, and click the link to Federal Directory. You will see the Federal Directory page, with links to each of the three branches of government.

2. Click the link to Executive Branch. You will jump to a list of departments and individual agencies.

3. Scroll down to the Department of the Treasury and click the link. You will see the Treasury Department's home page.

4. Click Browse to see a list of the Treasury's programs and.

5. Finally, click the link to Mint-Coins to see a description of currently available coins and medals from the U.S. Mint.

The process is about the same for any other agency, national park, or other activity of the federal government — start at http://www.info.gov and drill down through the branch and department until you get to the office you really want. In practice, this method may be better for browsing around than for moving directly to a particular Web site.

TIP There's another directory that may be a more efficient choice when you know exactly what agency you want to find: the Infomine site at the University of California (http://lib-www.ucr.edu/govinfo.html). It contains both a keyword search engine and an alphabetical Table of Contents with links to hundreds of topics. Because many subjects are the responsibility or interest of more than one agency, the topic and keyword directories will find more sites related to a topic.

One particular federal government Web site can save you a great deal of time and trouble, especially if you're one of those people who waits until the very last minute before preparing your income tax return. The Internal Revenue Service has a complete archive of downloadable tax forms that can be a lifesaver when you discover that you need some obscure form on the Sunday before April 15. You can find a list of every form and publication in the IRS catalog and links to sources for state forms at http://www.irs.ustreas.gov/prod/forms_pubs/index.html.

Other National Governments

The governments of many other countries also use the World Wide Web to share information with their citizens and anyone else who may want to visit their Web sites. Of course, most of a country's Web pages are in that country's national language, but a surprising number offer parallel sites in English.

For example, Figure 10-3 shows Statistics Finland's English-language home page (http://www.stat.fi/sf/home.html). It provides a link to the same page in Finnish (Suomeksi), along with additional links to pages in English with specific information. The Statistical Links page is especially useful because it contains links to other Web sites with similar information in about three dozen countries.

To find government information from a specific country, try one of these directories:

* **The Virtual Tourist** (http://www.vtourist.com/webmap). The Virtual Tourist is a map-based directory of Web sites around the world. To find information from a specific country, click the region of the world that includes that country and then follow the links until you get to a list of sites located in the country you want. Not all of the sites listed by the Virtual Tourist are official government sites.

* **The Yahoo! list of government sites** (http://www.yahoo.com/ Government/Countries).

* **The U.S. government's Government Information Xchange guide to Foreign Government Information** (http://www.info.gov/Info/ html/foreign_government.htm).

* **The Electronic Embassy** (http://www.embassy.org). The Electronic Embassy is a linked directory of Web sites maintained by national embassies in Washington, D.C. Many embassy Web sites contain basic

information about their countries, along with links back to other sites operated by their home governments.

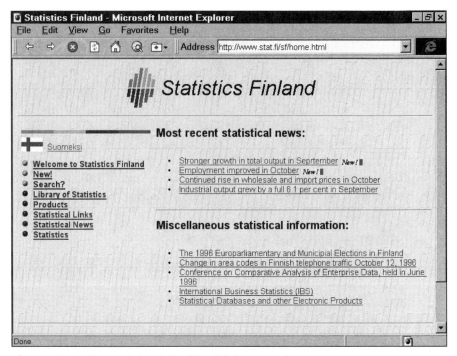

Figure 10-3   The Statistics Finland English-language home page.

Unfortunately, none of these directories is complete. In most cases, you might find links to just one or two sites in a country; but in many cases, you can follow links from those sites to other government sites in the same country. For example, the many agencies in the government of Malaysia have their own Web sites, but the Yahoo! directory lists only a handful.

To find more Web sites than those listed, follow these steps:

1. From the Yahoo! Government:Countries list (`http://www.yahoo.com//Government/Countries`), select the link to Malaysia@. You will jump to Yahoo's list of Malaysian government site.

2. The most promising item on the list is the Prime Minister's Department. Follow the links to the Prime Minister's home page.

3. Along with links to five years of speeches by the Prime Minister and other equally exciting items, there's also a link to Malaysia Information. Keep following likely-sounding links until you find the Government & Politics home page (`http://www.jaring.my/msia/govt/govt.html`), which has additional links to individual departments, ministries, state governments, and other agencies.

Obviously, the exact route to the information you want will be different for each country. But as a general rule, if you start with one of the worldwide directories, you can probably find an individual agency or department within three or four links.

State and Local Agencies

Finding a government home page for an American state, Canadian province, or other major region of a country is not much different from finding information from a national government: start with one directory and drill down to the specific page you want. To find a state, city, or county government, try one of these directories:

* The Public Technology, Inc., All Aboard guide to hundreds of city, town, and county home pages (http://pti.nw.dc.us/AllAboard.htm)
* Piper Resources' guide to State and Local Government on the Net (http://ww.piperinfo.com/state/states.html)
* The Library of Congress Internet Resource Page for State and Local Governments (http://lcweb.loc.gov/global/state/stategov.htm).
* The federal government Information Xchange includes a State and Local Governments page (http://www.info.gov/Info/html/state_government.htm) with both a clickable map and a text list of states
* USA CityLink (http://usacitylink.com)

If you can't find the place you want on one of these lists, try starting with the state or province and look for links to individual towns and cities, or use a search engine such as AltaVista to find all the pages related to the place in question.

Communicating with Elected Officials

Along with the lists of neighborhood schools and transit maps, many government Web sites also include lists of elected and appointed officials and automatic e-mail links to their mailboxes. When you click one of those links, your browser automatically opens your e-mail client, where you can write and send a message to the mayor, governor, or other official.

In some particularly enlightened places, the government may actually use the Web as a method for making meeting agendas and other very timely information available to concerned citizens. Once again, the city's home page is the place to start looking.

A few elected officials use their own personal home pages as one more way to convince their constituents that they're doing the job well enough to merit re-election. To find one of these pages, your best approach is to telephone the official's office and ask for a URL.

Election Information

During election campaigns, candidates' home pages are a new fact of political life. A good Web site might include the candidate's policy statements, a schedule of public appearances, and other information that a voter might want to decide whether or not to vote for that candidate.

You may find a candidate's URL in his or her printed campaign literature or in publications from the League of Women Voters and similar organizations. As an alternative, use the candidate's name for a keyword search with AltaVista or another search engine.

Other election Web sites are operated by political parties and by news media. On election nights, you can often find sites that provide detailed returns as the votes are counted. The news wire services, newspapers, and state or local election officials are all good places to look for the very latest numbers.

Interest Groups

Every imaginable political and social interest group is probably using a Web site to share information with its members and with interested outsiders. Some of these groups are out on the fringes, but many more are mainstream organizations, such as the AFL-CIO and the Red Cross. The Lycos subject list of Web sites (`http://a2z.lycos.com/index.html`) is a good place to start looking for the groups that interest you.

One less-than-obvious advantage of using the Web as a source for information about controversial groups rather than requesting it by mail or in person is that you can do it without calling attention to yourself — you don't have to let them add you to a mailing list or ask you for a contribution. If you want to receive more information or send a donation, that's your own business, but if you prefer, you can visit a Web site without any further obligation.

Health and Medical Sites

It's not a substitute for a visit to your doctor, but a tremendous range of medical information is available on the World Wide Web. Many hospitals, medical schools, and research institutions have Web sites with descriptions of various diseases and other medical conditions, advice for healthful living, and reports about recent research.

Some of these Web sites are targeted to medical professionals, whereas others are aimed at a more general audience. The amount of technical detail, complex language, and, unfortunately, the trustworthiness of each site is quite different. Because you can find everything on the Web from authoritative medical advice to advertisements for snake oil and "alternative therapies" of doubtful value, you should be extremely careful before taking any kind of action based on what you might see on your computer screen. As Dr. John H. Renner says in his In My Humble Opinion column on the Internet Health Watch Web page (http://www.reutershealth.com/ihw/):

> Because anyone can publish a Web page, bogus, inaccurate, and bizarre health information is sometimes masqueraded as authoritative and semi-scientific fact. Many pages have no known sponsor or origin of information. Also, there are no rules governing the links to other Web sites. As a result, even if the links are responsible or useful, the main information may be incorrect or misleading. It can be a daunting challenge to sort good, trustworthy medical information from well-packaged misinformation."

That said, here are some medical Web sites that appear to be reliable:

* **thrive@pathfinder** (pathfinder.com/thrive/). Part of the huge Time Warner Pathfinder Web site, thrive@pathfinder contains news about current medical developments; advice about cooking and nutrition, fitness, and sexuality; and an easy-to-use database of illnesses and conditions, symptoms, and prescription and non-prescription drugs. Thrive's medical information is written in clear English without a lot of dense technical medical language.

* **Reuters Health Information Services** (www.reutershealth.com). The Reuters Health Information Services (RHIS) uses the resources of the worldwide Reuters news service to offer a global, daily service that reports on major healthcare news. RHIS includes separate news files for consumers and medical professionals.

  The professional service, Reuters Medical News, includes 40 to 50 separate daily stories organized into 16 categories. The consumer service, Reuters Health eLine, is written in a style that is much easier for non-professionals to understand. RHIS also has links to the Internet Health Watch, which offers a doctor's reviews of other good, bad, and indifferent medical Web sites.

* **America's HouseCall Network** (http://www.housecall.com). America's HouseCall Network is a database of medical information supplied by the American Academy of Family Physicians, the National Health Council, and other organizations. The site includes access to information about many common medical concerns. This is a good source for answers to your medical questions, but the information on this or any other Web site should not be a substitute for a visit to your own doctor.

Travel

||t should not surprise you to discover that thousands of hotels, resorts, airlines, railways, auto rental agencies, and other tourist services and destinations have sites on the World Wide Web where you can learn about places to go, plan your itinerary, and even buy tickets and reserve hotel rooms.

Of course, you could do the same thing through a traditional travel agent. Most travel agents have stacks of brochures and guidebooks, but they don't always have specific answers about every place in the world that you might want to visit. Unfortunately, when you want to go someplace off the proverbial beaten path, a travel agent may know less about it than you do.

When you want to find out about, say, tourist facilities in Grik, Malaysia, the average American or European travel agent won't be able to offer much help. But a quick Web search will give you the names and descriptions of ten hotels and the Malaysian equivalent of a dude ranch (as shown in Figure 10-4).

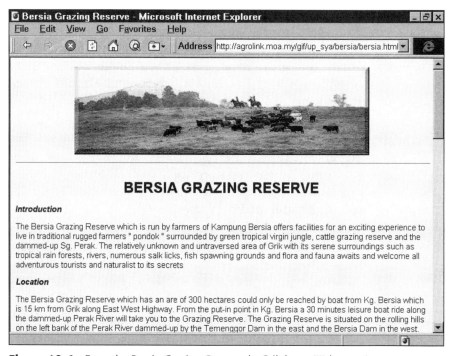

Figure 10-4   Even the Bersia Grazing Reserve in Grik has a Web page!

BE YOUR OWN TRAVEL AGENT

As an example of what you can find on the Web, here's my own recent experience: While I was writing this book, I took a short vacation to South Asia. The only hotels my travel agent in Seattle was able to suggest were parts of big, international chains that specialized in deluxe service for business people on expense accounts. Not the sort of place that I wanted at all.

After a few minutes on the Web, I found descriptions of several far less expensive hotels in all the cities I wanted to visit, including maps, pictures, and other information. The hotels I selected accepted my reservations by e-mail and returned confirmations within a few hours or less. The staff member of one hotel seemed so pleased that the Web site had actually produced some new business that I received an upgrade to the top-floor "executive club" at no extra charge.

Several kinds of travel-related information are available on the Web:

* Interactive, online travel guides with links to specific destinations and services.

* International travel guides, usually related to magazines or guidebook publishers.

* General information about destinations, provided by government tourist bureaus, chambers of commerce, and similar organizations.

* Specific information about an airline, railway, ferry boat service, hotel, resort, or other individual business or chain. Some sites offer little more than the contents of a hotel's brochure, whereas others can give you highly detailed advice about a possible destination or access to specific schedules, fares, and reservations.

A few Web sites can even provide some sense of an establishment's character. For example, `http://inthenet.sm/hg/hg.htm` is a page that describes a hotel and restaurant in the tiny, mountaintop republic of San Marino. The site includes descriptions of the hotel in four languages, a map, and pictures of a guest room and the hotel's dining room. It also contains an embedded audio file that plays a short segment from Vivaldi's *The Four Seasons*.

Each of the Internet-directory Web sites shows dozens of travel links, but most of the time, you will probably be better off with a keyword search engine rather than a list of topics because you probably have a general idea where you want to go before you start looking around the Web. Asking for specific information about "hotels in Tuscany" or "nature preserves" is much more effective than asking for something as general as "vacations."

Travel Destinations

Web pages that describe cities, resorts, or other travel destinations are all over the Web, so the best way to find something specific is to search for a keyword. For example, follow these steps to obtain information about tourist services in Santa Fe, New Mexico:

1. Go to one of the major Internet search engines, such as Lycos or Yahoo!.

2. Type the name of your destination (in this case, **"Santa Fe"**) in the keyword search field and click the Search button. The search engine will return a list of Web pages that match your keyword.

3. In this case, Excite found more than 50,000 matches for "Santa Fe." At the top of the list is the Santa Fe Convention and Visitors Bureau home page, shown in Figure 10-5 (`http://www.nets.com/santafe/`) with links to a calendar of events, maps, lists of hotels and restaurants and much else. As you move down the list of matches, you can find many more Santa Fe-related pages.

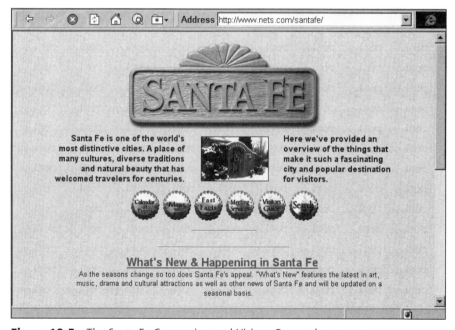

Figure 10-5   The Santa Fe Convention and Visitors Bureau home page.

If you don't find what you want the first place you look, try another link from the search engine. As a general rule, most search engines will probably list the Web pages with the most information about a destination in the first two or three pages of matching links.

Airline Web Sites

An airline's inventory of seats from Point A to Point B is absolutely worthless after an airplane leaves the ground with an empty seat. Therefore, the airlines set their prices to fill as many of those empty seats as possible. Many airlines use the World Wide Web to offer last-minute discounts.

The best airline sites on the Web have route maps, schedules, and online access to fares and reservations, along with information about destinations on their route systems and, sometimes, even some pictures of historic aircraft. For example, Alaska Airlines' home page (http://www.alaska-air.com) has a direct link to its reservations computer. To reserve a flight, follow these steps:

1. Jump to the Reservations page.

2. Type the names of your starting point and your destination in the From and To fields.

3. Choose the date and time you want to travel.

4. Click either the One Way or Round Trip button to send your request to the airline. After about a minute or two, you will see a new page that shows all the scheduled flights with available seats that meet your request.

5. Select the flights you want and follow the instructions on-screen to place your reservation and tell the airline how you want to obtain the ticket.

If you don't know or care which airline you want to use, try one of the services that isn't tied to a single airline, such as Internet Travel Network (http://www.itn.net), TravelWeb (http://www.travelweb.com/plane.html), or Trip Link (http://www.sys1.com/trip/). All three of these sites allow a user to enter a starting point, destination, and dates of travel and obtain a list of all available flights, regardless of airline.

Directories of Travel Sites on the Web

As I said earlier in this section, most travel information is best discovered with a search engine. But you may also want to take a look at a couple of general-interest travel Web sites:

* **Epicurious Travel.** From the publishers of *Conde Nast Traveler* magazine, the Epicurious Travel site (http://travel.epicurious.com) has links to a variety of travel services and news about special discount hotel and airline deals.

* **Travelocity.** Travelocity (http://www.travelocity.com) includes schedules for more that 700 airlines and reservations service for about 370 airlines, plus information about destinations, including thousands of hotels, restaurants, museums, and golf courses, and a link to Last Minute Deals offered by several airlines and rental car companies.

✳ **Search.com.** Under the Travel subject heading, Search.com has about three dozen links to other travel-related sites, including several automatic highway routing services.

Hobbies Online

No matter what your hobbies or other interests may be, there's probably a Web site (or several) and a community of other enthusiasts on the Web who share your passion for needlework, antique phonographs, or pet newts. Once you've found one of these Web pages, you can frequently follow links from that page to others with related information. Some hobby sites are maintained by other hobbyists, whereas others are more commercial sites provided by dealers of whatever the people who enjoy this particular hobby might need, such as crafts supplies, spare parts, or actual examples of the items themselves.

Once again, the place to begin is with a search engine. Type a description of the topic in the Search field and follow the links that come back from the search engine. For example, Figure 10-6 shows a site that I discovered with a search on the keyword *needlework*. This site contains a long list of links to other sites, many of which have additional links of their own. There's enough here to keep a curious quilter or embroiderer busy for weeks.

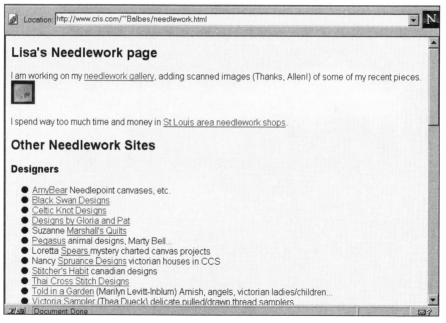

Figure 10-6 A needleworker's Web site with links to many other sites.

Similar sites exist for most other hobby topics. You may find catalogs, back issues of magazines, and sources of obscure, historical information along with related pictures and sound recordings.

Some of the items you may find when you run a search for a specialized topic are likely to be messages or articles from one or more Usenet newsgroups. Among the thousands of newsgroups, several hundred are devoted to hobby topics ranging from gardening to collecting model trains. In groups such as rec.antiques.radio+phono, rec.crafts.dollhouses, and dozens of others, participants share news and rumors, tips and techniques, and sometimes offer items for sale. It is not uncommon for a newcomer to a hobby to ask for advice ("Can anybody tell me how to rewire the armature on a 1937 Whizbang Model 42A?") or for more experienced people to describe their most recent projects and discoveries. In many cases, the single, best way to find some obscure bit of information is to post a question in an appropriate newsgroup.

NOTE AltaVista is a good choice for a search through newsgroups. To find relevant items in newsgroups, open the drop-down search field and select the Usenet option.

Unfortunately, most newsgroups have no quality control, so it's sometimes difficult to be certain that you're receiving reliable information; a self-appointed expert could very possibly post authoritative-sounding articles that are completely inaccurate. Of course, six (or sixty) other people will probably jump in and correct the mistake (sometimes with still more bad information), so you can gradually develop your own sense of who's reliable and who isn't.

With that warning in mind, it's worth the time and trouble to look for newsgroups that are devoted to your favorite hobbies and pastimes and spend some time reading recent articles. If the information looks worthwhile, you may want to consider checking for new articles every few days (or even more often for a really active group).

Personal Web Pages

Some people believe that the Internet and the World Wide Web are changing the world. If that's true, one of the biggest changes is that they make it possible for anybody with an Internet connection to become a *content provider*. Because production and distribution costs are low, just about anyone can create his or her own Web page.

Of course, that means that thousands of personal Web pages are out there that are not particularly interesting. With the possible exception of your own grandchildren, very few (if any) people will want to spend time looking at a page with nothing on it except pictures of your cat. Smart and funny as your cat may be, it's still a cat. That may seem obvious, but plenty of personal Web pages don't seem to have much more content than that.

However, there are also plenty of personal pages that are as entertaining or useful as anything created by a big corporation. Many college professors have created home pages about their academic specialties; advanced hobbyists have posted information about their collections; and any number of people have produced lists of links to other pages that they like for one reason or another. Along with the junk, some personal pages are among the most unusual, the most helpful, and the most amusing things anywhere on the Web.

All of the warnings that apply to any Web site apply even more to personal pages: just because it's on the Web is no guarantee that the information there is accurate. When you're reading a personal page that discusses politics, religion, or some other controversial subject, you should assume that the person who created the page has a particular point of view to promote; don't automatically accept everything you see as even-handed and objective.

One example of a good personal home page related to a hobby is the Folk Music home page (`http://www.jg.org/folk/folkhome.html`), which includes links to a couple hundred other pages related to folk music, including concert schedules, discographies, places to order instruments, recordings and songbooks, and much else related to traditional folk music.

BONUS

Finding Personal Web Sites

In practice, there are only a couple of reasons why you might want to visit a personal Web page: either you know the person who created it, or it has some content that interests you. It really doesn't make much sense to look for personal pages just because they are personal pages.

Therefore, you're likely to find the pages you want to visit in one of three ways: somebody gives you the URL of his or her page, you find a link to the page from another Web site, or you find it through a keyword search engine such as AltaVista.

If a member of your family tells you that he or she has just created a home page, or if you learn about one in a magazine or an online newsgroup, viewing the page is just a matter of typing the URL in your browser's address field. Just as it does for any other URL, the browser will find the server that contains the page you request and display it on your screen.

TIP   As always, it's essential that you get the URL exactly right, including any odd punctuation marks. In particular, you're likely to see a tilde (~) in some personal URLs. In the UNIX operating system, the tilde is a way of skipping part of the path between the server address and a directory that may be four or five layers down. The server replaces the tilde with a specific path that leads to the home page of the user's account. If you see a tilde in a URL, go ahead and use it, but if the URL includes a detailed path, don't try to replace it with a tilde.

When you search for a topic with a search engine, many of the sites you're likely to find may be personal sites. For example, an AltaVista search on *folk music* produces a list of links that includes both personal and commercial pages.

It can also be productive to run a search for the name of the person you want to find. If he or she has a home page (or if that person's name shows up on any other page, for that matter), you'll probably find it with a keyword search engine. This can be a great way to find old friends, school or college classmates, and distant relatives about whom you might never have known otherwise.

Other sources for pointers to personal home pages include signature blocks in e-mail and news articles. Many people include their URLs along with other ways to contact them in every message they send. When you see an article in a newsgroup that seems especially well-written or useful, you may want to take a look at the originator's home page to find out what else they have to say.

And finally, many access providers and online communities have set up directory pages with links to the home pages created by their customers. If you just want to spend some time looking at personal pages, one of these directories might be a good place to start.

To find pointers to service providers, follow these steps:

1. Jump to The List, a directory of Internet service providers around the world, at `http://thelist.com`.

2. Click one of the directory types to choose a state, province, or country directory.

3. Find a likely-looking access provider and jump to its home page.

4. Look on the home page for a link to Our Customer's Home Pages, XYZcom User Pages, or some such description. Click that link.

5. When you see a list of subscribers, choose the personal pages you want to visit.

Not all the service providers in The List have directories of their subscribers' pages, but many do.

Summary

The World Wide Web has hundreds of thousands of separate sites, with information and services related to almost every imaginable topic. You can consult a library catalog, find information and documents from local, state, and national government agencies, obtain advice about health and nutrition, and plan a trip to just about anywhere in the world. Whatever your hobby or other interest might be, you'll probably find a wealth of information online to support and encourage your obsession.

This chapter provided pointers to some of the places on the Web that may be related to your particular interests and suggestions for finding others. In general, the search engines and topical directories are the best place to start looking for just about anything; if you know where to look, you can probably find exactly what you want, along with dozens of similar things that you had never known about before.

CHAPTER ELEVEN

COMPUTER
RESOURCES

IN THIS CHAPTER, YOU LEARN THESE KEY SKILLS

J ust about everybody in the computer business has a Web site. If you think about it, this makes perfect sense, because everyone who uses the Web also uses a computer. Therefore, the World Wide Web is an excellent channel for distributing product information, software upgrades, and patches. It also provides a good way for users to communicate with manufacturers when they need help installing or using their products.

Besides the "official" information supplied by manufacturers, the Web is full of additional, technical information from individual users, groups, and other organizations who want to share their knowledge with other people. Not uncommonly, these secondary sites have better information and more detail than the ones maintained by the people responsible for the original product. This chapter tells you how to find information on the Internet that can make it easier to use your computer.

The Web as a Troubleshooting Tool

Here's an all-too-common scenario: your twelve-year-old nephew comes to visit and spends two hours in front of your computer, keeping your neighborhood safe from space aliens. When you turn on the machine after he goes home, the computer beeps nine times, but nothing shows up on-screen. Or maybe you buy a new accessory for your computer, but you find nothing in the instruction book about making it work. Or, even worse, you inherit a five-year-old computer widget from a friend or relative, with no information about installing it.

Obviously, you need help. You could try calling the manufacturer's technical support center, but the last time you tried that, you spent 38 minutes on long-distance hold, listening to new-age banjo music before anybody answered your questions. And three months later, you're still waiting for the support person to return your call with the specific information you requested.

If you know where to look, you can probably find the solution to many computer problems somewhere on the Web. It may not be quite as easy as handing the problem to an experienced technician, but when nobody will take your calls, being able to solve it yourself is a useful alternative.

And if you're really ambitious, you might even try looking at some of the Web sites that offer support for your particular computer *before* it breaks. You'll find explanations of all those special features and functions that you've never exactly understood and downloadable programs that will make your computer a great deal easier to use.

In practice, the Web and other online resources are especially useful when you're looking for that one specific fact that is keeping you from true computer happiness: the obscure command sequence, the special printer driver, or the exact words and numbers that you have to use when you configure a new program or a new piece of hardware. When you need more subjective information, actually talking to someone who can lead you through things is often better. But even then, a well-written description of the solution to your problem can be a close second-best.

Hardware and Software Support

So, you've tried all the obvious things to make your computer and software do what you want it to do: you've asked the resident 12-year-old in your house for help; you've called your friend who has been messing with computers for ten years; you've even looked in the instruction manual. What now? It's time to look for help from the manufacturer.

To find a manufacturer's home page on the World Wide Web, try http://www.*name of company*.com (for example, if you want to reach MegaGlobal

Data Systems, try `http://www.megaglobal.com`). If that doesn't work, use the name of the company as the keyword in a search engine. Try one of the subject-based services, such as Lycos, Excite, or Yahoo! first; if that doesn't find what you need, go to AltaVista, where you'll find every Web page that contains the company's name anywhere in its text.

Most computer-industry Web sites include both marketing information for people who haven't yet bought a company's products and technical support for those who have. Let's look at several examples ranging from large to relatively small.

A Very Large Web Site: Microsoft

As you might expect, the Microsoft Web site (`http://www.microsoft.com`) is huge. It contains hundreds of separate pages and thousands of downloadable files related to all their products. As Figure 11-1 shows, it has many separate sections, with information about individual products, archives of software for download, news releases and new product announcements, and apparently, everything else they could think of.

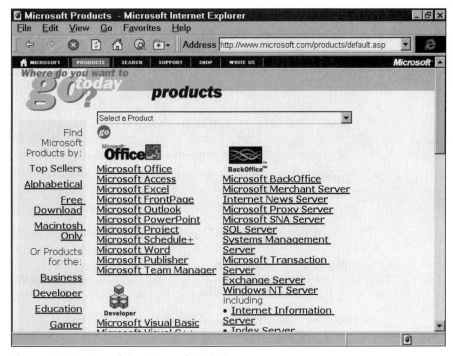

Figure 11-1   Part of the Microsoft Web site.

For example, if you want to find help on using a Microsoft product, follow these steps:

1. Go to the Microsoft Web site at `http://www.microsoft.com`.

2. Click the link to Support. You will see the page like Figure 11-2.

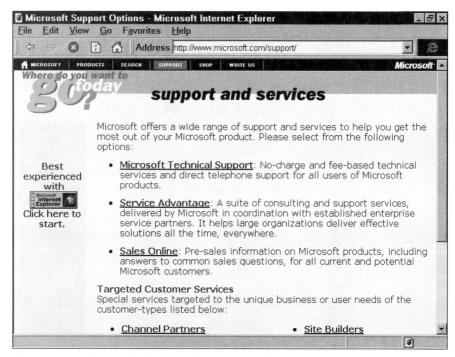

Figure 11-2   The top-level Microsoft Support Web page.

3. Choose the option that sounds like it will lead you to a solution to your problem. If you have a specific problem, try the Knowledge Base, where you can search for fixes to known issues. If you need a printer driver or an update to your software, try the download section.

If you're using Windows 95, you may want to download the free Windows 95 Power Toys set, which includes more than a dozen small programs that provide minor but useful tweaks to the Windows desktop.

To get a copy of this package, follow these steps:

1. Create a new folder called Power.

2. Jump to `http://www.microsoft.com/windows/software/powertoy.htm`. You will see the page shown in Figure 11-3.

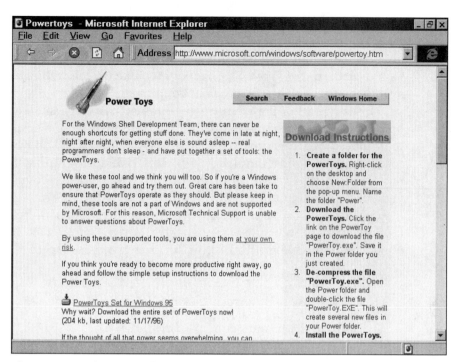

Figure 11-3 The Microsoft Windows 95 Power Toys Web page.

3. Read the descriptions of the programs in the package. You can download the whole package or, if you prefer, you can select the individual components that you want to install. Unfortunately, the descriptions aren't always completely clear, so you may want to go ahead and install everything and then remove anything you don't expect to use.

4. Click the link to the program you want to download. When your browser asks what you want to do with the downloaded file, tell it to store it in the new Power folder.

5. Close your browser and disconnect from the Internet.

6. Open the Power folder and double-click the file you just downloaded. The compressed .EXE file will expand and create several new files.

7. To install an individual program, right-click on a .INF file and choose the Install option.

A Smaller Site: Seagate Disk Drives

Here's another scenario: your son-in-law replaces the disk drive in his computer and gives you the old one. The label on the drive says Seagate, with a model number, but you don't have any instruction book or other information. How do you install it?

Seagate's Web site (http://www.seagate.com) contains product data sheets for all of its current products, but more importantly, it also includes downloadable copies of the Installation Guides for every drive that's likely to be useful with a modern computer. These guides include all the information you need to install your new-old drive into your computer.

This is typical of the Web sites maintained by many small and medium-size hardware and software vendors. You can find instructions for performing common procedures, answers to frequently asked questions, and copies of product specifications on most manufacturers' sites, along with links to file archives that may contain new versions of software that may have become available since you bought the original product.

Of course, in an ideal world, you'd never have to look for this kind of information; everything would work perfectly right out of the box. But we're talking about computers, where nothing works exactly as you expect.

Here's the generic procedure for finding information from a manufacturer's Web site:

1. Use a search tool such as Excite or Yahoo! to find the site you want to visit.

2. Jump to the manufacturer's home page.

3. Look on the home page for a link to the information you want. If it's not there, look for a Site Index, search field, or something else that might lead you to the specific page you need to find.

Another type of downloadable program that is becoming very common on the Internet is the pre-release *beta test* version of new software products. In exchange for the use of these programs, the developers want you to tell them about any bugs that you might discover. The software developer encourages regular users of a program to try new and (perhaps) improved versions to find problems before the product goes into commercial release. If your comments and bug reports are particularly useful, a software developer might add you to its list of "official" beta testers and send you free copies of its future products.

If you like that sort of thing, testing beta software can be fun, but remember that you're dealing with pre-release programs that may still have major problems. If your business depends on the documents and reports that come out of your computer, you should let somebody else do the software testing.

Shareware Collections and FTP Archives

Manufacturers aren't the only people who distribute software through the Internet. There's a long tradition of users and third-party software developers making programs available at little or no cost. Some of these programs are *freeware*; the developer gives them away as a contribution to the community, or as a way to create a demand for their other products. Others are *shareware* offered on a try-before-you-buy deal; if you like the program, you're expected to send the developer a fee.

Many of these programs are add-on utilities that solve specific problems or add new features and functions to existing programs. Others are separate application programs. And, of course, many of the most popular shareware programs are games.

You'll probably discover that some of these "helpful little programs" are solutions for problems you've never detected, but if you discover one or two programs that eliminate some of the minor irritations connected with using a computer, the search is definitely worth the time and trouble.

For example, here are some of the most popular shareware categories:

* **File compression.** To save disk storage space and transmission time, most programs in online software archives are distributed in compressed form. That's why you will see so many downloadable files with .ZIP file extensions. Before you can use one of these programs, you must restore the files to their original, uncompressed form. Programs such as PKZIP and WinZip enable a user to create new, compressed files and open previously compressed files.

* **Anti-virus.** Unfortunately, a few files in public download archives may contain viruses that can do serious damage to your computer. The responsible archive-keepers check their files for viruses before they make them available for download, but it's still a good idea to use an anti-virus program for reassurance.

* **File viewers and players.** Before you can display an image file on your screen or play a sound file through your sound board and speakers, you must run that file through a program that recognizes the file format. Because you can find graphic files on the Internet in any of 20 or 30 formats, you ought to have at least one utility on your computer that will let you see what the image looks like. Two of the best shareware graphics viewers are LView and Paint Shop Pro.

* **Internet applications and tools.** The best of the freeware and shareware Internet programs are at least as good as the ones that you can buy at your local software emporium. Some are even better. You will find many of these tools on the computers of almost every serious Internet user.

You're already familiar with at least two of these programs — Microsoft Internet Explorer and Netscape Navigator. Both programs are essential tools for navigating around the World Wide Web. Many other, more specialized Internet programs are available that are clients for specific Internet protocols, such as FTP, Telnet, and news. All the file archive sites have extensive collections of Internet tools available, but the best places to look are the two specialist sites: TUCOWS (The Ultimate Collection Of Winsock Software) and Stroud's Consummate Winsock Applications List.

CAUTION: DOWNLOADING MAY BE HAZARDOUS TO YOUR (COMPUTER'S) HEALTH!

This is a good place to include a warning about downloading software from strangers. It's an unfortunate fact that installing software obtained through the Internet is one of the most common ways to infect your computer with a virus that could destroy all the data on your system (and ruin your whole afternoon).

Therefore, you should install and use an anti-virus filter program to test every program that you download. Three good ones are McAfee Viruscan, Norton Antivirus, and Thunderbyte Anti-Virus. The McAfee and Norton products are widely available through retail software dealers. You can download an evaluation version of the Thunderbyte program from their Web site at `http://www.thunderbyte.com`.

If you know the name of a shareware program, you can probably find a copy with a search engine. But more often, you may identify a problem or just want to look around to see what's out there. For that kind of search, your best bet is one of the shareware Web sites that offers descriptions and downloads hundreds of programs.

Many of these file archives include both shareware and freeware; understanding the difference is important. Shareware is software that the developer distributes at no charge, but if you use the program after a short evaluation period, you're expected to send the developer a payment. Most shareware operates on an honor system, but some programs automatically stop working after a month or two unless you obtain a registration code from the publisher. Freeware, on the other hand, is just what the name suggests: it's free. The software developer does not expect any kind of payment for freeware programs.

Some of these collections are limited to a single topic, such as Internet tools or graphics, whereas others are more general. Either way, the best download archive sites include reviews of each program and comparisons between programs that promise to perform similar jobs.

General-Purpose Shareware Collections

The best places to start looking for programs to download are the large file archives that gather software from hundreds of sources and organize them by category. Most of these sites are supported by advertisers.

You have two ways to use a software archive; either search for a specific program or browse through the descriptions of many programs and sample the ones that sound most interesting.

These collections have a lot of overlap among them, but it's a good idea to look at several because each may have a few programs that are not available from any other sites.

SHAREWARE.COM AND DOWNLOAD.COM

Shareware.com (`http://www.shareware.com`) and Download.com (`http://www.download.com`) are services of C|net, the same people responsible for Search.com and several other Internet-related Web sites. As the name suggests, Shareware.com (Figure 11-4) specializes in shareware; the Virtual Software Library search tool maintains a database of more than 160,000 files.

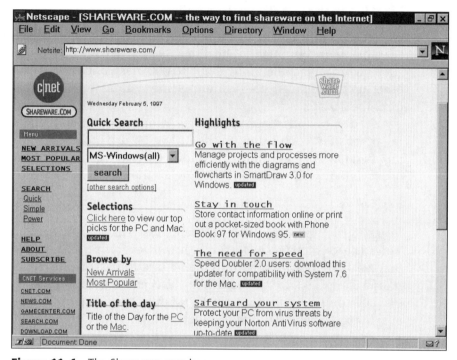

Figure 11-4   The Shareware.com home page.

Download.com is primarily a source for commercial files, including demonstration versions of shrink-wrap programs; upgrades, patches, and drivers for existing programs; and selected shareware and freeware programs. Some files may be available from both services.

JUMBO

Jumbo (`http://www.jumbo.com`) organizes almost 100,000 shareware and freeware programs into more than two dozen categories. Jumbo doesn't offer as much descriptive information about each program as some sites, but it has one of the largest catalogs.

WINSITE

Winsite (`http://www.winsite.com`) claims to be "the planet's largest software archive for Windows shareware." Winsite is the weakest of the major archives in graphic presentation, but it has features that suggest some careful thought has gone into the archive's design. When you click a filename from one of the Winsite lists, you jump to a page that lists the estimated download times at different modem speeds and offers direct links to documents (such as read-me files and manuals) within the compressed file. When you're considering a file for download, these text files can give you many more details than the one- or two-sentence descriptions found in a download directory.

ZDNET SOFTWARE LIBRARY

ZDNet is an offshoot of the Ziff-Davis magazine empire, which includes a long list of popular computer publications. The ZDNet Software Library (`http://www.hotfiles.com/`) includes only about 10,000 files, so it's not as large as some of the other archives, but it does contain some unique items that are only available from the ZD site.

ZD also provides more subjective information about each file than some of the other sites. Each listing in the ZDNet library includes a one- to five-star rating. In addition, you can find Roundup Reviews in which an editor evaluates five or six similar programs and recommends the best of the lot.

FILEPILE

ExecPC's FilePile (`http://filepile.com`) looks like a definition of the word *shovelware*. The creators seem to have thrown everything they could find into this archive — shareware programs, demo programs, satellite TV schedules, graphic image files (GIFs), hardware drivers, screensavers, sound files, and even files for antique computers that use the CP/M operating system. If you can't find a specific file someplace else, there's a good chance that it is someplace in this archive of more than a million files.

Internet Tools

All the shareware archives have sections that offer tools for obtaining specialized services through the Internet. But the best places to look for Internet programs are the sites that specialize in them — such as Stroud's Consummate Winsock Apps List and The Ultimate Collection of Winsock Software (TUCOWS). You can find more information about these programs from either of these sites, described in more detail later in this section, than from any of the general-interest shareware sites.

When you're ready to move beyond your Web browser to explore some other features and services the Internet has to offer, these collections are the best place to look for newsreaders, FTP clients, stock ticker programs, weather forecast programs, Telnet programs, and about 30 other categories of specialized Internet services. Both sites have very similar lists — it's very rare to find a program on one that isn't listed on the other as well. After watching both sites for a while, you get the impression that the first thing each site-keeper does every day is to look at the other site to see if the competition has discovered something that he has missed.

STROUD'S CONSUMMATE WINSOCK APPLICATIONS LIST

Forrest Stroud's CWSApps List (http://www.stroud.com) uses a one- to five-star rating system for each program in about three dozen categories, with separate lists in each category for Windows 3.1 and Windows 95 programs. As Figure 11-5 shows, each listing includes links to a detailed review and to the software developer's own pages for downloads and more information. If the same publisher has released other, related programs, the listing also provides direct links to Stroud's descriptions of those programs.

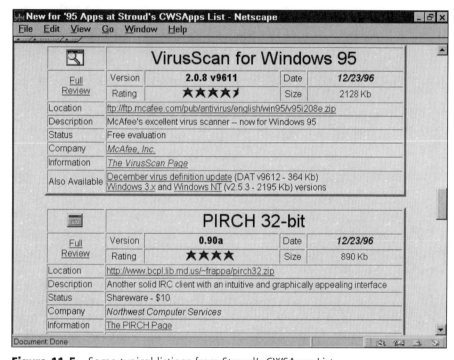

Figure 11-5 Some typical listings from Stroud's CWSApps List.

TUCOWS

TUCOWS, The Ultimate Collection of Winsock Software (http://www.tucows.com), has just about all the same files as the Stroud List, but it downloads most of them from their own servers rather than from the developers' home sites. In practice, this isn't likely to make much difference because the files in both locations are identical. Unlike Stroud's, which is limited to Windows programs, TUCOWS has a separate list of downloadable Internet tools for the Macintosh.

Each TUCOWS listing includes a rating of up to five Holstein cows and a link to the developer's home page, but it provides no detailed reviews or comments about individual programs. Figure 11-6 shows a typical listing.

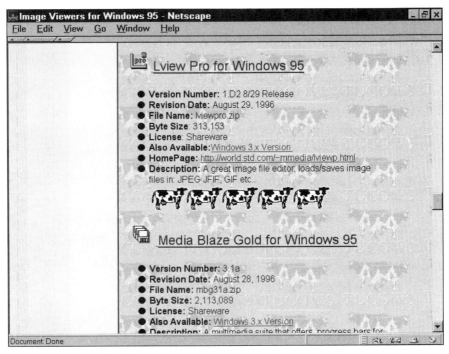

Figure 11-6 A TUCOWS program listing.

User Groups

L ong before the Internet became a universal information source, computer users met to exchange war stories and programs and to present a "united front" to the software and hardware manufacturers who depended on them for repeat business. Many user groups have established libraries of programs and other resources, and some offer as much informal support as the manufacturers themselves. When a manufacturer disappears or moves away from an older product, other users are sometimes the only place to look for help.

User groups exist for just about every type of computer and most popular software products. If you have questions about a particular program, an obscure type of system, or if you want advice from somebody who isn't interested in selling something, a user group can be a great place to start. And as you become more adept at using your own computer, you may want to give back some of your knowledge and experience by answering questions from other people.

Some user groups are local organizations that hold meetings where members can listen to resident and guest experts, exchange rumors and gossip about their favorite hardware and software, and sometimes preview new products before they're released to the general public. Other user groups are national or international, with hundreds or thousands of members. Many manufacturers use their products' user groups as a direct channel to communicate with many of their best and most loyal customers (who are sometimes also their most vocal critics). Today, many user groups maintain their own Web sites, with libraries of useful files, patches, and add-on programs and lists of answers to frequently asked questions (FAQs).

WEB PATH Two good places to look for links to user groups on the Web are the **User Group Connection** (`http://www.ugconnection.org`) **and Yahoo!'s Directory of User Groups** (`http://www.yahoo.com/Computers_and_Internet/Organizations/User_Groups/`).

Newsgroups

There's one more place on the Internet where you can find help with your computer: newsgroups. If you can find a newsgroup devoted to a particular type of computer or software product, you will probably find people there who can answer your questions. In addition, many manufacturers keep at least one eye on the newsgroups related to their products, so you might get answers directly from their tech support people.

The most difficult part of using a newsgroup can be finding the right one; there are more than 15,000 user groups, and the names are not always models of clarity. This is especially true in the technical topics, where the groups are organized into hierarchies that apparently make sense to somebody.

In general, the newsgroups where people discuss computer topics have names that begin with *comp.*, followed by additional words (or abbreviations) that describe the specific topic. For example, there are groups called comp.apps.spreadsheets, comp.laser-printers, and comp.os.ms-windows.apps.word-proc.

NOTE If you're looking for information about a Microsoft product, you should also look in the microsoft.public.*** hierarchy. Microsoft has established more than 200 separate groups, each devoted to a single product.

Before you jump in with both feet and ask a question in a newsgroup, it's a good idea to read the messages that other people have posted. If you can find an answer, don't bother posting the same question again; the answer won't change and the regular participants are probably tired of seeing it. In many newsgroups, you can find a document called a FAQ (short for *frequently asked questions*) that lists the most common problems faced by inexperienced users. In some newsgroups, somebody posts the FAQ as an article every month or two; in others, you will see articles with instructions for obtaining the document via e-mail or through the Web.

BONUS

More Internet Tools and Toys

M any people are quite happy to just use a Web browser, maybe an e-mail client, and two or three other basic client programs in their cyberspace explorations. They're more interested in the things they can find on the Internet than the methods they must use to reach them. But for other people, the process of moving around the Web is just as exciting as the destination. If you're part of that second group, plenty of dandy new programs are out there for you.

Many new Internet client programs and accessories appear on the Stroud and TUCOWS lists every week or two. A few are must-have advances over anything previously available, but others are little more than one-trick ponies that are good for an entertaining evening or two. As long as you have a relatively up-to-date Web browser, and maybe a separate e-mail client, you can get along without most of these programs. You don't need them to navigate the Web. But if you want to enhance your plain vanilla Web browser or play with some of the other services available through the Internet, the programs in this section are a good place to begin.

Oil Change

Oil Change is a shareware utility that automatically compares the installed versions of other programs on your computer to the most recent versions available from the software developers. When it discovers an out-of-date program, it lists all currently available updates, patches, and new drivers, and explains what each update will do for you.

When you select an update, Oil Change downloads it from the manufacturer and installs it on your system. You can download a limited version of Oil Change from http://www.cybermedia.com/products/oilchange/ochome.html. The full version, which supports hundreds of additional programs, is available from Cybermedia for about $40.

Oil Change is a relatively inexpensive way to keep up with changes to your application programs. Many of these changes probably won't make any difference to the way you operate your computer, but finding just one or two patches or a revised driver can help you avoid many hours of misery.

When you start the program, Oil Change scans your system to identify all of the programs currently installed. Figure 11-7 shows the results of an Oil Change scan in an Applications and Drivers list. Under each application that Oil Change recognizes, it lists all available updates.

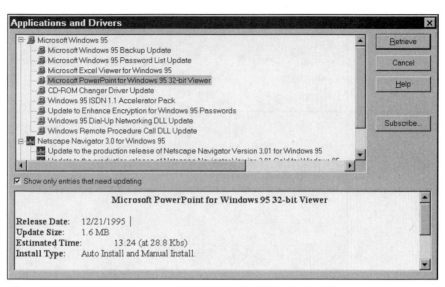

Figure 11-7 The Oil Change Applications and Drivers list.

Select an update to display a description in the bottom half of the dialog box. To install an update, click the Retrieve button.

FTP Explorer

When downloading files from FTP archives, you don't need to use a separate FTP client program, because you can use your browser to do the same task. However, the FTP protocol method is faster when you transfer files because it doesn't exchange as many handshaking signals as a browser. FTP Explorer is a share-ware FTP client with a screen layout and command structure very similar to those in other Windows 95 applications. It's available for evaluation at http://www.ftpx.com.

Figure 11-8 shows FTP Explorer connected to the FTP archive at the University of North Carolina. The left pane of the window shows the archive's file structure, whereas the right pane shows individual files within the current folder. The program displays messages in the bottom pane as it receives them from the server.

To connect to an FTP archive, follow these steps:

1. Click the Connect button in the toolbar or select **Tools** → **Connect**. The Connect dialog box shown in Figure 11-9 appears.

2. Select the archive from the list on the left side of the dialog box or type the address of the archive in the Host Address field.

3. Make sure that the Anonymous option is active.

4. Click the Connect button.

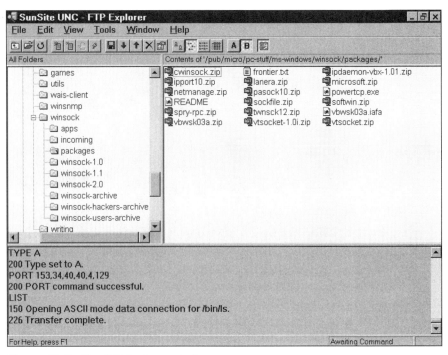

Figure 11-8 The FTP Explorer window.

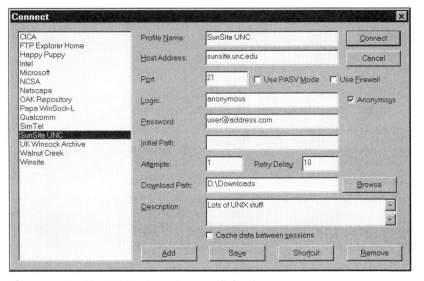

Figure 11-9 The FTP Explorer Connect dialog box.

Like Windows Explorer, FTP Explorer displays files as large or small icons, or as a list of files with or without details.

To transfer a file from the archive to your default download folder, either double-click the icon, select **File** → **Download**, click the Download button in the toolbar, or drag and drop an icon to your desktop.

The Internet Chess Club

Users started playing chess across the Internet just a few months after the first academic computers were connected in 1969. The Internet Chess Club (ICC—http://www.chessclub.com) carries on this tradition with a Web site that supports more than 15,000 games on a busy day. At any time of the day or night, you can log in to ICC and find a ready opponent close to your own skill level, from beginners to Grandmasters and International Masters.

BlitzIn Chess is a Windows chess client for Windows 95 (Figure 11-10) that displays your own moves and those of your opponent as they occur. It's available for free download from ICC.

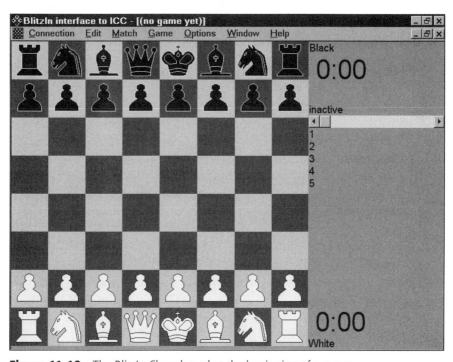

Figure 11-10   The BlitzIn Chess board at the beginning of a game.

NetCheckers

If chess is too complex for you, how about checkers? Pillar Software's NetCheckers is a combined client and server that connects directly via the Internet to another player using the same program. You can download NetCheckers from http://www.pillarsoft.com/.

The program doesn't include a place to find other players, so you'll have to connect directly to an opponent who's also using NetCheckers.

To connect to another player and start a game, follow these steps:

1. Both players connect to the Internet.

2. Start NetCheckers. The game window in Figure 11-11 appears.

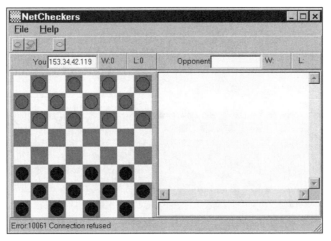

Figure 11-11 The NetCheckers board.

3. NetCheckers displays the IP address for your current connection in the You field directly above the board. Obtain your opponent's IP address (by telephone or e-mail).

4. Click the Start button in the toolbar. The player who hits the Start button first gets the black pieces and the first move.

5. The other player clicks the Join button and types the opponent's IP address in the Connect dialog box. That player gets the red pieces.

6. To exchange messages during the game, type text into the pane at the bottom right and press Enter. The text appears in the message area to the right of the board.

Summary

The World Wide Web is full of information about computers and software. Almost every hardware manufacturer and software developer has a Web site, and many other sites are run by user groups. Still other unofficial sites are devoted to most of the popular systems and programs. Other Web sites contain huge archives of free and low-cost software that can make your computing life easier and more pleasant. If you can't find the help you need on a Web site, you can probably find somebody in a newsgroup who knows the answers to all your questions.

CHAPTER TWELVE

COMMERCIAL WEB SITES

IN THIS CHAPTER YOU LEARN THESE KEY SKILLS

FINDING PRODUCT INFORMATION ON THE WEB
PAGE 212

BUYING PRODUCTS ON THE WEB   PAGE 215

INVESTING THROUGH THE WEB   PAGE 228

TAKING ADVANTAGE OF PRIVATE SALES THROUGH THE
WEB   PAGE 229

12

T he Internet and the World Wide Web started out as communication tools
for academic researchers and computer professionals, but they're rapidly
becoming mass media. Like radio, which started out as a way for ships to
talk to shore stations, businesses are exploiting the Web as yet another way to
promote and sell their products. The banner advertisements you see on many
Web pages are just one form of this commercialization of the Web.

Advertising on the Web may or may not be a good thing, but it's here. The
big corporations and advertising agencies are spending serious money on Web
content and design. And just as the ads can be more interesting than the editorial content in certain magazines, many commercial Web sites are among the
best things on the Internet.

X-REF   This chapter contains descriptions of some of the things you can find on
commercial Web sites, including product descriptions, catalogs, online
auctions, and financial brokerage transactions. Of course, these aren't the
only commercial sites that appear in this book; some of the travel sites in
Chapter 10 and the computer support sites in Chapter 11 exist at least in
part as promotional exercises for the companies who create them.

But the sites in this chapter are more blatant; they're purely commercial. Both the Internet and the Web were created as channels for people to share information and ideas, but most commercial sites are not concerned with sharing anything; they exist to convince you to buy something.

That doesn't make them bad. When you're trying to choose a new refrigerator, looking for a bargain on computer equipment, or searching for a book that's not available at your local shopping mall, a commercial Web site can save a tremendous amount of time and trouble. But it's extremely important to remember that advertising on a Web page can be just as aggressive and just as misleading as anything you might see on television.

Finding Product Information

Like it or not, everybody is a consumer. Whether it's kitchen appliances, cars, groceries, clothing, or books, you're going to buy something. Hundreds of businesses have placed information about their products on the Web. If you're looking for information about a specific product, or if you want to find out about items within a specific category, manufacturers' Web sites are a good place to start looking.

In some cases, you may want to use the Web to find and compare similar products within the same category. At other times, you might be searching for very specific information about a particular product. Either way, you most likely can find what you want on the Web, but the search techniques will be quite different.

Searching for a Category

The best ways to run a category search are to use Web directories that have listings for that category or a keyword search in one of the Web search engines. For example, if you're a golfer, you may decide that it's time for a new bag. Your local pro shop carries two types, but neither is exactly what you want. So, you turn to the Web.

To find descriptions of golf bags on the World Wide Web, follow these steps:

1. Jump to a Web directory. For this example, use Yahoo! (`http://www.yahoo.com`).

2. Type "golf bags" in the search field and press Enter. Yahoo! returns a list of more than 30 site matches, including Web sites maintained by makers of custom bags, bags made of ostrich skin, and an assortment of special designs such as the "dual-strap carrying system."

3. Jump to each site that sounds as if it may contain useful information related to the type of product you want.

Subject searches like this are not always as extensive as other keyword searches, so you may not find every possible site related to the category you want. Therefore, running similar searches through more than one directory service is a good idea. You'll probably discover sites that the first search engine missed with each additional directory you try.

Finding Specifications and Product Data

You can also use the Web to research major purchases. For example, if you've decided it's time to replace your old refrigerator, you can look on the Web for product information from General Electric, Whirlpool, and the other major icebox manufacturers. Of course, you're probably not going to consider plunking down your money for a major purchase like a refrigerator or a car just because you found a picture on a Web page. But by using the lists of features and specifications on makers' Web sites to narrow your search to a few makes and models, you will be able to reduce the amount of time you'll have to spend talking to high-pressure sales people. As an informed consumer, you won't be as distracted by irrelevant features as you might be when you're staring at 38 different refrigerators all lined up at the store.

Today, the most common type of product information you're likely to find on the Web is still related to computers. But this is changing rapidly. Web sites are also available for everything from laundry detergent (http://www.clothesline.com) to orange juice (http://www.floridajuice.com) to musical instruments (http://www.g2g.com/steinway/). Within another year or two, you can expect to see many more new Web sites for just about every imaginable type of consumer and industrial product.

Yellow Pages Searches

Even if a business doesn't have a Web page, it almost certainly has a telephone. Therefore, you can probably find just about any business in a classified telephone directory. It should not surprise you to learn that that Web has several, nationwide Yellow Pages directories.

You know how the Yellow Pages works. Listings are organized by type of business, so you can look in one place to find all the bookstores, pretzel benders, or picture framers in town. The online yellow pages directories work exactly the same way, except that they aren't limited to a single metropolitan area unless you specify a geographic area for your search.

These yellow pages directories contain business listings for the United States:

* **Big Yellow.** Big Yellow (http://bigyellow.com) is a service of NYNEX, the regional telephone company in New York and the New England states. Big Yellow includes both business and residential directory databases and links to many other, more specific directories.

* **BigBook.** BigBook (http://www.bigbook.com) offers a similar directory service that provides a great deal more information in each listing, including a map, driving directions, and comments about the business from other BigBook users. However, it's also a lot slower than Big Yellow

* **GTE SuperPages.** GTE SuperPages (http://yp.gte.net) is one more nationwide, classified directory. Like BigBook, it provides a map that shows the location of a business and detailed driving instructions that allow you to specify your own location as well as that of the business you want to find. Figure 12-1 shows the route it recommended from Seattle to a nursery outside of Morton, Washington.

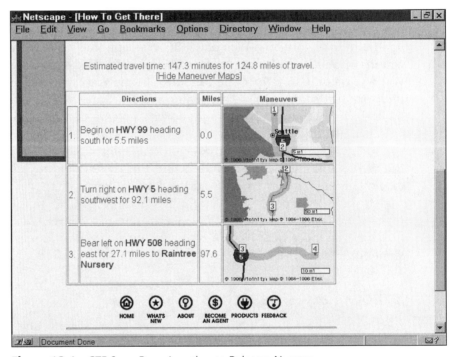

Figure 12-1 GTE SuperPages' routing to Raintree Nursery.

* **AT&T Toll-Free Internet Directory.** As the name suggests, the AT&T Toll-Free Internet Directory (http://att.net/dir800) is a searchable list of businesses that have toll-free telephone numbers. Unfortunately, the directory is limited to businesses that obtain their telephone service from AT&T, so many companies are not listed, even though they do have toll-free numbers.

For similar searches in other parts of the world, Big Yellow Global (http://bigyellow.com/global) is a good place to start. Organized by continent, it contains links to directory services in about three dozen countries.

Buying Stuff Through the Web

Information isn't the only thing you can obtain through the Web. Many businesses have set up sites where people can order airline tickets, books, computer equipment, fancy foods and wine, and clothing, among other things. *Electronic commerce,* as this kind of transaction is known, is not always a better method than ordering from a printed catalog, let alone walking into a retail store, but it does offer some advantages:

* **Convenience.** You can order groceries through the Web and have them delivered directly to your door. You can compare offerings from many suppliers in minutes without leaving your own desk. And you can discover a huge variety of products that you may not otherwise know about.

* **Inventory.** A very large bookstore may have 150,000 different titles in stock, but a well-organized online bookseller such as Amazon.com can maintain a database of more than a million books. If you're looking for an obscure book or recording or a regional food specialty that's not available at the local mall, you can probably find it from an online supplier.

* **Personal service.** Many high-end retailers use the Web to reach customers who are not able to come to their stores. Major department stores such as Nordstrom (`http://www.nordstrom-pta.com`) and Bloomingdale's (`http://www.bloomingdales.com`) will put you in touch with a "personal shopper" through the Web who will offer specific suggestions based on your own interests, style, and budget.

* **Access to foreign suppliers.** On the Internet, a computer on another continent is as easy to reach as one in your own town. Therefore, you can order handmade, wool sweaters from Australia, Tibetan rugs from a dealer in Nepal, and chocolates directly from a confectioner in Switzerland. And if you live in a country where local prices are high, you may be able to save a substantial amount by ordering books or computer equipment from overseas.

* **Unique items.** If you collect antiques, rare books, handcrafts, or other one-of-a-kind items, you've probably seen everything your local suppliers have to offer. A search through the World Wide Web will probably point you to some excellent new sources. Many specialist dealers have placed their catalogs on Web pages, where you can find pictures and descriptions of thousands of collectibles.

* **Special prices.** By ordering directly from manufacturers and discount outlets, you may find quality equal to what you find in high-priced retail stores, at a fraction of the cost. But remember to add the cost of shipping before you decide that you've discovered a real bargain. Other merchants use their Web sites as a convenient way to distribute lists of

surplus, overstock, and discontinued items, special sales, and other hot offers. Because adding one more page to an existing Web site doesn't cost very much, some specials can be extremely good deals.

Of course, there are a few drawbacks to buying things through the Web. Unlike a retail store where you can examine the merchandise before you buy it, you may sometimes receive things that are not exactly as they were described. And some completely unscrupulous businesses may take your order and never send anything at all. That's one of the reasons you should use a credit card to pay for your order — if there's a problem, you can tell your bank to cancel the transaction.

But in general, the proportion of honest merchants to any other kind is about the same on the Web as it is anywhere else. All the same rules apply to electronic commerce as to any other kind; just because somebody has created a Web site, that doesn't automatically make them any more or less reliable than any other business.

Catalog Shopping

Each of the general-interest Web directories includes a list of catalog sites, but the search engines are not always the fastest way to find a specific type of product catalog — when you enter a keyword like *quilts*, you may find several thousand matching pages, but most of them will be hobbyist home pages where people are more anxious to share information than to sell a product. You'll probably find a lot of interesting sites with a keyword search, but there are better ways to look for catalogs.

SIDE TRIP

USING CREDIT CARDS THROUGH THE WEB

Some people are concerned about the security of sending credit card numbers through the Internet. Isn't it possible for somebody to steal the number as it passes through all those computers between yours and the merchant's? It's technically possible, but it's extremely unlikely — it's probably no more dangerous than handing a credit card to the cashier at an all-night gas station or to the server in a restaurant.

If you do have doubts about security, most Web sites offer an alternative way to make contact — either a telephone number or a postal address. And, of course, you should carefully examine your sales slip and monthly statement to make sure that you haven't been overcharged, but that ought to be standard practice with any kind of charge account.

CATALOGS OF CATALOGS

One good approach is to search for *catalogs* in one the directory services, such as Yahoo! or Lycos. For example, Yahoo! returns almost 3,000 listings (including many duplicates) in 24 categories, ranging from apparel to volleyball. But you may have even better results if you try one of the "catalog of catalogs" sites.

One of the best is Buyer's Index (http://www.buyersindex.com), shown in Figure 12-2. Buyer's Index is a specialized search engine with a database of more than 4,000 mail order catalogs and Web sites. In other words, when you receive the results of a search for catalogs in a particular category, you won't have to sift through several hundred irrelevant listings to find what you want. For example, a search in Buyer's Index for *quilts* produced a list of just 18 catalogs and Web sites. Obviously, this is considerably less than the 3,000 quilt pages identified by Yahoo!, but all of them are actual dealers.

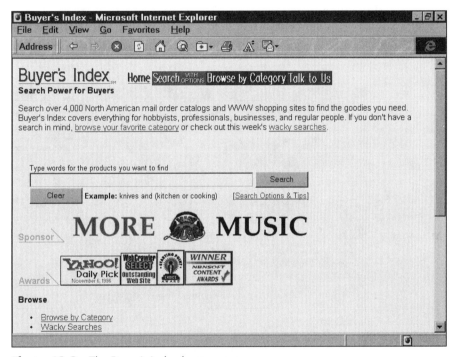

Figure 12-2   The Buyer's Index home page.

If you know exactly what you want to order, you can enter a very specific description in the Search field and get back a list that's limited to suppliers who actually carry the product you want.

The Catalog Site (http://www.catalogsite.com) is another "catalog of catalogs" with a slightly different approach. Although it does list a few companies who sell through the Web, the vast majority of the catalogs listed at The Catalog Site are the old-fashioned, ink-on-paper type.

AN INSIDE LOOK AT THE CATALOG TRADE

For true catalog addicts, Media Central's Catalog Age Web site (http://www.mediacentral.com/CatalogAge) is a chance to look behind the industry's curtains to learn how the business *really* works. It's also a great place to learn about new and unusual catalogs (both print and online) that you might not otherwise find. Even if you're not in the business, the monthly Cybercritic feature is worth a look. It's a review of some cataloger's Web site, written from a would-be consumer's point of view.

SHOPPING GUIDES

If you prefer to limit your shopping to Web sites rather than printed catalogs, the All-Internet Shopping Directory (http://www.webcom.com/tbrown) is a good place to start. As Figure 12-3 shows, it's a collection of links to commercial Web sites around the world.

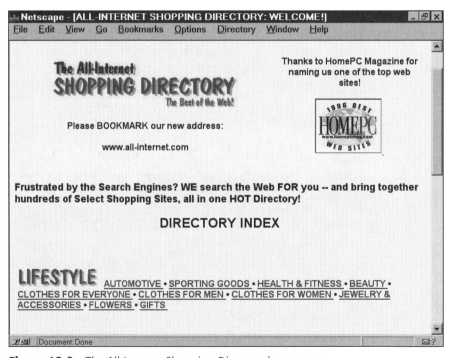

Figure 12-3 The All-Internet Shopping Directory home page.

Book Buying Online

Finding and buying books through the Web is quite different from buying sweaters or hand tools because there are so many different titles out there. Several online booksellers have created databases that include several times more books than any real-world bookstore could possibly keep in stock. And if you're looking for books that have not been published in your own country, ordering books through the Web is much faster and more convenient than trying to find a source by mail or telephone.

AMAZON.COM

Amazon.com is one of the Internet's early success stories. Without maintaining an inventory of its own, it offers access to just about every book currently in print in the United States. When you order, Amazon.com gets the book you want from a distributor and ships it out within a couple of days. Most books sell for at least 10 percent under the list price. Bestsellers and daily specials are even less.

At least that's the way it works most of the time. If Amazon.com can't find the book in any of its distributors' warehouses, it will order it directly from the publisher, which may mean that you'll have to wait several weeks or more to receive it. If that's likely, Amazon.com notes it in the description of the book. They charge full price for special-order titles.

The Amazon.com site has much more to it than just a simple catalog. If you enter a subject, title, or author, the search engine takes you to a list of matching titles. Click the one you want for a description like the one shown in Figure 12-4. To order a copy of the book, click the Add This Book to your Shopping Basket button.

If you don't know exactly what you want, Amazon.com's editors can help point you to new and interesting books in 40 different categories. They'll even let you sign up for an e-mail notice when Amazon.com gets new books that you might want to know about.

BOOK STACKS UNLIMITED AND BOOKSERVE

It was inevitable that other booksellers would try to duplicate Amazon.com's success selling books through the Web. Both Book Stacks Unlimited (http://www.books.com) and BookServe (http://www.bookserve.com) offer services similar to Amazon.com — including author, title, and subject searches, reviews from readers and editors, and discount prices.

WALK-IN BOOKSTORES WITH WEB SITES

The online mega-booksellers are a great convenience, but they can't match the kind of personal service that a good independent bookstore can provide. Unlike the national chains, independent bookstores are essential to the intellectual life of the cities they serve and much more willing to promote new writers who haven't yet developed commercial reputations. If you prefer to buy your books from a traditional bookstore, several good ones will accept orders through their Web sites.

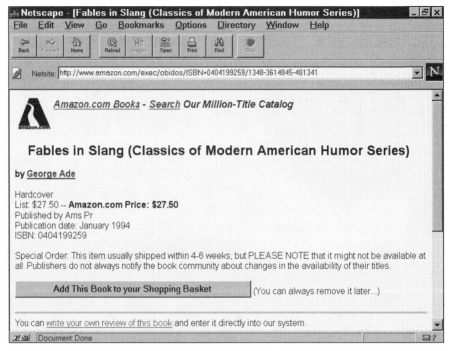

Figure 12-4 An Amazon.com book description.

The independent booksellers described in this section should provide a good place to start looking. If you want even more choices, the American Booksellers Association's Web site includes a directory of links to bookstore home pages at `http://www.bookweb.org/directory/202.html`.

ELLIOTT BAY BOOK COMPANY
Located in Seattle's Pioneer Square neighborhood, the Elliott Bay Book Company bookstore (`http://www.elliottbaybook.com/ebbco`) has an extremely knowledgeable staff and more than 150,000 titles on its shelves. Its Web site includes lists of staff recommendations, bargain books, and local Seattle authors.

THE UNIVERSITY BOOKSTORE
The other great Seattle bookstore is the University Bookstore (`http://www.bookstore.washington.edu`) at the University of Washington. The University Bookstore stocks more than 150,000 general and reference books in approximately 750 subject categories. Unlike most other online booksellers, this one doesn't charge for shipping and handling.

CODY'S BOOKS

Cody's Books main store (http://www.codysbooks.com) in Berkeley, California, has more than 140,000 books in stock, and they're all listed in a searchable, online database. The Web site also includes lists of new and recommended books and bestsellers.

POWELL'S BOOKS

Powell's Books (www.powells.com) in Portland, Oregon, is the largest bookstore in the United States. Because its sells both new and secondhand books, you can often find things at Powell's that may not be available from a place that limits itself to current titles. Powell's Web site allows customers to search quickly through more than a million new and secondhand books.

TATTERED COVER

The Tattered Cover bookstore (http://www.tatteredcover.com) in Denver has more than half a million books in stock. Tattered Cover doesn't have an online inventory database, but they will accept inquiries and orders through their Web site.

A CLEAN WELL-LIGHTED PLACE FOR BOOKS

With several stores in and around San Francisco, A Clean Well-Lighted Place for Books (http://www.bookstore.com) has more than 90,000 titles. You can search an online inventory database and order books directly from the home page.

FOREIGN BOOKSELLERS

Unfortunately, Amazon.com and its competitors are limited to books published in the United States. If you're looking for a book from some other country, you may have better luck trying a bookseller in that country. The following sections list some sites you can try, arranged by country.

AUSTRALIA

The Australian Online Bookshop (http://www.bookworm.com.au) will ship Australian books anywhere in the world. They offer a 10 percent discount on all orders, not including shipping.

BRITAIN

Blackwell's has been shipping books by mail from their Oxford book shop for many years. Blackwell's on the Internet (http://www.blackwell.co.uk/bookshops) offers a BookSearch service and separate listings for dozens of categories.

Waterstone's is a chain of book shops in Britain, Ireland, and the United States. Its Web site (http://www.waterstones.co.uk) offers most of the books published in Britain, but it adds very hefty shipping charges for overseas delivery.

The Gairloch Bookshop (http://www.catalyst-highlands.co.uk/book/shop) is a specialist in books about Scotland.

CANADA

Duthie Books in Vancouver (http://www.duthie.com) operates the International Virtual Bookstore, with more than 80,000 current and backlist titles in over 150 subject areas. The Web site's search engine enables customers to search for books by title, author, or subject.

Canada's Internet Bookstore (http://www.canadabooks.com) is a Canadian service similar to Amazon.com. It offers special discounts on bestsellers and Canadian award winners.

Canada's Virtual Bookstore (http://cvbookstore.com) specializes in books by Canadian authors and publishers. In addition to the usual search engine, its Web site also offers a browsing section with reviews and excerpts of new releases. Most books are offered at a discount, and customers collect bonus points with each purchase that they can trade for free books.

La Grande Ourse (http://www.cybersmith.net/ours) offers French-language books, CD-ROMs, and videos through a Web site that conducts business in both French and English.

GERMANY

Osiandersche Buchhandlung (http://www.osiander.de) offers a Web-order service for German books.

IRELAND

Fred Hanna's Bookstore in Dublin (http://www.adnet.ie/hannas) specializes in books from Ireland. Hanna's offers online searches, reviews, and a special courier delivery service for American customers.

The Ireland Bookstore in Dundalk (http://indigo.ie/~spc) offers fewer titles than Hanna's, but its prices are a bit lower.

ITALY

La Bancarella International Bookstore in Trieste offers books from all over the world. Its Web site (http://www.interware.it/bancarella) offers an online catalog of more than 300,000 items in both Italian and English.

Liberia Rinascita (http://www.rinascita.it/rinascita_web/rinascita_libr/rinlibringl.html) is another Italian bokseller that has more than 100,000 titles in its database.

MEXICO

Liberias Gandhi (http://www1.gandhi.com.mx) offers books from Mexico and other Spanish-speaking countries. Its Web site offers searches by author and title.

NEW ZEALAND

New Zealand Books Online (http://www.nzbooks.co.nz) is a catalog of New Zealand books, with sections devoted to new releases, best sellers, book reviews, and more.

SINGAPORE

The Singapore Bookshop (`http://www.bookshop.canadasia.com.sg`) specializes exclusively in books about Singapore and by Singapore authors. It takes orders through the Web site and accepts payment by credit card or check in U.S., Canadian, or Singapore dollars.

For links to booksellers in other countries, take a look at the Yahoo! directory under *name of country*:Business:Books.

USED AND RARE BOOKS

Locating secondhand and out-of-print books is a very different kind of challenge. Because no central warehouse exists where a retailer can obtain old books easily, finding a book that was originally published in 1927 rather than 1997 is a lot more difficult.

Before the Web came along, secondhand booksellers sent their customers printed lists of books currently on their shelves and advertised in trade publications like *The Antiquarian Bookman*. To find a particular book, a buyer had to search through pages and pages of lists, usually in very tiny print. Those methods are still used, but many booksellers have also placed their catalogs on Web sites. To find an out-of-print book on the Web, you still have to spend some time looking through catalogs, but you can automate much of the search process.

In fact, finding an old book can be an excellent test of your Web-searching skills. As an example, let's look for a copy of *Apples of New York*, by S.A. Beach, published in 1905.

USE A WEB SEARCH ENGINE

The first place to try is a Web search engine such as AltaVista or HotBot that can look for a specific string of text within millions of Web pages. Follow these steps to use AltaVista to search for a book:

1. Open the AltaVista main page (`http://www.altavista.digital.com/`).

2. Type the title of the book in the search field and click the Submit button. If the title has more than one word, use quotation marks around it. The search engine returns a list of matching Web pages, including one from a bookseller.

To search for the specific title within the catalog, follow these steps:

1. Select Edit → Find from within your browser.

2. Search the bookseller's Web page for *Apples*.

Aha! Here's a copy of *Apples of New York* for sale.

ANTIQUARIAN BOOKSELLERS' CATALOG SEARCH SERVICE

The next place to look is the Antiquarian Booksellers Association of America's ABAA-booknet Catalog Search service at `http://www.clark.net/pub/rmharris/abaa.html`. The ABAA maintains a searchable database of some of its members' catalogs, along with a separate list of links to hundreds of additional online catalogs of old and rare books.

When the ABAA Catalog Search finds a listing that fits your specifications, it gives you a link to the top of a bookseller's catalog rather than the specific listing you requested.

Therefore, you must follow these steps to find a particular book title:

1. Jump to the catalog you want to search.

2. Select `Edit` → `Find` in your browser to search for the title, author, or subject within the list.

Unfortunately, not all the linked catalogs are in the database, so it can be productive (if tedious) to look through each one separately. If the database search doesn't find the book you want, go to the ABAA's list of book dealers on the Internet and start looking through individual catalogs. Once again, the browser's Find command will save you a great deal of time.

If you're browsing for books on a particular topic rather than searching for a specific title or author, start with the ABAA's list of "dealers by specialty."

STILL MORE PLACES TO LOOK FOR BOOKS

Searching through catalogs that you find through the ABAA list will probably keep you busy for a couple of weeks, but it's not the only place to find second-hand books. Another good starting place for a book search is the Excite directory of Used, Old, & Rare bookstores (`http://www.excite.com/Subject/Shopping/Bookstores/Used_Old_and_Rare/`). A few of the booksellers on this list are also in the ABAA directory, but many of the largest are not.

Buying Music through the Web

Books and records (including compact discs and cassettes) have some things in common that make them good prospects for sales through the World Wide Web: they're relatively small objects, and there are thousands of individual titles. Outside of a few large cities, it can be extremely difficult to find anything except the current top hits, especially if you're looking for something obscure. Several music retailers have identified this opportunity and tried to take advantage of it.

CDNOW

CDnow (`http://www.cdnow.com/`) says it's the world's largest music store. It's certainly a well-organized Web site, with a search engine that accepts names of artists, album titles, individual songs, record labels, and audio samples from many records. You can display the results of a search in alphabetical order, by date, or according to CDnow's own ratings of each performer's best work. For those music fans who want to keep up with the latest and greatest, CDnow offers separate lists of best sellers and new releases.

For music lovers with specialized interests, the feature that makes CDnow particularly valuable is the amount of detail it provides about each artist. For example, Figure 12-5 shows the discography page for the American folk and blues singer Odetta. Each listing includes the year a record was first released, a rating (one to four stars), a list of tracks on the CD or tape, and links to a picture of the album cover and to short audio samples of each song.

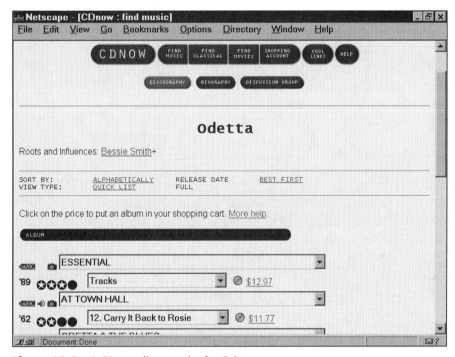

Figure 12-5 A CDnow discography for Odetta.

At the top of each discography page, CDnow has a link to a more detailed biography of the artist, links to Similar Artists and to other artists who were Roots and Influences. You can use these links to find new musicians that you might not know about but whom you're likely to enjoy.

GLOBAL ELECTRONIC MUSIC MARKETPLACE (GEMM)

GEMM is a database of almost a million new and used CDs, LPs, and related material from more than 700 retailers. When you enter the name of an artist, album, or record label, GEMM returns a list of matching items available from the participating dealers. For example, Figure 12-6 shows the result of a search for Odetta. Because this list includes both current and out-of-print releases, it's substantially longer than CDnow's discography on the same subject. Each item on the list is a link to the dealer who provided that listing. To order a recording, click the link and follow the specific instructions provided by each dealer.

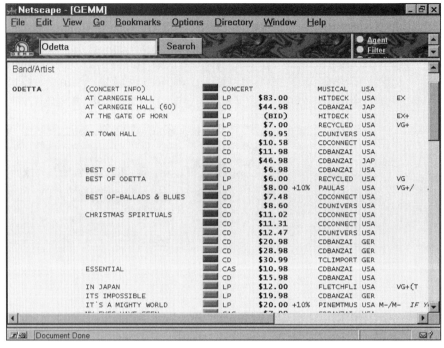

Figure 12-6   The product of a GEMM search for records by Odetta.

Antiques and collectibles

Books and records are not the only kind of collectible items sold through the Internet. Dealers in antiques and other one-of-a-kind collectibles also offer their merchandise on Web pages.

By now, you can probably guess the method for finding a specific type of item: use a search engine. The more specific your keywords, the better your chance of finding exactly what you want.

For example, follow these steps to find antique dealers who have Japanese Sumida pottery to sell:

1. Open the AltaVista search engine at `http://www.altavista.digital.com`.

2. Type **"sumida pottery"** (including the quotation marks) in the search field. AltaVista returns a handful of links.

3. Click each link to examine the site.

4. Many of the linked sites will probably be catalogs with several items in a list. Select `Edit` → `Find` to locate the specific item you want. In this case, the dealer has linked a photograph to each listing in an auction catalog. Figure 12-7 shows the dealer's picture of a Sumida pitcher.

Figure 12-7 A Sumida pitcher sold through an antique dealer's Web site.

If you prefer non-directed browsing through antique dealers' Web sites, the Antique-I-Net directory (`http://www.antique-i-net.com/ANTLINKS.htm`) contains links to more than 500 sites, including those specializing in things like corkscrews, typewriters, and jukeboxes.

Auctions

In addition to conventional merchants who offer things for sale at fixed prices, the Web is also home to several auction houses. An online auction works just like any other auction: if you're the highest bidder, you get the item.

The most common items in online auctions are slightly-out-of-date computer equipment. If you know exactly what you're getting, and if you don't mind buying last year's model, you can find some great bargains — but you'll probably have to spend an entire afternoon configuring your system to make the new widget work properly. Other Web auction houses sell antiques and collectible items such as toys, dolls, and works of art.

Table 12-1 lists some places to look for auctions on the Web.

TABLE 12-1 Auction Sites on the Web

Site	Wares	URL
A&A AUCTION GALLERY	Antiques, collectible glassware, fine art, and so on	http://www.bonk.com/auctions
AUCTION SALES	Mostly computer hardware and software, but also lists miscellaneous electronic stuff	http://www.auction-sales.com/
EBAY	Classified listings, mostly from individuals	http://www.ebay.com
ONSALE	Computers and consumer electronics from liquidators and manufacturers	http://www.onsale.com
VANDERMADE & COMPANY	An online flea market with all kinds of odd stuff for sale	http://www.vandermade.com
WORLD WIDE AUCTION	Collectibles, jewelry, art, coins, and stamps	http://www.wwauction.com

Investing Through the Web

Another type of commercial transaction that often can be easier and less costly to transact through the Web than via traditional channels is investment in stocks, bonds, and other securities. If you do your own research rather than taking advice from a broker, you can save a substantial amount in commissions by using one of the discount brokerages that accepts buy and sell orders through the Web. Financial trading through the Web is a rapidly growing new business. Because you must establish a continuing business relationship with a stockbroker, buying stocks and bonds is more complicated than ordering a book or a compact disc. Each online broker offers a slightly different set of services and has a different commission structure, so it's important to look at several before setting up your own account.

For information about setting up a brokerage account through the Web, go to these sites:

ACCUTRADE	`http://www.accutrade.com`
BULL & BEAR SECURITIES	`http://www.bullbear.com/`
CERES SECURITIES INTERACTIVE	`http://www.ceres.com`
EBROKER	`http://www.ebroker.com`
E*TRADE	`http://www.etrade.com`
CHARLES SCHWAB (E.SCHWAB)	`http://www.eschwab.com`
JACK WHITE & COMPANY	`http://pawws.secapl.com/jwc/`
K. AUFHAUSER & CO.	`http://www.aufhauser.com`
PC FINANCIAL NETWORK	`http://www.pcfn.com`
QUICK & REILLY	`http://quick-reilly.com`

Additional brokerage firms, including some of the large, well-established traditional companies are also introducing trading services through the Web. To find a current list of services, look in the Yahoo! directory under Business and Economy:Companies:Financial Services:Investment Services:Brokerages:Online Trading.

Private Sales

One more type of Internet commerce I want to discuss is private, noncommercial sales between individuals. It's not uncommon to buy and sell things through newsgroups and other online conferences.

The most common places to find this kind of deal is in the "marketplace" newsgroups specifically devoted to buying and selling and in newsgroups and mailing lists dedicated to hobby topics. For example, if you want to buy or sell a car in New Jersey, the newsgroup nj.market.auto is the place to look. If you're looking for a tuning capacitor for an RCA Radiola built in 1925, try rec.antiques.radio+phono.

Before you post an article in a newsgroup offering something for sale, it's extremely important to make sure that the other people who participate in that newsgroup consider this kind of informal advertising to be appropriate. If they don't, you'll probably hear about it in no uncertain terms. As a general rule, don't post a "for sale" article in a newsgroup or mailing list unless you have some positive indication that it would be welcome there. (Such an indication may just be other people posting similar messages or the newsgroup's charter specifically noting such items as acceptable.)

Some of the other newsgroups where buying and selling are welcome include the ones with the word "marketplace" or "forsale" in their names, such as rec.music.marketplace.vinyl, which contains lists of old phonograph records for sale, and uwash.forsale, devoted to items for sale at the University of Washington.

All the rules for doing business with strangers apply to transactions through the Net. Don't send money or goods if the deal doesn't sound legitimate; if it sounds too good to be true, it probably is. Don't assume that everybody is as honest and honorable as you, and don't send more money to a complete stranger than you can afford to lose. The vast majority of online transactions are entirely unremarkable, but unfortunately, there are a few people out there who are trying to take advantage of unsuspecting victims.

BONUS

Reminder Services: Keeping Track of Special Occasions

A computer is a fine tool for remembering important dates such as family birthdays and anniversaries. It can automatically give you advance notice about special occasions that take place on the same date every year, so you can mail those gifts and greetings that will convince your elderly aunt that you're always so thoughtful.

Of course, many people (including your aunt) have been doing this for years with a paper calendar. But letting a computer send you a message in advance may be more effective, because you don't have to remember to actually look at that calendar every day. As long as all that technology is available, you might as well use it.

Commercial reminder services exist that charge a small amount of money every year to send you postcards or some other form of notice a week before important birthdays and other occasions, but several Web sites offer similar services that will do the same thing via e-mail for free.

Remember that things change constantly on the World Wide Web. If you use one of these services to keep track of important dates, you should make sure the same information exists in some other form, such as a paper calendar. "I missed your birthday because my database was the victim of a hostile takeover" is an awfully lame-sounding excuse.

Candor's Free Reminder Service

One of the simplest of these services is a demonstration of Candor Technologies' Web-based database services. Follow these steps to use Candor's free Reminder Service:

1. Jump to Candor's Reminder Service home page at `http://www.candor.com/reminder/`. The interactive reminder page shown in Figure 12-8 appears.

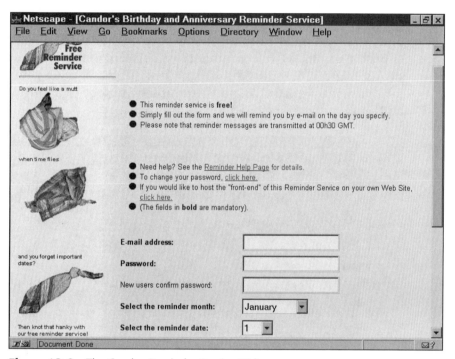

Figure 12-8 The Candor Reminder Service Web page.

2. If this is the first time you have used the service, choose a password and type it into both of the Password fields. If you have used the service before, just type your password once. You will use this password if you want to see a list of currently active reminder requests.

3. Type the address where you want the reminder service to send you a message into the E-mail Address field.

4. Use the drop-down menus to select the month and day when you want to receive this reminder message.

5. Select an option from the Remind Me menu to specify whether you want the reminder service to send you a message on the day of an event, a day or two before the date, or a week or two in advance.

6. Select either the Once only or Every year option.

7. In the message field, type the exact text of the message you want the reminder service to send you.

8. Click the Add Reminder button.

Remind Me!

The Remind Me! service operated by a Chicago florist (http://www.gbs.com/ flowers/remind.htm) offers the same kind of e-mail reminder as the Candor service. However, it can be configured to send you the same reminder once a week or once a month, as well as annual and once-only messages.

As Figure 12-9 shows, the input screen asks for similar information in a different format. Type the date and text of the message you want to send yourself, and select the message interval.

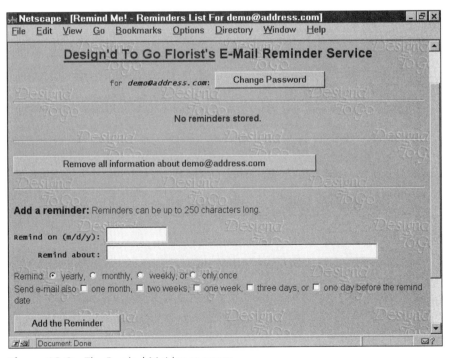

Figure 12-9 The Remind Me! input screen.

THE REMINDER

The Reminder (http://www.magellan.net/reminder) is one more free e-mail notice service. It tracks public holidays and special personal events and sends e-mail any specified number of days, weeks, or months in advance.

Summary

Thousands of businesses use the World Wide Web to offer information about their products and sell everything from computer equipment and books to hot sauce and antiques. Some retailers accept orders directly from their Web sites, whereas others provide catalogs, inventory databases, and other methods of locating hard-to-find items. Still others operate ongoing auction sales and automated stock brokerages.

Electronic commerce is still in its infancy, but it's probably as safe to use a credit card or charge account through the Web as to buy things over the telephone or across a counter. Ultimately, you can expect secure servers to make online transactions as common as the printed catalogs that clog your mailbox today.

BEYOND BROWSING

The Web is more than just words and pictures. This section tells you how to use the Web to see and hear multimedia programs and radio stations, to exchange messages with other people around the world, and to participate in virtual communities.

Stephen Gainer didn't know what to expect when he walked into the Harvard University auditorium the night of October 5, 1995. A friend had recruited him to videotape the Annual Ig Nobel Prize Ceremony, an awards presentation that honors people around the world for achievements that "cannot or should not be reproduced." The ceremony, sponsored by the Annals of Improbable Research (AIR), includes such awards as the Chemistry Prize, once given to a fellow who set the world record for igniting a barbecue grill in three seconds (using charcoal and liquid oxygen), and the Prize for Art, which went to the inventor of the plastic pink flamingo.

But it wasn't the awards that confused Gainer that night — it was his role in the broadcast. "What I didn't realize was that it was being televised directly on the Web," Gainer says. Armed with an S-VHS camera borrowed from the local cable station, a Sun workstation, a convicted felon (Robert T. Morris, who was convicted some years ago for creating the infamous worm that ultimately shut down the entire Internet), and the then-fledgling CU-SeeMe software, Gainer and the crew broadcast a direct feed from Cambridge, Mass., to the world.

The revolutionary CU-SeeMe software, the commercial version of which is available from White Pine Software (http://goliath.wpine.com), was developed as an experiment at Cornell University. Basically, the software enables live audio and video communication between two or more people on the Web. To increase transition speed and decrease the amount of resources it uses from your computer, CU-SeeMe uses a technique called *Frame Differencing* to read the picture and repaint only that which moves on-screen from one frame to the next (the background stays the same). "It's still very jerky but works for its purpose," Gainer says.

This must require some pretty hefty hardware, right? Wrong. "The technology has changed drastically since the Ig Nobel broadcast," Gainer says. "Sure, we used a Sun Workstation, but that was a year and a half ago. Now any two people who have cameras, average computers, and the software can teleconference — and the software is cheap." At $99, White Pine has indeed made teleconferencing accessible to almost everyone.

Gainer says the concerns about the Web making folks anti-social couldn't be further from the truth. "It's had a very positive influence on my life. Most of my family is in another state — we used to talk on the phone only about once a month. Now we e-mail constantly. And I see CU-SeeMe completely revitalizing personal communication. If anything, the Web makes you more interesting. There's more information right in your living room than you'd ever need — and hey, you can watch the Ig Nobels," Gainer laughs.

CHAPTER THIRTEEN

PLUG-INS, ADD-ONS, AND MULTIMEDIA AUDIO SERVICES

IN THIS CHAPTER YOU LEARN THESE KEY SKILLS

13

When the earliest Web pages were created, they consisted of nothing but text, with the occasional link to a picture that a separate program would display. Much has changed since those days. Today, many Web pages include scrolling text, embedded sounds, animated images, and direct access to programs that can perform even more complex tasks. It's entirely possible to create a Web site that offers both real and virtual bells and whistles.

The latest versions of both popular Web browsers include many of the tools necessary to take advantage of these features and functions. However, many additional programs are available that you may need for certain specialized services or obscure formats. This chapter explains how and where to find these add-on and plug-in programs, and how to integrate them with Netscape Navigator and Microsoft Internet Explorer.

The most important thing you need to understand about these enhancements to your Web browsers is that they're transparent — your browser will automatically load these fancy effects without any special action on your part. You can think of these functions as being a little like a new television channel: When the station goes on the air, you won't have to do anything special to receive it along with all the other channels you've been watching for years.

One special form of plug-in adds sounds to the words and pictures that you see on your screen. This chapter also tells you how to install and use audio plug-in programs, and where to find live and recorded radio programs, news events, and concerts that are available from hundreds of Web sites around the world.

Java

When you run a conventional program such as a word processor or a Web browser on your computer, the program files necessary to run that program are located on your own system. Even if you transfer a data file through the Internet from a server, you load that data into a local program. If you don't have a copy of the appropriate program (for example, if somebody gives you a diskette full of financial data formatted as a Microsoft Excel spreadsheet, but you don't have a copy of Excel), you're out of luck.

Java is a programming language that was originally created by Sun Microsystems for application programs that are located on a network server rather than on your own computer. When you request a Java data file, the server transfers both the file you requested and an application (called an *applet* in Java) that you need to use the data. It doesn't matter what kind of computer you're using, because Java client programs are available for many different platforms. As long as you have a browser or other client that recognizes Java, the applet will work with that client. For example, the stock tracking program shown in Figure 13-1 uses Java to load the applets it needs to obtain and display the current value and past performance of individual stocks.

Java applets can do almost anything, from adding a spinning globe or a bouncing logo to a simple Web page, to downloading and displaying a complex, multimedia, sound-and-video extravaganza, to providing live, real-time access to an airline reservation system that a passenger or travel agent can use to select a specific seat (http://www.somewhere.com/demos/midwest/booking/airline.html).

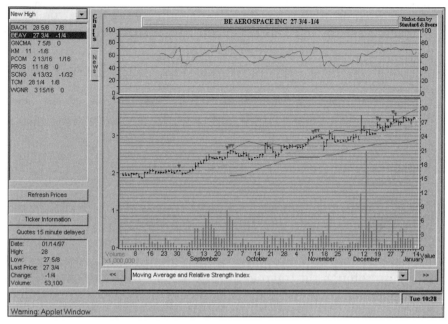

Figure13-1 A typical Java site: Wall Street Web.

For one more demonstration of a Java-enabled, interactive Web site, let's take a tour of pubs in Edinburgh, Scotland through a Web site that automatically follows the position of your mouse cursor:

1. To begin the tour, jump to `http://www.electrum.co.uk/pubs`.

2. Click the word Start to jump to the next page. Move your cursor over each of the people in the picture to see a message from that person.

3. Choose a guide and click his or her picture. For this tour, choose Gordon, the gentleman in the middle, to visit some historic pubs.

4. The Java applet in this site makes each page interactive — when you move your cursor over an interactive spot, the image changes. Move your cursor around the map to see descriptions of each of the pubs. Click a pin to visit a pub.

5. Move your cursor around the picture. When you find an interactive spot, such as the pub sign or the front door, the spot will light up and Gordon will tell you something about each feature. You can enter the pub by clicking the door.

From your perspective as a user, Java can add a great deal to the experience of using the Web without requiring you to find and install additional application programs on your own computer, because your Web browser automatically recognizes and loads Java applets as it needs them. In the long run, Java programs may make it possible to use a much simpler and less expensive computer (without any disk drive at all) to do many of the things you now do on your system, because you will download *all* your application programs as you need them rather than store them locally.

In the meantime, Java is one of those things that you should know about, even if you don't have to do anything special to use it. To see more demonstrations of the very latest Java applets, take a look at the Gamelan directory (`http://www.gamelan.com/index.shtml`).

ActiveX

So, Java will make everyone happier, wealthier, and improve our lives in every way, right? That's not the way Microsoft sees it. If all of you start using programs created with Java, you won't have to buy all those expensive Microsoft application programs because you'll download the programs you need through the Internet instead. So, Microsoft has introduced their own set of technologies, called ActiveX, that does many of the same things as Java, but it also integrates them into local application programs.

Microsoft has promised to make ActiveX an *open standard,* which means that the details will be available to anyone who wants to make a browser or other client program that recognizes ActiveX controls. Microsoft is also adding ActiveX controls to its application programs, including Word, Excel, and Office 97. The Microsoft Internet Explorer Web browser already includes the software necessary to display and play Web pages and other files that include ActiveX. Because many Web site developers are using ActiveX, Netscape has also added it to Netscape Navigator.

Plug-in Browser Enhancements

Java and ActiveX are deluxe tools for enhancing Web pages and distributing specialized services to users, but they're not the only ways to add animated images and special effects to a Web site. Dozens of other programs are available that can also incorporate audio, video, and interactive functions into the pages displayed by your Web browser. As a group, these programs are known as *plug-ins*. Both Netscape Navigator and Microsoft Internet Explorer can recognize most (if not all) these programs.

The basic difference between plug-ins and Java applets or ActiveX controls is the location of the software. Java applets live on a server and download to your computer only when you need them; the software for plug-ins must already be on your hard drive before you download data that requires that plug-in.

You may see three different kinds of plug-ins:

* Embedded plug-ins that place an image within a rectangular frame as part of a larger Web page

* Full-screen plug-ins that open in a separate page of their own
* Hidden plug-ins that run in the background

When you installed Internet Explorer or Netscape Navigator, you also installed some of the most commonly used plug-ins. To see a list of the plug-ins currently installed with your copy of Netscape Navigator, follow these steps:

1. Open Netscape Navigator.

2. Select Help → About Plug-ins . A list of installed plug-ins like the one in Figure 13-2 will appear.

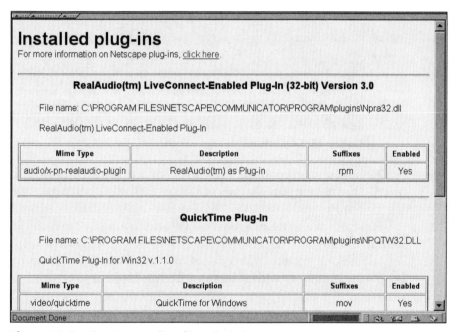

Figure 13-2 The Netscape list of installed plug-ins.

Installing a Plug-in

Before your browser can start a plug-in program, that program must be installed on your hard drive. That's not a serious problem, however, because you can download all those programs for free from the Net. You don't have to worry about loading a program until you need it, because just about any Web site that uses a plug-in will also have a link to a source for the plug-in program.

For example, one of the most common plug-in multimedia formats is Macromedia's Shockwave. The first time you try to open a page that uses Shockwave, Netscape will open a new browser window that contains its Plug-in Finder with a link to the Macromedia site (Figure 13-3), from which you can download a version of the Shockwave plug-in.

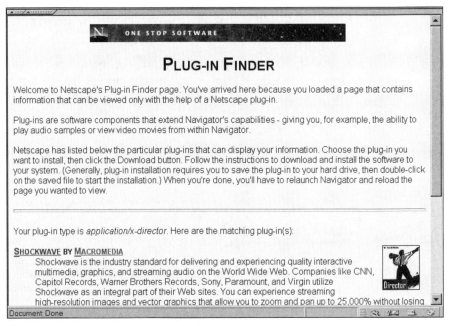

Figure 13-3 Netscape's Plug-in Finder.

After you download the plug-in, install it just as you would any other program. The installation routine will automatically configure your browser to recognize the new plug-in.

A similar sequence of events occurs when you use Microsoft Internet Explorer to link to a site that uses a plug-in format you haven't already installed. You will see a message window that offers to download the new program; when you install the plug-in, it will configure Internet Explorer to recognize it.

Testing Your New Plug-in

After the installation is complete, the easiest way to test it is to go back to the original page that you tried to visit before installing the plug-in program. If you want to try a different site or additional sites that use the new format, try the plug-in developer's home page. Most developers include links to their own and their users' pages that use their products. Look for a link called "gallery" or "demonstration."

Sources for Plug-ins

In most cases, you won't need a plug-in until you try to visit a site that uses that plug-in. But if you want to install one or more additional plug-ins in advance, you can use the Netscape guide to Third Party Inline Plug-ins, shown in Figure 13-4 (`http://home.netscape.com/comprod/mirror/navcomponents_download.html`) to link to just about every known plug-in developer. Although this is a Netscape site, you can safely use it with Microsoft Internet Explorer if that's your chosen browser — the plug-ins will work with either browser.

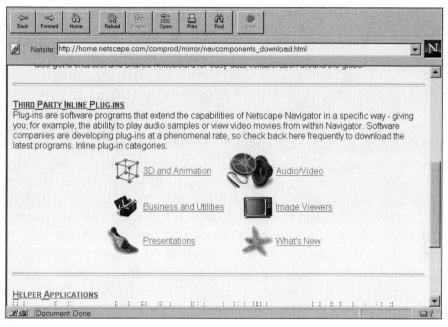

Figure 13-4 The Netscape guide to plug-in programs.

NOTE It doesn't make a great deal of sense to visit Web pages just because they use a particular plug-in; that's sort of like choosing a restaurant based on the brand of frying pan the chef uses to cook your meal. The content of a Web site is much more important than the tools you must use to get that content.

Using Plug-ins

An important fact to remember is that a plug-in program won't do anything until you download and install it; unlike a Java applet, it won't automatically install itself. And after you have installed a plug-in, it remains on your hard drive until you uninstall it.

TIP You may tie up a lot of disk space with an assortment of plug-ins, some of which you may never use, so it's a good idea to look at your system once in a while and delete all the plug-in programs you haven't used more than once. If you ever need them again, it will be simple enough to download and install new copies.

Listening to the Internet

Anything that can be converted to digital form can also be distributed through the Internet. That includes computer programs and documents, of course, but it also includes live and recorded sounds. The same digital recording of a Mozart symphony that can be stored on a compact disc also can be transmitted through a data communication network such as the Internet. Radio stations, government agencies (including live pickups from Congress and several state legislatures), record companies, and independent producers are just a few of the organizations that have created Web sites that include audio with the usual words and pictures.

As far as the Internet goes, no real differences exist among document files, graphic images, and sounds. They're all just strings of data bits. But each file type uses a different kind of application program to convert those bits back into words, pictures, or sounds. Downloading files from the Internet to your computer is easy, but you won't be able to view or play those files unless you have the right software. To listen to sound files, your computer must also have a sound card and a pair of external speakers or headphones (you could get by with just one speaker, but sound boards are set up for stereo, so you may as well use two).

Converting sounds to data bits uses a *lot* of bits. To get one minute of full, high-fidelity stereo sound comparable to what you get from a compact disc, you need about 10MB. If you're using a 28.8 Kbps modem, it would take more than 5 minutes to transfer 1 minute of sound to your computer, or more than an hour to transfer a 12-minute sound clip.

You have a couple of ways to get around this problem. If you reduce the quality of the sound — use one mono channel instead of two stereo channels, eliminate some of the highest frequencies, or accept more distortion — you also reduce the number of bits needed to store or transmit the sound file. But even if the sound quality resembles what you hear through a telephone, it still takes more than a minute to transmit a minute of sound through a modem.

To reduce the amount of time needed to transmit a sound file without losing the audio quality, the file can be *compressed* when the computer stores it or transmits it and restored to its original form on playback. Several compression methods are fast enough for an audio server to transmit live events as they take place.

Compression techniques are getting better, but unless you have a high-speed network connection to the Internet, they're not up to the quality of an uncompressed (but very large) sound file. The people who distribute audio through the Web have to face a trade-off: either force would-be listeners to wait a long time to download high-quality sound or give them immediate access to lower-quality sound.

In practice, your computer handles audio files much like the way it handles graphic images and other specialized formats: you need a separate client program or plug-in for each file format. Clients for some of the most popular formats are included with Netscape Navigator and Microsoft Internet Explorer; others are available from the developers for free download through the Internet.

As with the other multimedia formats described in this chapter, your Web browser will automatically recognize the format of each audio file and use the right client program or plug-in to decode the file and send it to your computer's speakers. Almost every Web page that includes links to audio files also has a link to a source for the plug-ins needed to listen to those files.

Some audio files are embedded in Web pages and start playing as soon as the browser receives them, whereas others are separate downloads that you can either play immediately or store on your hard drive for playback later.

Downloading an Audio File

Downloading an audio file is fairly simple. For example, the debates on the floor of the Washington State Legislature are available on the Web using a system called RealAudio.

To listen to them, follow these steps:

1. Point your browser to TVW, the Washington State Public Affairs Network (http://www.tvw.org). You will see the home page shown in Figure 13-5.

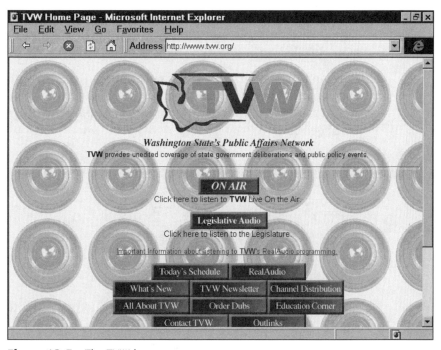

Figure 13-5 The TVW home page.

2. Click the Legislative Audio button. You will see a schedule of committee hearings and sessions of the state House and Senate, with a link to each one (Figure 13-6).

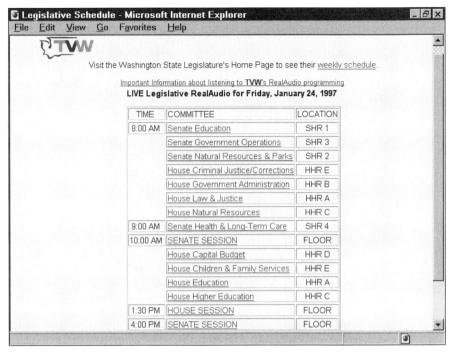

Figure 13-6 The Washington State Legislature schedule.

3. Click the link to the session or hearing you want to hear. You will see more detailed agendas of the session or hearing you requested.

4. To listen to a session or hearing, click the RA (for RealAudio) icon. Your browser will download the streaming RealAudio file, open an external RealAudio player (Figure 13-7), and start to play the program through your speakers.

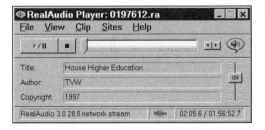

Figure 13-7 The RealAudio control panel.

5. Use the slider on the right side of the RealAudio window to raise or lower the volume.

Other content providers use different audio-encoding methods, but they all work in a similar manner to RealAudio:

1. The server downloads the sound file to your computer.

2. The browser loads the sound file into an external audio player or a plug-in.

3. The audio player decodes the file and sends the sound to the speakers.

Adjusting the Volume

Many sound-file players have their own volume controls, but others depend on the Windows Volume Control program.

To raise or lower the volume in Windows 95, follow these steps:

1. Click the Start button to open the `Start` menu.

2. Select `Programs` → `Accessories` → `Multimedia` and click `Volume Control`. You will see the Volume Control window (Figure 13-8).

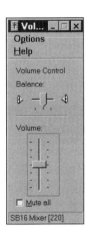

Figure 13-8   The Windows Volume Control window.

3. Move the Balance slider to the left or right to adjust the relative volume between the two speakers.

4. Move the Volume slider up to increase the volume in both speakers or down to reduce the volume.

Directories of Audio Services

The software developers who produce the various Internet audio formats all expect to make their money by selling servers to content providers. To create an audience for their customers, they give away the client programs and plug-ins (if this approach sounds familiar, it should; it's the same approach that Microsoft uses to sell Web servers). Because they want to create as much demand for their products as possible, developers have created a directory Web site with links to other sites that use their format.

RealAudio

The most widely used audio format is *RealAudio* from Progressive Networks. Their TimeCast directory site at `http://www.timecast.com` provides links to dozens of radio stations, concerts, and special events around the world, organized by category.

StreamWorks

It's not as common as RealAudio, but many radio stations use the *StreamWorks* format from Xing Technologies to transmit a continuous broadcast to the Web. StreamWorks is especially popular with content providers that want to supply pictures along with their streaming audio programs. The StreamWorks Content Guide Index at `http://www.xingtech.com/content/sw2_content.html` includes most of the content providers who use StreamWorks servers.

TrueSpeech

TrueSpeech is yet another streaming audio format used by several hundred broadcasters and other content providers. Its Site Index is located at `http://www.dspg.com/cool.htm`.

Shockwave Audio

Macromedia's *Shockwave Audio* is used by several major record companies, including Warner Brothers, Capitol, and MCA Records. The Shockwave Gallery is at `http://www.macromedia.com/shockwave/epicenter/index.html`.

Internet Wave

The *Internet Wave (IWAVE)* audio format was created by VocalTec, who offers free encoder and server software along with the IWAVE player. As a result, this format is used by several tiny record companies and other low-budget groups to offer samples of their work on the Web. You can find a directory of IWAVE sites at `http://www.vocaltec.com/sitesdt.htm`.

Live Events

Once the software developers figured out how to transmit audio files through the Internet as fast as the server can receive them, it became possible to use the Web to distribute live events as well as prerecorded files. Unless you have a high-speed connection to the Internet, you probably won't want to listen to much live music this way, but the sound quality is quite acceptable for speech and special events, even if the speakers occasionally sound like they're under water for a few seconds.

In particular, online audio is a great way to keep track of such things as news events, press conferences, public hearings, and legislative debates without needing to travel across town or across the country to attend in person. It may not be practical for broadcasters to provide more than brief sound bites from all the events happening in Washington, Ottawa, or London, but many of those events are available, complete and unedited, through the Web.

In the following sections, you will find pointers to some of the best sources for live events online.

TimeCast

RealAudio's TimeCast directory (http://www.timecast.com) includes a Live Guide that provides links to RealAudio feeds from both live events and radio programs. Other pages in the TimeCast Web site provide more detailed listings of individual, RealAudio program services, many of which don't show up in the Live Guide list.

NetGuide

NetGuide's (http://www.netguide.com) daily directory of live events is not as extensive as TimeCast's list, but it hits a few events that TimeCast misses. NetGuide also includes *chat sessions* in which the guest answers questions through a keyboard rather than a microphone.

AudioNet

AudioNet (http://www.audionet.com) distributes programs in RealAudio format from more than 150 radio stations and disseminates play-by-play information from more than 150 high school, college, and professional teams, along with live concerts and coverage of special events. The AudioNet home page (Figure 13-9) provides direct links to current and upcoming events and to recordings of recent programs from its archives.

Listening to the U.S. Government

Live and recorded events from all three branches of the U.S. government are available through the Web. Some of the best places to start looking and listening are listed in the following sections.

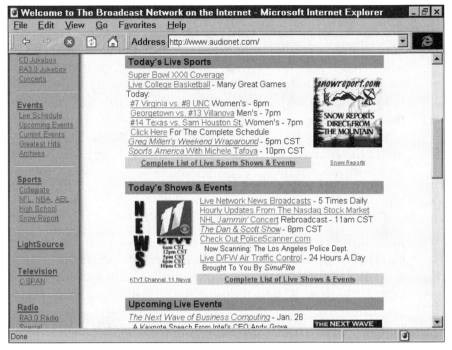

Figure 13-9 The AudioNet home page.

FedNet

FedNet (`http://www.fednet.net`) is a terrific service that offers live audio feeds from the floors of the United States Senate and the House of Representatives, all the individual House and Senate committee hearings that take place every day in Washington, D.C., and press conferences from the Senate and House Radio/TV Galleries. Figure 13-10 shows a FedNet description of a Senate committee hearing.

C-SPAN

C-SPAN is primarily a cable TV service, but it also has a strong presence on the Web at `http://www.c-span.org`. Live audio coverage from both of C-SPAN's cable TV channels are transmitted through the Web Monday through Friday from 10 a.m. until 8 p.m. Eastern Time. C-SPAN's daily programs include news conferences, round table discussions among journalists and Washington newspapers, and live, gavel-to-gavel pickups from the Senate and House.

Besides the broadcast feeds, the C-SPAN Web site offers additional, special-events broadcasts that are not carried on either of C-SPAN's TV channels. Some events carried by C-SPAN overlap those on FedNet, but checking both sites is worthwhile because each covers events that the other misses.

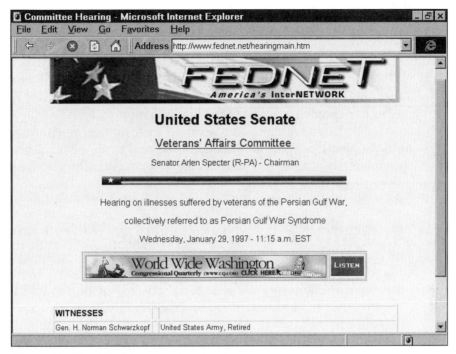

Figure 13-10 A FedNet committee hearing.

Oyez Oyez Oyez: The Supreme Court Online

The Supreme Court doesn't allow live broadcasts of its public sessions, but oral arguments and opinion announcements have been recorded since 1955. Oyez Oyez Oyez: A Supreme Court WWW Resource (`http://oyez.at.nwu.edu/oyez.html`) at Northwestern University is an archive of recordings that includes many of the most important cases to come before the court in the last 30 years, taken from the National Archives. The material on this site is historical rather than current, but some arguments make for fascinating listening.

Agencies and Departments

A few federal agencies and departments have started to set up their own, live audio feeds of official proceedings and specials events, and you can expect more to jump on the same bandwagon in the near future. Appropriately, one of the first agencies to do so is the Federal Communications Commission, the agency responsible for regulation of telecommunication services. You can listen to public announcements of commission actions and press conferences at `http://www.fcc.gov/realaudio`.

State and Local Governments

Some states and cities have followed the C-SPAN model to broadcast live sessions from the state legislature or city council on cable TV and the Internet. The TVW service in Washington state (`http://www.tvw.org`), described earlier in this chapter, was one of the first and most extensive of these sites.

When new Internet audio services such as this are introduced, it usually receives plenty of publicity in newspapers and other media. If you don't see anything advertising the service, call the city council office or the local League of Women Voters.

Services for Serious Audio Junkies

Don Marquis wrote a wonderful short story about a man who was a glass eater — he started out eating the occasional crystal goblet, but eventually he ended up in the gutter, chewing on cheap crockery. Some people may have a similar problem listening to Web sites. You might start by listening to an occasional college basketball game or a newscast from Ireland and later discover that you've spent an entire afternoon following a hearing before a Senate subcommittee. That's probably okay; but when you find yourself listening to an air traffic control center or a police radio in a city a thousand miles away, it may be time to turn off the computer and go for a long walk.

If you really want to listen to police calls, PoliceScanner.com (`http://www.policescanner.com`), provides continuous, live audio feeds from police and fire department radio conversations in Dallas and Los Angeles, with the promise of other cities to come.

WEB PATH If the PoliceScanner page interests you, you'll want to explore the links also. Must-see Web sites for those who follow law enforcement.

If you want to listen to something even less exciting than police calls, the SimuFlite Training International Web site offers live, air-to-ground conversations from the Dallas/Fort Worth Air Traffic Control center.

Radio Stations

More than 2,000 radio stations have Web sites. Many of these sites contain little more than schedules and promotional information about the station's broadcasts, but several hundred stations also feed their on-air programs to the World Wide Web. As a result, a listener in California can hear live news from WBAL in Baltimore and Radio Finland in Helsinki, interviews and comedy from the Canadian Broadcasting Corporation, or music from around the world on TNL Radio in Sri Lanka, Radio Conquistador in Santiago, Chile, and the Austrian Broadcasting Company in Vienna.

As the technology improves, the prospect of *webcasting* will have a huge impact on the nature of broadcast radio. When a program maker is not restricted by the limited range and high cost of distribution by radio, it will become practical to create special-interest channels that would not attract enough listeners to support a traditional radio station. Within a few years, you can expect to see new "Internet radio stations" that broadcast nothing but polka music or poetry readings. In the meantime, you can use your computer to listen to stations and program services that are not available on your radio.

The best directory of Internet radio stations comes from WMBR at the Massachusetts Institute of Technology (http://wmbr.mit.edu/stations), shown in Figure 13-11. This list includes just about every known station with a Web site, whether or not it offers live audio. Those stations that do have an audio connection are identified with a lightning bolt next to their listings.

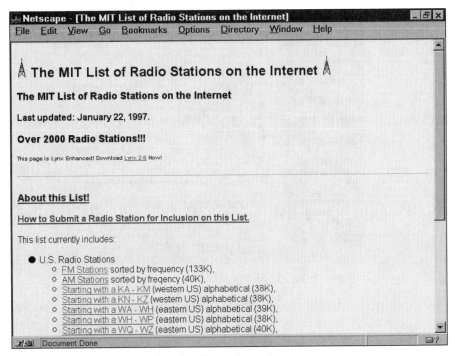

Figure 13-11   The WMBR list of online radio stations.

 WEB PATH **For another list limited to stations with live transmissions to the Web, try the RadioTower directory at** http://www.radiotower.com.

In addition to the individual stations included in the MIT and RadioTower directories, several major national and international radio networks also distribute their programs through the World Wide Web. In general, the networks have more money to spend on production than any single local station, and their programs are frequently among the most interesting things on the Net.

One of the best is the Canadian Broadcasting Corporation (CBC). Starting at the CBC Radio home page (`http://www.radio.cbc.ca`, shown in Figure 13-12), you can listen to live, RealAudio transmissions of CBC Radio (the news and information channel), CBC Stereo (the classical music and variety channel), Radio Canada International (the international shortwave service that broadcasts in seven different languages), and to archives of recent newscasts and public affairs programs. You can also follow the links to Radio-Canada for live pickups from the network's French-language services.

Figure 13-12 The CBC Radio home page.

In the United States, CBS Radio has the strongest Web site of any commercial network (`http://www.cbsradio.com`). It includes RealAudio archives of various network talk shows, commentaries, and special programs. The specials have included things like full-length drama from the old CBS Radio Mystery Theatre and a 60th anniversary tribute to the soap opera *The Guiding Light* (which started on radio), direct from the Museum of Television and Radio in New York.

ABC Radio doesn't offer as many programs on the Web as CBS, but it does provide hourly newscasts, sports reports, and commentaries around the clock. You can find them at `http://www.abcradionet.com`.

The noncommercial National Public Radio network (`http://www.npr.org`) also has an extensive online archive that includes its two daily news programs, *Morning Edition* and *All Things Considered,* going back to 1995.

Monitor Radio, another noncommercial service (Figure 13-13), is also available on the Web with hourly newscasts 24 hours a day, Monday through Friday, and an hour-long news magazine from the *Christian Science Monitor*. Look for Monitor Radio at `http://www.csmonitor.com/monitor_radio/monitor_radio.html`.

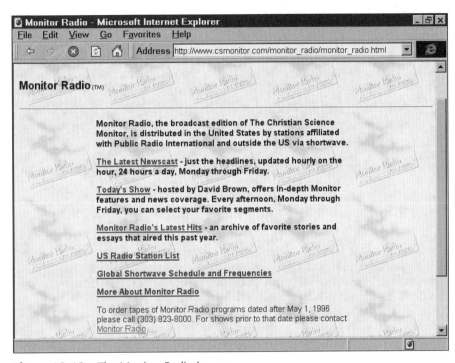

Figure 13-13 The Monitor Radio home page.

For international radio services, two directories supply links to most of the world's active Internet broadcasters. The Radio Netherlands list of Colleagues in International Broadcasting (`http://www.rnw.nl/en/pub/hitlist.html`) shows major national radio services and related agencies and organizations around the world. The World Radio Network (`http://www.wrn.org/audio.html`) is a RealAudio relay service for about 20 different broadcasters. Both sites are good places to look for links to online audio services.

More Java Web Sites

Thousands of Web site developers are using Java to add interactive features and functions to their pages. In another year or two, a site that includes a Java applet won't be any more remarkable than one with a graphic image. But today, developers are still experimenting with the new technology. This section contains descriptions of a few of the more interesting early demonstrations.

The Interactive New York Subway Map

The Interactive New York Subway Map (http://www.transarc.com/afs/transarc.com/public/brail/html/transit/) is a Java applet that identifies the most direct route between any two stations on the New York City subway system.

To request directions, follow these steps:

1. Find the location of the station where you want to start your journey on the map, and click the name of the station.

2. Click the name of the station closest to your destination. A Route Display window opens with specific instructions.Garden Planner

Garden Escape's Garden Planner (http://www.garden.com/) is a Java site that you can use to design the layout of your garden. You can place your choice of flowers, vegetables, or other plants anywhere on the grid, move each plant to any location, and create a Bill of Materials that you can take to your nursery (or order directly from Garden Escape).

Summary

Java, ActiveX, and other plug-in programs add special functions to your Web browser by incorporating clients for new and unconventional file formats. These functions may include animated images, interactive images that change their appearance when you move your mouse over them, downloadable programs, and direct links to other application programs, which may be located on your own system or anywhere else on the Internet.

The World Wide Web is not limited to words and pictures; it can also store live and recorded sound in computer files and transmit them through the Internet. Therefore, many Web sites include some form of audio along with text and images. Downloading a sound file to your computer is no different from transferring any other type of file from a server.

To listen to a sound file that you receive from a Web site, you need a sound card and a pair of speakers or headphones, plus a plug-in program for your Web browser that can recognize the audio file format. Fortunately, those plug-ins are easy to find; you will see links to their developers on almost every Web site that includes an audio file.

The developers of each major audio format maintain a directory of Web sites that use their servers. Those directories are a good place to start looking for audio on the Web. For directories based on content rather than file format, take a look at the NetGuide and AudioNet sites.

Among the audio services that you can find on the World Wide Web are live pickups from the U.S. Congress, recorded arguments before the Supreme Court, and police radio traffic from several American cities. Several hundred local radio stations and national networks also offer newscasts, live program feeds, or archives of past programs through the Web.

As the technical quality of audio-through-the-Web improves, the number and variety of program services will increase. Within a few years, you can expect to see (or hear) all kinds of specialty music programs ("all bluegrass, all the time"), live concerts and special events from around the world, and other new program formats that we haven't even thought about today.

And what about video? It's on the way. Although your computer probably won't replace your kitchen radio or living-room television anytime soon, it will take up much of the time you spend today with both of those older appliances. Five hundred cable TV channels? Please. How about five million Web sites?

CHAPTER FOURTEEN

VIRTUAL COMMUNITIES

IN THIS CHAPTER YOU LEARN THESE SKILLS

Virtual communities are classic examples of the law of unintended consequences. The Internet was created as a channel for researchers to exchange technical information, but almost as soon as it went into use, the people exchanging that information started forming a community whose members were playing chess and space war through the network, exchanging recipes, and developing friendships with people who had never occupied the same physical space.

In his book *The Virtual Community: Homesteading on the Electronic Frontier* (Addison-Wesley, 1993), Howard Rheingold defines virtual communities as "social aggregations that emerge from the Net when enough people carry on ... public discussions long enough, with sufficient human feeling, to form webs of personal relationships in cyberspace." In other words, a *virtual community* is a group of people who develop a social relationship based on their contact through the exchange of electronic messages.

This chapter contains descriptions of a handful of virtual communities and instructions for finding others that may be closer to your own needs and interests. All of the communities in these examples use the Internet (most are accessible through the World Wide Web), but other communities have formed in CompuServe, America Online, and other online services and through private bulletin board systems such as FidoNet.

Virtual communities take many forms. Some are made up of scientific researchers, hobby groups, or fans of a musician or author who share information about a specific subject. Others are more like cocktail parties or neighborhood taverns, where many conversations about unrelated topics take place at the same time. Still others exist as support channels for people who share a particular political or religious philosophy, or who have common experiences with a disease or other personal problem. Some virtual communities communicate through interactive Web sites, others use Usenet newsgroups or mailing lists, and others require special client software programs or remote access to a host computer.

Like any other social group, a virtual community can develop a shared set of values, traditions, and customs. Until you join one, you may find it difficult to believe that a community based on typing can be anything like one in which people interact in other ways. Of course, the experience is not exactly the same. But the friendships that you develop online are just as real, and the effect on your life can be just as profound. When you discover a comfortable and sympathetic virtual community, it can quickly begin to feel like your online home.

Be aware that "meeting" and "getting to know" someone electronically offers the cloak of anonymity that can be both intriguing and deceptive. Share personal information cautiously, keeping in mind that virtual personalities may be more or less fictitious.

One more attraction of participating in a virtual community may not be quite so obvious: because the Internet extends to all parts of the world, a virtual community may include people who share interests but live far apart. Therefore, the members of a community can learn about conditions and customs that may be very different from their own. For example, during the months leading up to the handing over of Hong Kong to China, members of Electric Minds — a Web site discussed later in this chapter — have been able to follow developments from the perspectives of people living in Hong Kong.

In emergencies, community members often mobilize to provide assistance to other members in need. When a member of one such community died suddenly, others in the same city moved quickly to take care of her dog. After an earthquake, people inside the affected area used online conferences to relay messages to concerned relatives when long-distance telephone lines were unavailable. And during political uprisings, participants on live Internet Relay Chat channels sometimes have been able to supply information to the rest of the world more quickly and in more detail than the conventional news media.

The communication medium used by the virtual community varies from one group to the next. Some Web communities use conference software, in which every message becomes a permanent part of the conversation because it's added to the end of the topic. When the next participant comes along, five minutes or three hours later, the earlier comments are still there to provide a context for later additions.

Other communities use a live chat system in which all active participants see your comments as soon as you type them. Conversation on a chat system tends to move more quickly and spontaneously than a conference, but this medium does not offer as much opportunity for users to carefully consider their responses before adding them to the fray.

Regardless of the technology you use to reach other members of a community, the social phenomenon is the same.

SeniorNet

SeniorNet was established in 1985 as a way to bring older adults together through computers and online communication. Today, SeniorNet operates conferences on the World Wide Web and through America Online and The Microsoft Network. It also supports about 100 SeniorNet Learning Centers and researches the use of computers by older adults.

The SeniorNet RoundTables (http://www.seniornet.org/cgi-bin/WebX) are organized into a couple of dozen topics, with a handful of separate discussions in each one. Some RoundTable discussions are devoted to serious subjects, such as Health Matters and Current Events, but many others contain more lighthearted conversations about travel, cooking, and gardening. In one section, members help each other with computer problems, and in another section, they share pointers to favorite Web sites and newsgroups. One of the liveliest conferences is the SeniorNet Cafe, where the discussion is not limited to any specific topic. Figure 14-1 shows a SeniorNet conversation.

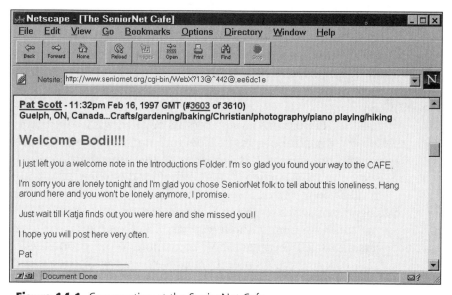

Figure 14-1 Conversation at the SeniorNet Cafe.

Members of SeniorNet use their computers to extend their contact beyond local friends and family to others who share similar interests and an impatience with the "geek-speak" language common in so much other online communication. These users are informed, intelligent people who don't want to learn a new technical language to talk about the news, their gardens, or their grandchildren. SeniorNet provides a place on the Web where they can find supportive, nonpatronizing conversation

The Well

The Well (the *Whole Earth 'Lectronic Link,* originated by the same people responsible for the Whole Earth Catalogs) is a conference service that attracts a mixture of articulate computer experts, Grateful Dead fans, young- and middle-aged professionals – most of whom would deny being anything like yuppies – and survivors of the 1960s counterculture. The Well is based near San Francisco, and many of its members live in and around the Bay Area, but most of The Well's conversations are not restricted to a single geographic region. More than 200 conferences on The Well play home to discussions about computers, current events, books, music, parenting, and many other topics. Because many journalists also are active on The Well, the discussions that take place there often have influence reaching far beyond its 10,000 or so subscribers.

A single conference might have more than a dozen active topics, each with 20 or more new messages every day. Each conference has one or more hosts who are responsible for encouraging new participants, keeping the discussion on-topic, preventing personal attacks, and generally moving the conversation forward. A good host can play an important role in pulling together the participants in a conference to form a community.

The depth of knowledge among The Well members sometimes is quite astonishing. When somebody posts an obscure question about almost any subject in the Experts on the Well topic, it's not unusual to see a detailed answer within an hour.

The Well discussions can be serious or filled with light banter, depending on the subject. For example, in the Cooking conference, regulars are always sharing recipes and techniques, but they also bounce around topics such as "What's the oldest food in your kitchen?" and "What kind of cheese did you eat today?"

In addition to the ongoing conferences where each set of comments is added to the end of a series of previous entries, members of the Well exchange one-to-one messages via e-mail and live *sends,* which enables users to conduct real-time conversations. All these elements contribute to the strong feeling that The Well is a real place where its members can interact with each another in a variety of ways.

Like other active virtual communities, The Well has produced its share of social events in "meatspace." Informal Well gatherings are held in Boston, New

York, Chicago, Seattle, and Denver in addition to the several events that take place every month in the San Francisco area.

 WEB PATH The Well is accessible through the Web at http://www.well.com. You can also reach The Well via a Telnet link to well.com, which connects you to a text-based conferencing program called Picospan. Many Well regulars consider Picospan much more flexible and easy to use than the Web interface, although it can be more difficult to learn. The Well has several pricing plans, depending on the type of access you use.

Electric Minds

Electric Minds (http://www.minds.com) is a Web site that has been carefully designed to create a community around discussions of technology and culture. Along with conference topics related to communities, computers, media, and similar subjects, Electric Minds also offers live conversations and interviews with technologists, futurists, and other experts in the Minds Palace. It also hosts interactive activities designed to build and maintain the sense of community.

Electric Minds is a relatively new service, but it looks like it's off to a good start. The organizers of Electric Minds seem to be more than a little blatant in their efforts to turn their participants into a community, and their fascination with Internet culture and technology may not appeal to everyone. But many users find much of the conversation in Electric Minds worth the time and effort of participating.

Finding Other Online Communities

Dozens of other virtual communities exist on the Web and still more use other Internet services, such as mailing lists and newsgroups. Some have a regional focus, such as Echo in New York City (http://www.echonyc.com) and The Spring in Austin, Texas (http://www.spring.com). Others, including ParentChat (http://www.talkcity.com/chat) and TravelTalk (http://www.traveltalk.com), are dedicated to specific topics. Each of these communities has its own personality, traditions, and local customs.

The Virtual Community Center at Electric Minds is a very good place to begin your quest for an online home. It includes links to a long, subjective list of conferences, mailing lists, live chats, newsgroups, and other communities, with a profile and other essential information about each of them. For example, the regional conference based in Seattle is called Drizzle.

TIP If you want to limit your search to more-or-less mainstream discussion forums on the Web, try the search tool at Forum One (`http://www.ForumOne.com`). It offers an indexed catalog of more than 40,000 topics in forums operated by newspapers, magazines, and non-profit organizations. Forum One is not an exhaustive list of every forum and conference on the Web, but it does provide a good single point of access to the services it follows. When the search tool takes you to an interesting discussion thread, spend some time exploring other discussions in the same forum or conference. If it seems like a comfortable place to join in the conversation, add the top-level page to your list of favorites or bookmarks.

Forum One also offers its own list of the forums it rates as the best in several major topic categories.

BONUS

Other Places to Find Virtual Communities

The Web isn't the only place to look for virtual communities. Many communities have grown within Internet newsgroups, mailing lists, and online services. You won't be able to join these communities with a Web browser, but that shouldn't make any difference; the community is much more important than the technology. The human animal seems driven to create communities – virtual and otherwise – with whatever resources are at hand.

One of the oldest and largest systems that support such groups is Minitel, the French electronic telephone directory service. Minitel was started by the French telephone system as an inexpensive alternative to the high cost of distributing ink-on-paper telephone directories to every telephone subscriber. It has grown into a worldwide service that offers more than 25,000 channels of information, business services, and online chats in French, English, and other languages to more than 7 million users.

In France, almost all Minitel subscribers use a free, stand-alone terminal, but users in other parts of the world can reach Minitel through the Internet, using special, free client software that you can download from `http://minitel.fr`. There's a per-minute charge for access to Minitel services that varies from around 14 cents for e-mail and chat to about $2 for specialized, professional databases.

The original purpose of the Minitel network was to reduce the cost of providing telephone directories, but the people who received Minitel terminals quickly discovered that they could also use them to set up chat channels where several users could conduct live conversations through their keyboards. Today, it's not uncommon to find more than 3,000 active chat sessions operating at the same time. Of course, most of these chat sessions are in French, but you should be able to find others in English, Dutch, and other European languages.

 Minitel is most interesting to students of the French language and people looking for a non-American perspective. However, at $9 an hour, it quickly can turn into an expensive hobby. Serious Minitel addicts can accumulate bills of more than $500 a month (or the equivalent in francs).

Access to still other virtual communities is one of the few obvious reasons to use America Online, Prodigy, or CompuServe as your gateway to the Internet. All three services offer conferences dedicated to particular topics and chat sessions that may have no specific focus but which offer a comfortable place to hang out. Many of these chats and conferences have grown into lively groups with all the same social characteristics as any other virtual community.

For example, some of the most active communities on America Online are operated by The Motley Fool (AOL keyword FOOL), shown in Figure 14-2. The Fool offers an assortment of information and advice for investors, including several thousand separate message boards devoted to individual stocks. Each of these message boards provides an opportunity for people who want to follow a company's stock to share their knowledge of that company – explanations of the company's product or business, recent developments in their industry, and other information that can help other readers make informed decisions.

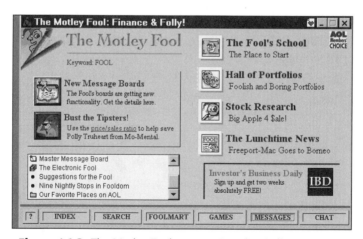

Figure 14-2 The Motley Fool area on America Online.

Of course, many of the items in a public conference for sharing information and advice about the stock market may not be absolutely reliable; they're supposed to be a starting point for your own research rather than an infallible source of great stock tips. But the regular participants in many of the Fool's message boards have all the characteristics of a virtual community. The participants know one another and provide a supportive environment for community members. For example, when one or two people on a message board attend a shareholders' meeting, they write up the highlights (and offer their own subjective thoughts) for the benefit of others who may not have been able to attend. When a company announces a major new contract, it's likely that somebody will post the press release to that company's message board.

Most of this content is just basic investment research, but by sharing information with other members of the community, the pool of data can be greater than any single small investor can find on his own. Assuming that an informed investor will make better decisions, people who follow the Motley Fool's message boards may have a better idea when to buy or sell.

Virtual communities come in many forms. Some are made up of nothing but bored suburban teenagers or enthusiastic quilters; others may include people with very different backgrounds and interests. But regardless of the topics they discuss and the technology they use to participate, these communities can be rewarding social experiences.

Summary

Virtual communities are the social groups that grow out of electronic conversations through the Internet and other computer communication services and technologies. Some virtual communities are closely focused on subject matter, which may be highly technical or based on a shared interest in an author or entertainer. Others provide opportunities for members to discuss a variety of topics. Individual members of a virtual community may be thousands of miles apart, but their relationships are just as real as the ones they develop in a neighborhood social club or tavern.

Over time, a virtual community can become as complex and as close as any other group of people. When one member of a virtual community faces a personal crisis, it's not unusual for people who may have never met except online to rally 'round with support, encouragement, and other forms of help. Many participants consider the regular members of a conference or chat group as some of their best friends.

CHAPTER FIFTEEN

ELECTRONIC MAIL: EXCHANGING MESSAGES WITH THE WORLD

IN THIS CHAPTER YOU LEARN THESE KEY SKILLS

With a few exceptions, the World Wide Web is a one-way medium: the content creators use the Web to distribute information, but a Web page is not a particularly efficient way to exchange information between individual users. Electronic mail, also known as *e-mail*, is a much better approach.

Sending and receiving e-mail is just as important a part of the overall Internet experience as browsing the World Wide Web. If you think of the Web as a one-to-many service, like broadcast radio and television, then e-mail is closer to a one-to-one service for sending and receiving personalized messages, like the telephone.

E-mail is the process of exchanging messages and data through computer networks. Most of these messages are transmitted as text, but you can also send them as audio or video recordings or as copies of handwritten or printed notes. Using gateways between the Internet and other networks, you can send and receive messages to and from millions of other people.

Most e-mail messages contain text, but many also include *attached files*. An attached file is a document, data file, or program that comes along with the text. When you receive a file as part of an e-mail message, you can handle the file exactly the same way you would treat a file that arrived on a floppy disk.

This chapter provides a general description of the Internet e-mail system and specific information about the e-mail client programs that come with Netscape Navigator and Microsoft Internet Explorer. It also discusses Eudora, a separate e-mail program that you may want to consider as an alternative to the one supplied with your browser.

How E-Mail Works

Just as you need a Web browser to view pages on the World Wide Web, you must have a mail-handling program to send and receive e-mail. Like any other type of client program, a mail client exchanges commands and messages with a server. In practice, the mail client on your computer talks to two servers – one for sending outbound mail and another for receiving incoming mail.

When you send an e-mail message, your message travels from your mail client program through a series of computers and networks to the recipient's mailbox on a *mail server*. The next time the recipient checks for new mail, the server relays your message to the recipient's computer. Just as you can place a telephone call from your kitchen to any telephone number in the world, you can send an e-mail message to just about any e-mail address, even if that address is an account on a completely different system.

Electronic mail is a *store-and-forward* system, rather than a direct connection to the recipient's computer. The message that you type into your mail client program travels to a *post office server*, which routes the message through the Internet to the recipient's mail server. In other words, a message travels from one server to another, where each server holds it until the server can relay the message to the next server along the line. In most cases, it takes less than a minute for a message to travel from your post office server to the recipient's mail server, but it sits in a mailbox at that server until the recipient checks for new mail.

Every e-mail message includes a *header* at the beginning of the message. The mail servers use the information in the header to route the message to its ultimate destination, and the recipient's mail client uses it to identify the source of the message. The header also includes the names and addresses of the sender and the recipient, the date and time the message was sent, a subject line assigned by the person who created the message, and a lot of internal routing information that means much more to the servers and clients than it will to you or me.

A mail client program, also called a *mail reader,* performs several functions:

* It provides an editing platform where you can create new messages.
* It transfers outgoing messages to a post office server.
* It obtains incoming messages from a mail server.
* It displays the content of received messages.
* It stores copies of incoming and outgoing messages.

Figure 15-1 shows the path of an e-mail message from sender to receiver.

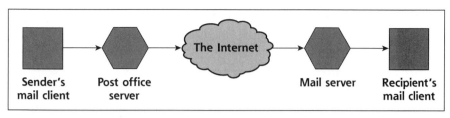

Figure 15-1 The progress of an e-mail message.

Assuming that you're using either Microsoft Internet Explorer or Netscape Navigator as your Web browser, your Internet service provider probably processes mail with the Simple Mail Transfer Protocol (SMTP) and Post Office Protocol No. 3 (POP3) protocols. Therefore, you need an SMTP/POP3 client program to send and receive your mail. Both of the major browsers come with their own mail programs, but if you prefer, you can install a client from another source, such as Eudora by Qualcomm. There's no rule that requires you to use the mail client from the same company that created your Web browser; if you like Netscape's browser and Microsoft's mail client, or if you prefer the Microsoft browser and the Netscape mail program, go ahead and use them.

The major exceptions are the online information services (CompuServe, The Microsoft Network, America Online, and Prodigy), and local area networks that use their own mail systems. If you're connecting to the Internet through one of these services, you'll have to use the mail client provided by that service. If you're not sure what kind of server handles your mail, ask your network administrator or the service provider's support center.

The latest versions of all three mail clients – Navigator, Internet Explorer, and Eudora – share several common features:

* **Address books.** A personal *address book* is just what the name implies: a list of names and addresses of people to whom you send e-mail messages. If you select a name from your address book, you won't have to type the recipient's full address.

* **Spell checking.** After you compose a message, you can use the message editor's built-in spell checker to find and fix misspelled words.

* **Paste as quotation.** When you reply to a message, including excerpts from the original message is often convenient, so your recipient has some kind of context for your comments. The usual method for quoting in an e-mail message is to start every line you quote with a > mark, so your message might look like this:

```
>This is a quotation from the original message.
>This is more of the original message.
This is my reply to that message.
```

* **Text formatting.** If the recipient of your message is using a mail client that recognizes formatting, you can align the text, indent paragraphs, and specify the typeface, style, and color of your text. However, most e-mail clients ignore formatting instructions, so you shouldn't take the time to use them unless you know your recipient can recognize them.

* **Multiple mailboxes.** All three programs place newly received messages in a folder called *Inbox* and hold messages that are ready to send in another folder called *Outbox*. You can create additional folders to organize your e-mail messages by date, recipient, subject, or any other criteria you want to establish.

* **Signatures.** Many users include a short signature block at the end of an e-mail message with the sender's name, e-mail address, and other information. You can create a standard signature block that your e-mail client can automatically insert into all your messages.

During installation of your mail client (either with a browser or separately), the setup routine asks you for the addresses of your outgoing (SMTP) and incoming (POP3) servers and for your account name and password. Your ISP should give you this information when you establish your account. If you can't find the piece of paper that contains these addresses, ask your service provider or network administrator for help.

Using Microsoft Internet Mail

Internet Mail is the Windows 95 e-mail client program supplied with Microsoft Internet Explorer. Like Internet Explorer itself, the mail program is free. If you didn't obtain it along with the Internet Explorer software, you can get the software from Microsoft's Web site at `http://www.microsoft.com/ie/download/`. Follow the download instructions to specify Internet Mail and News for Windows 95 & NT 4.0.

Receiving e-mail with Microsoft Internet Mail

Internet Mail can wait for you to check your mailbox for new mail manually or it can automatically check for new mail on a regular schedule. To check mail manually, click the Send and Receive button in the Internet Mail toolbar (Figure 15-2).

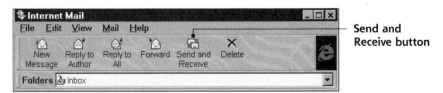

Figure 15-2 The Microsoft Internet Mail toolbar.

To instruct Internet Mail to check for mail regularly, follow these steps:

1. Select ⬚ **Mail** ⬚ → ⬚ **Options** ⬚. The Options dialog box opens.

2. Click the Read tab. The dialog box in Figure 15-3 appears.

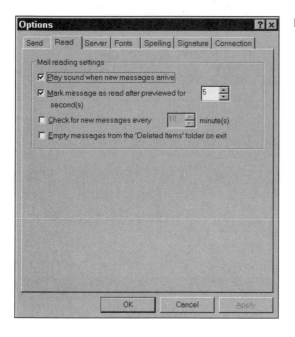

Figure 15-3 The Internet Mail Read Options dialog box.

3. Click the box next to the Check for new messages every *xx* minutes option to place a check mark there.

4. Use the up- and down-arrow buttons to instruct the program how often you want to check for new mail.

5. Because you will probably run the mail client in background while you do other things on your computer, place a check mark in the Play sound when new messages arrive check box by clicking it.

6. Click the Apply button.

7. Click the Connection tab. The dialog box in Figure 15-4 appears.

8. Select the Connection option you normally use to connect your computer to the Internet. Internet Mail will use the option you select to connect to your mail server.

When Internet Mail receives new messages, it places them in your Inbox folder (Figure 15-5). New messages appear in **boldface type**, with sealed envelope icons to their left. After you read a message, the typeface changes to normal type, and the icon looks like an opened envelope.

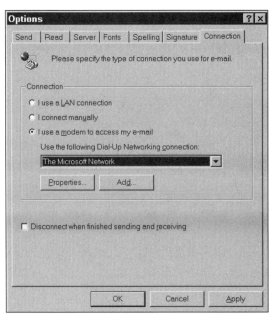

Figure 15-4 The Options Connection tab.

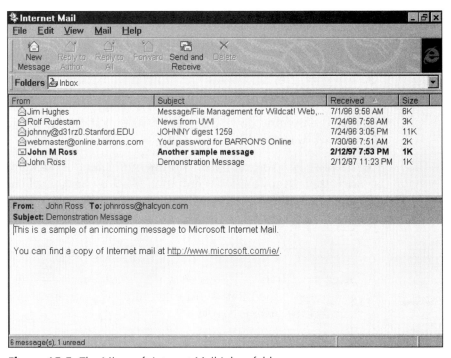

Figure 15-5 The Microsoft Internet Mail Inbox folder.

To read a message, select it from the list. The text of the message appears in the preview pane at the bottom of the Internet Mail window. To see the message in a separate window (Figure 15-6), double-click the listing for that message. In practice, you can do just about everything from the preview pane that you can do from a message window, so you probably won't need to open messages in their own windows very often, unless you want to see the text of more than one message at one time.

Received messages remain in your Inbox until you do something with them. As a result, your Inbox will quickly fill up with old messages. If a message is unimportant, you can delete it; otherwise, you can transfer messages to other folders.

To move a message to a different folder, follow these steps:

1. Select the message you want to move from the list of messages in the current folder.

2. Select **Mail** → **Move to** and choose the destination folder from the submenu, as shown in Figure 15-7.

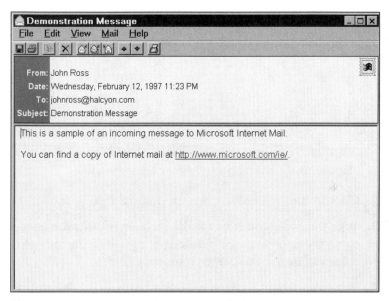

Figure 15-6 The Internet Mail message window.

Figure 15-7 The Move to submenu.

TIP   To place a copy of a message in a new folder without deleting the original, use the Copy to command instead of Move to.

Creating and Sending Messages

To compose and send a message with Internet Mail, follow these steps:

1. Click the New Message icon in the Internet Mail toolbar or select ⏎ Mail ⏎ →
⏎ New Message ⏎ . The New Message window shown in Figure 15-8 appears.

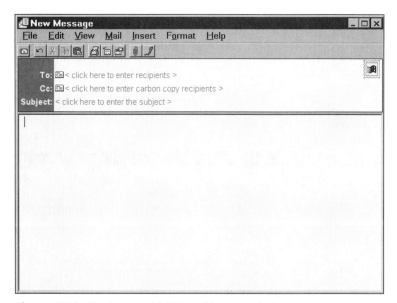

Figure 15-8 The Internet Mail New Message window.

2. Click in the To: field to open an address field.

3. Type the e-mail address for the recipient of this message. To send the same message to more than one recipient, separate the addresses with commas, or use the Cc: (carbon copy) field.

4. Tab down to the Subject: field and type a brief description of the message's content.

5. Tab down to the large pane in the lower portion of the window and type the text of your message.

6. Select ⏎ Mail ⏎ → ⏎ Check Spelling ⏎ or press F7 to spell check your message.

7. After you complete the message, click the Send button in the toolbar, select ⏎ File ⏎ → ⏎ Send Message ⏎ , or press Alt-S. The program moves the new message to your Outbox folder.

8. You can send each message to your mail server as soon as you have created it, or if you prefer, you can hold several messages in your Outbox and send them all at once. To send all the messages in your Outbox folder, click the Send and Receive button in the main Internet Mail toolbar, select `Mail` → `Send and Receive`, or press Ctrl-M.

NOTE To attach a file to your message before you send it, click the Insert button in the toolbar or select Insert→File Attachment. To import a text file into the body of your message, select Insert→Text File.

Using Netscape Messenger

Netscape's mail client, Messenger, is part of the Netscape Communicator package that also includes Version 4 of Navigator. You can buy Communicator as a commercial product through retail channels or you can download it from Netscape's Web site at http://home.netscape.com/. Earlier versions of Navigator also came with mail clients, but those clients did not have all the features in Messenger.

WEB PATH Messenger has links to the Four11 and Bigfoot online directory services. You can search for an e-mail address in either of these databases by clicking a button on the message editor's toolbar.

Receiving E-mail with Netscape Messenger

You can configure Netscape Messenger to check for new mail on a regular schedule or you can connect to your mail server and look for new mail right now, either by clicking the Get Mail button in the toolbar or pressing Ctrl-T. When Messenger receives new messages, it places them in the Inbox folder.

Communicator uses a set of *thread windows* like the one in Figure 15-9 to display the contents of your Inbox, Outbox, and other folders. Each thread window contains a message list that displays details about every message in the current folder. The thread window displays new messages in **boldface type** and with a sealed envelope icon until you read them.

Thread windows can list all messages in a single column or indent replies under the original message, as shown in Figure 15-10. A series of replies and the replies to those replies is called a *thread*. Click the button at the upper-left corner of the message list to toggle between a conventional list and a threaded list.

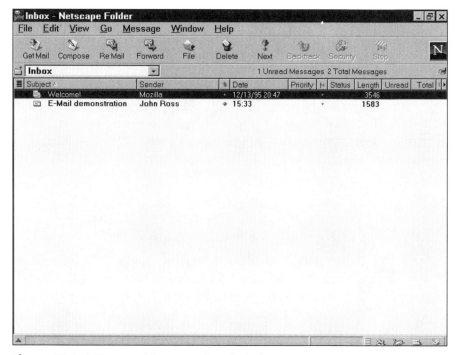

Figure 15-9 A Netscape Messenger thread window.

Click to toggle
between a
conventional
list and
threaded list

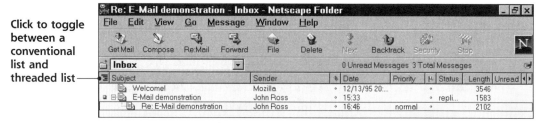

Figure 15-10 A threaded list of messages.

To read a message, select it from the list and click the control at the bottom-left corner of the window to display the message contents in the message area (Figure 15-11). If you would rather read it in a separate window, double-click the listing for that message.

Click to show/
hide the
message area

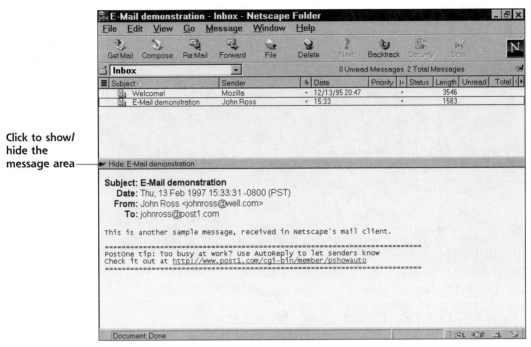

Figure 15-11 A thread window with the message area visible.

To move a message to a different folder, select `Message` → `File Message` and select the destination folder from the submenu. To create a new folder or sub-folder, follow these steps:

1. Open the drop-down list of folders at the top of the thread window.

2. Select mail at the top of the list. The Netscape Message Center window appears (Figure 15-12).

3. Select `File` → `New Folder`. The User Prompt window appears.

4. Type the name of your new folder and click OK. The new folder appears at the end of the list of folders.

5. To make the new folder a subfolder of another folder, drag and drop it to the folder you want to be the top-level folder.

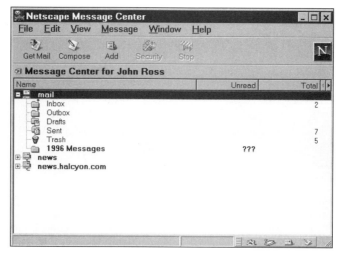

Figure 15-12 The Netscape Message Center window.

Creating and Sending Messages

To create and send a new e-mail message, follow these steps:

1. Click the Compose button in the toolbar or press Ctrl-M. The Message Composition window appears (Figure 15-13).

2. Type the recipient's e-mail address in the To: field.

3. If you want to send a copy (Cc:) or blind copy (Bcc:) of this message, click the To: button to open a menu with those addressing options.

4. To select a name from your address book instead of typing it, click the Address button in the toolbar.

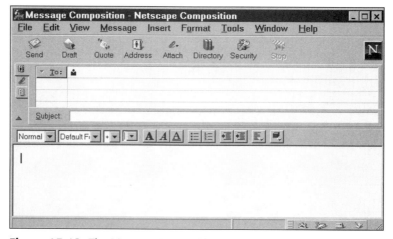

Figure 15-13 The Message Composition window.

5. Tab down to the Subject: field and type a subject line for this message.

6. Tab down to the message field and type the text of your message.

7. To attach a file to this message, click the tab with a paper clip icon on the left side of the address field, click inside the blank field, and select the file from the directory.

8. When the message is ready to transmit, click the Send button in the toolbar.

Using Eudora

Eudora is yet another e-mail client program that many users like better than either Internet Mail or Messenger. Originally developed at The University of Illinois/Champaign-Urbana as a Macintosh program, Eudora (whose name was inspired by Eudora Welty's story, *Why I Live at the P.O.*) is now owned by Qualcomm, whose other products consist mostly of wireless communication hardware. Qualcomm offers two versions of Eudora:

* **Eudora Light**, available at no charge from `http://www.eudora. com/ light.html`

* **Eudora Pro**, sold through retail channels (you can also order it directly from Qualcomm, but the price will probably be lower at a discount software store or in a catalog)

WEB PATH You can download a free 30-day trial version of Eudora Pro from `http: //www.eudora.com/prodemo/`.

Both versions of Eudora use the same approach to sending and receiving e-mail, but as you would expect, the Pro product has many features that are not included in the free program. The most important additional features are as follows:

* Text formatting
* Filters that can direct mail into specific folders automatically (based on the content of the header or message text) and send an automatic reply
* Built-in spell checker
* Multiple signature blocks
* Support for multiple e-mail accounts
* Address book with postal addresses and voice and fax telephone numbers
* Free technical support for 90 days

The free Eudora Light package probably includes all the features you need for sending and receiving mail. However, you may want to try the 30-day trial version of Eudora Pro to see if any of the additional features seem useful enough to justify spending the money for a permanent upgrade.

Organizing Folders

Eudora stores messages in mailboxes, which can be grouped into folders. You can create mailboxes and folders to arrange messages by date, by topic, by sender or recipient, or any other method you want to use. Note, however, that Eudora displays mailboxes in alphabetical order, which can be confusing if you're trying to work with a list of mailboxes in some other kind of logical order, such as a folder for each month.

Eudora displays its hierarchy of folders in a pane at the left side of the program window, as shown in Figure 15-14. You can open a different folder by double-clicking the folder's name. To move a message to a different folder, drag and drop the listing for the message on the name of the destination folder.

To create a new message mailbox, select ` Mailbox ` → ` New ` and enter the name you want to assign to it in the dialog box (Figure 15-15). To create a new folder, select the Make it a Folder option.

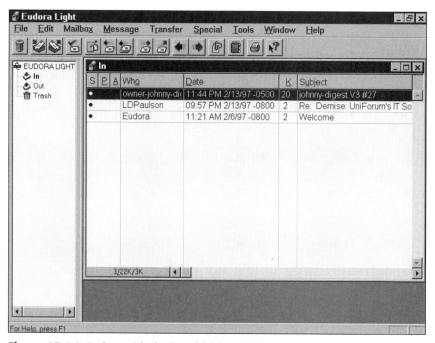

Figure 15-14 Eudora with the list of folders visible.

If you don't want to use the list of folders and mailboxes, right-click inside the directory pane and select Hide. To restore the pane, select ` Tools ` → ` View ` Mailboxes.

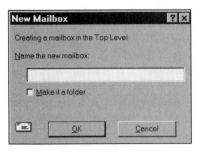

Figure 15-15 The New Mailbox dialog box.

Receiving Messages

Like the Netscape and Microsoft mail clients, Eudora can automatically check for new mail on a preset schedule or in response to a user command. Unless an active filter directs it somewhere else, all new mail goes to the Inbox folder, as shown in Figure 15-16. To read a message, double-click the listing to open a new window.

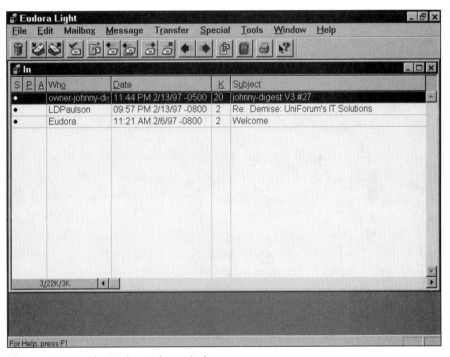

Figure 15-16 The Eudora Inbox window.

Creating and Sending Messages

Eudora can automatically send a new message as soon as you complete it or hold it in a message queue and send several messages in a batch. To set this option, follow these steps:

1. Select [Tools] → [Options].

2. Select Sending Mail from the Category list. The Options dialog box in Figure 15-17 appears.

3. To send messages as soon as you finish them, make the Immediate send option active. To place messages in a queue for sending in a batch, make Immediate send inactive.

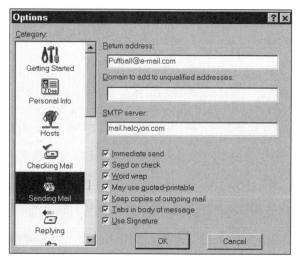

Figure 15-17 The Sending Mail Options dialog box.

To compose a new message, follow these steps:

1. Click the New Message button in the toolbar or select [Message] → [New Message]. The message editor window appears (Figure 15-18).

2. Move your cursor to the To: field and type the e-mail address of the recipient of this message or click the Address Book button on the toolbar to select a name from your address book.

3. Tab down to the Subject: field and type a subject line for this message.

4. If you want to send copies (Cc:) or blind copies (Bcc:) of this message to other people, tab down to those fields and type the recipients' addresses or select them from your address book.

5. Tab down to the lower pane of the window and type the body of your message.

6. To attach a file to your message, click the Attach File button (the one with the paper clip) from the toolbar, select [Message] → [Attach File], or press Ctrl-H.

New Message button

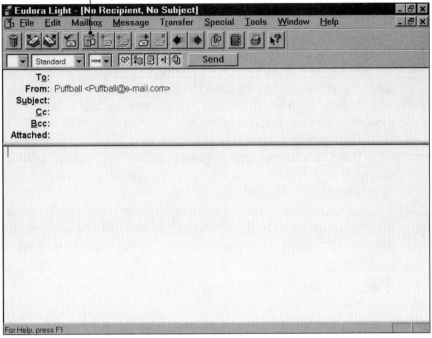

Figure 15-18 The Eudora message editor window.

7. When the message is ready to send, click the Send button or the Queue button.

To send the messages waiting in your message queue, select `File` →
`Send Queued Messages` .

BONUS

Internet Mailing Lists

M ost of the time, you will use e-mail to exchange private messages with specific people: you send a message, the recipient sends back a reply. But you can also use a mailing list to send the same message to many recipients. Internet mailing lists can be used to distribute news bulletins and promotional announcements to many interested parties quickly and efficiently. They can also support discussion groups in which any participant can send a message to the mailing list manager, which automatically re-sends it to everybody on the list.

Commercial Mailing Lists

Many businesses and organizations use Internet mailing lists to send periodic announcements to their customers or members. For example, several airlines use mailing lists to distribute special offers for bargain fares. If you're able to plan a trip at the last minute, you can sometimes learn about some excellent deals (such as a coast-to-coast round trip for less than $200). For information about signing up for airline e-mail lists, take a look at Epicurious Travel's Airfare Bargains on the Internet Web page at `http://travel.epicurious.com/travel/c_planning/02_airfares/intro.html`.

Other commercial mailing lists are maintained by retailers and mail-order businesses to send special offers to regular customers and people who sign up through the company's Web site.

Mailing lists also are an excellent way for special-interest groups to send up-to-the-minute news to their members in daily or weekly bulletins. Look for information about subscribing to such lists in your organization's printed newsletters.

Participatory Mailing Lists

Commercial mailing lists are a one-to-many service. The people who keep the list use it to send the same message to dozens (or thousands) of recipients. Depending on the value of the information they send you, the messages you receive from commercial mailing lists can be either tremendously interesting or little more than junk mail.

But another type of mailing list may be more useful to you than an offer for cheap tickets to Memphis or a special offer on slightly out-of-date software: the many-to-many list. These many-to-many lists support discussion groups among people who share an interest in some specific topic. Some of these lists may reach people around the world who want to share information about a technical or scholarly subject, whereas others simply may be a way for people within a single metropolitan area to plan a monthly Chinese dinner. A few very large lists may reach a huge number of subscribers, but mailing lists of between 10 and 1,000 people are much more common.

When one person sends a message to the list, everyone on the list can read that message. Therefore, mailing lists can be a channel for continuing conversations where everyone has seen the previous comments and has a chance to offer their own ideas.

Finding a Mailing List

Many times, the best way to learn about a mailing list is by rumor; somebody may mention it in a public newsgroup or at a professional, hobby, or social gathering. If you hear about a mailing list that sounds interesting to you, send an e-mail message to the person who told you about it and ask how to join.

One of the most common types of mailing list servers is the LISTSERV. To search the master list of LISTSERVs, send an e-mail request to listserv@listserv.net. The subject line of your request should be blank, and the body of the message should contain this text:

```
list global nnn
```

Use the search string you want to use in place of nnn. For example, to search for mailing lists about quilts and quilting, type **list global quilt**.

For a linked list of LISTSERV mailing lists in a Web site, sorted by description, name, subject, or sponsoring organization, try the directory at `http://www.tile.net/listserv/index.html`.

Another good place to look for mailing lists is the directory of Internet mailing lists at `http://www.liszt.com/`. Liszt is a database of more than 65,000 separate lists. It includes college alumni groups, people interested in playing the trombone, journalists, and thousands of other topics. You can use the search engine at Liszt's Web site to find specific topics, or you can browse through dozens of lists of general mailing list categories.

To request information about the content, focus, and local customs of a particular list, send a request to the administrative address for that list with this command in the body of the message:

```
info list name
```

If the server is set up for automatic response, you should receive a reply within a few minutes that contains the details you need to decide whether or not you want to join, as well as instructions for adding your name to the mailing list.

NOTE **The computer that receives your request will respond automatically, so you should copy this format exactly. Don't add any polite extras, such as "Thanks for your help." Nobody will ever see your note, and it just confuses the computer.**

Joining a Mailing List

To join a mailing list, you must send a request to an administrative account on the list server. Sometimes this account has an address like majordomo@host.edu or listserv@host.com, but the addresses of other administrative accounts may be something more specific, such as quilt-request@list.org. The important thing to remember is that you won't use the same address to send messages to the list.

Regardless of the type of mailing list server, you can always obtain instructions for joining by sending an e-mail with no subject line and just the word "help" in the body of the message to the list's administrative address. The return message that explains how to join a list will also tell you how to remove your name from that list.

Some mailing lists are open to anybody who wants to join, but many others are limited to qualified members. The information you receive in response to your help message will give you the specific requirements for that list.

For example, the Cider Digest is a mailing list for people interested in making apple cider. It's a *digest* because the list server sends messages in batches rather than automatically re-sending each message as soon as it receives it.

The Cider Digest list includes people who operate commercial cider businesses, hobby cider makers who buy fresh apple juice and let it ferment in the cellar, and academic experts on apple production and fermentation. Over the course of a year, it will contain requests for help ("My cider is still cloudy after five months. What should I do?"), discussions about specific apple varieties ("Does anybody have any experience using a blend of winesaps and Granny Smiths?"), and news about the commercial cider market.

Like every other mailing list, the Cider Digest has two addresses: one for requests to join, and another for posting messages to the readers of the list. To add your name to the Cider Digest mailing list, send a request (with your own e-mail address) to cider-request@talisman.com.

Using an E-mail Filter

When you join a mailing list, you will probably want to store the messages you receive from the list in a separate location from the one you use for other personal or business mail. If your e-mail program can filter your messages, it's a good idea to configure it to recognize mail from each list server and place it in a different mailbox or folder. All the mail programs described in this chapter (except Eudora Light and older Netscape mail clients) include automatic message filters.

Because mailing lists are not as easy to find as newsgroups and Web sites, they're one of the great hidden resources of the Internet. As a source of timely information and a point of contact with other people who share your interests, a mailing list can be one more important way to keep up with news about almost any subject. However, joining an active mailing list can be like opening a floodgate; some of them produce dozens of new messages every day. If you want to maintain any kind of life away from your computer, don't try to join two or three dozen new mailing lists right away. A much better idea is to subscribe to one list at a time; if you can keep up with the new mail, try one or two more until you reach the saturation point. Remember that the information on a mailing list does you no good at all if you don't have the time to read it.

Summary

E-mail makes the difference between participating in a worldwide community and using the Internet as a consumer of information and services supplied by other people. You can use Internet e-mail to exchange messages with millions of users around the world.

To send and receive e-mail, you must use a client program that sends outbound messages to a mail server and receives incoming messages from a post office server. Both Netscape Navigator and Microsoft Internet Explorer come with e-mail client programs that share almost identical feature sets. A third alternative with a slightly different approach to the same objectives, Eudora, is available for free from Qualcomm. All three programs include message editors for new messages, mail readers, and configurable, file-management functions.

Just as the content of Web pages is more important than the browsers you use to read it, your choice of e-mail programs is purely a matter of personal taste. After a few weeks or less, you will ignore the program and concentrate on the messages you send and receive. The content of those messages and the process of communicating with other people are what's really important about e-mail.

Over time, you may discover that you have created a close friendship with people you've never seen. The people who meet through online conferences, newsgroups, mailing lists, and other communication channels have formed communities as strong and as important to their lives as those friends and neighbors you meet face to face.

DISCOVERY CENTER

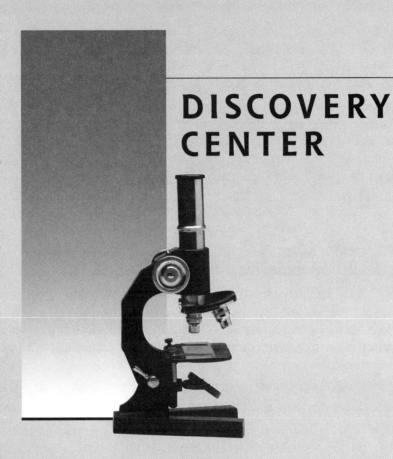

The Discovery Center serves as a handy reference to the most important topics discussed in this book. Here you will find quick summaries of information about connecting to, navigating, and finding particular information on the Web. These summaries include page numbers to guide you to the parts of the book where you can find more detailed information on that topic.

CHAPTER 1

How the Internet will widen your horizons (page 14

The Internet connects millions of computes in all parts of the world. World Wide Web pages from Europe and Asia are just as easy to read through the World Wide Web as those from your own town or city.

The Web includes sites with information about just about every imaginable topic. You can use the Web to visit museums, follow athletic teams, shop for books and clothing, and exchange political opinions and recipes. If those subjects don't excite you, just look around the Web. There's sure to be something else that does.

How you can meet new people through the Web (page 15)

Many Web sites contain interactive conferences where you can send and receive messages and participate in discussions of thousands of different topics. Other Internet services — including newsgroups and e-mail mailing lists — are forums for continuing conversations and platforms for virtual communities of people who share the same interests.

How you can keep up with the world through the Web (page 19)

Hundreds of radio stations and newspapers use the Web to distribute their stories and programs. If you're interested in following news that's not covered locally, or if you want to see and hear more details and analysis, the Web can bring you news reports from reporters and editors around the world.

You can also use the Web to read specialty and trade magazines and newsletters for almost any business or industry. If you want to follow trends or become an informed consumer, the Web places a wealth of valuable information on your computer's screen.

CHAPTER 2

What is the Internet? (page 27)

The Internet is the worldwide "network of networks" that connects millions of computers through *backbone* networks. Any computer connected to the Internet can exchange messages and data with every other computer on the system.

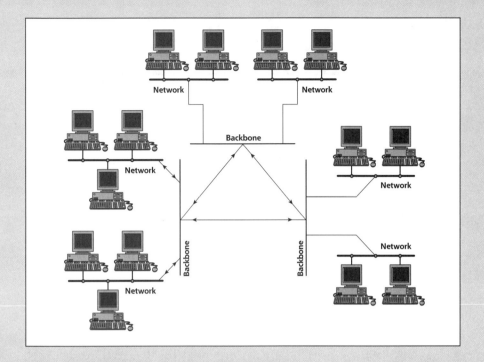

Working with Internet addresses (page 29)

Every computer connected to the Internet has a unique address. In the United States, most addresses end in a *domain* that identifies the type of organization using the address. For example, business.com is a business, college.edu is an educational institution, and bureaucracy.gov is a government agency. Addresses in the rest of the world usually end in a geographical domain, such as dim-sum.hk for Hong Kong or lutefisk.no for Norway.

Servers and clients (page 31)

Almost all communication through the Internet occurs when a *client* program on one computer sends an instruction to a *server* on another computer. The server may respond by sending or receiving a file, running another program, or performing some other action.

Each client-and-server combination uses a *protocol* that specifies the signals, formats, timing, and types of data that the two programs exchange. The most commonly used Internet protocols include the following:

* Mail
* News
* File Transfer (FTP)
* Access to a distant host computer (Telnet)
* The World Wide Web (HyperText Transfer Protocol)

CHAPTER 3

To use the World Wide Web, you need a computer with a modem and access to a network connected to the Internet.

A computer used for browsing the World Wide Web should include the following:

* A 486 or Pentium processor
* At least 16MB of RAM
* A hard drive with at least 1,000MB space
* A 15-inch or 17-inch color monitor with dot pitch of .28 mm or less

If you inherit an old computer that doesn't have all the features you need, you may still be able to use it for browsing the Web, with a few additions and changes. But if the upgrades cost more than about $500, you should consider buying an inexpensive new system instead. The most effective improvements you can make to an old computer are as follows:

* Replace the processor
* Add more memory
* Install a bigger hard drive
* Install a 3.5-inch diskette drive

A modem converts between digital data from a computer and audio signals that can travel through the public telephone system. Your modem should have these features:

* At least 28.8 Kbps data transmission speed (14.4 Kbps if it's a gift)
* Internal or external for a desktop computer; external on a PC Card for a portable
* Meets the V.34 standard (V.32bis for 14.4 Kbps)

CHAPTER 4

How to choose an Internet service provider (page 58)

Several types of businesses offer access to the Internet. Each has specific advantages.

National and international service providers:

* Large, well-established companies
* Local telephone numbers in many locations
* Competitive, flat-rate service with unlimited hours

Local and regional service providers:

* Local telephone numbers for technical support
* More personal service

Online information services (America Online, CompuServe, Prodigy, Microsoft Network):

* Additional proprietary content and services
* Easy to set up new accounts
* Nationwide dial-in access

CHAPTER 5

How to choose a Web browser (page 69)

To explore the World Wide Web, you must use a client program called a *Web browser*. The two most popular browsers are Netscape Navigator and Microsoft Internet Explorer. Both are available as free downloads through the Internet and in commercial versions from software retailers. Both programs have very similar feature sets and are about equal in speed and ease of use.

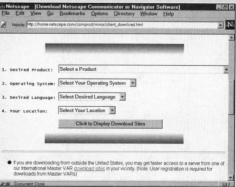

How to configure Netscape Navigator (page 73)

1. Select [Options] → [General Preferences].
2. Click the Colors tab to select background and text colors.
3. Click the Fonts tab and then click one of the Choose Font buttons to change the typefaces.
4. Use the other tabs to change other options.

How to configure Internet Explorer (page 75)

1. Select [View] → [Options] and click the General tab.
2. Select the colors you want to use for text, background, and visited and unvisited links.

How to change your start page (page 76)

Netscape Navigator:

1. Select [Options] → [General Preferences] and click the Appearance tab.
2. Type the URL of the page you want to use in the Browser Starts With field.

Internet Explorer:

1. Jump to the page you want to use as your start page.
2. Select [View] → [Options] and then click the Navigation tab.
3. Select [Start Page] in the [Page] menu .
4. Click the Use Current button.

CHAPTER 6

How to use Uniform Resource Locators (page 85)

The Web uses URLs to identify individual Web pages and other files. A URL has this format: *type://address/path*. The *type* for Web pages is http:// , so the URL for IDG Books' Worldwide Web site is `http://www.idgbooks.com`.

To jump to a new Web page, type the URL for that page in your browser's Location or Address field.

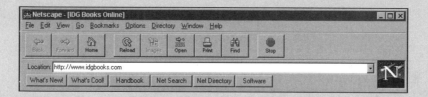

How to use hot links (page 87)

Many Web pages have hot links to other locations on the Web embedded into text or pictures. Hot links in text usually appear in a contrasting color. To jump to the target of a hot link, click the link.

How to retrace your steps through the Web (page 90)

To jump to the last Web page you visited, click the Back or Forward button in your browser's toolbar.

How to keep a list of Web pages you want to visit again (page 91)

To add the current Web page to Netscape's list of bookmarks, select Bookmarks → Add Bookmark. To add the current Web page to Internet Explorer's list of favorites, select Favorites → Add To Favorites.

CHAPTER 7

How to construct a keyword search (page 104)

To use a Web search engine, enter the word or name you want to find in the Search field. To search for a phrase, place quotation marks around the phrase. To search for Web pages that contain more than one keyword, use a plus sign (+) in front of each word. For example, **+apple +cider**. To exclude Web pages that include a keyword, use a minus sign (−) in front of that word. For example, **+apple +cider −vinegar**.

Where to find search engines (pages 104–107)

Yahoo!	http://www.yahoo.com
Excite	http://www.excite.com
AltaVista	http://www.altavista.digital.com
Lycos	http://www.lycos.com
WebCrawler	http://www.webcrawler.com
HotBot	http://www.hotbot.com

Infoseek	http://guide.infoseek.com
Search.com	http://www.search.com
MetaCrawler	http://metacrawler.com

Where to find Web guides (page 110)

Netscape Destinations	http://home.netscape.com/escapes/index.html
EINet Galaxy	http://galaxy.einet.net
LookSmart	http://www.looksmart.com
The Huge List	http://www.thehugelist.com
NetGuide	http://www.netguide.com
The Scout Report	http://rs.internic.net/scout/report
Eye on the Web	http://www.eyeontheweb.com
Maple Square	http://maplesquare.sympatico.ca

CHAPTER 8

Where to find online newspapers (page 129)

| Newslink | http://www.newslink.org/news.html |

Where to find online news services (page 131)

MSNBC	http://www.msnbc.com
CNN Interactive	http://www.cnn.com
Time Daily	http://www.pathfinder.com/time
Nando.net	http://www.nando.net
New Jersey Online	http://www.nj.com

Where to find news directly from wire services (page 135)

The Associated Press	Through member newspapers' Web sites, including www.abqjournal.com, www.dallasnews.com/, www.freep.com/the_wire/
United Press International	www.clari.net/iap
Reuters	http://www.reuters.com/reutersnews
Agence France Press	http://www.afp.com/monbref/monbrefva.html
ITAR-TASS	http://www.itar-tass.com/news.htm
The Press Association	http://www.pa.press.net
Kyodo News	http://www.kyodo.co.jp

Where to find news reports selected from many sources (page 141)

Top News   `http://topnews.com`
New Century News   `http://www.newcentury.net`

Where to find radio and TV news on the Web (page 143)

National Public Radio   `http://www.npr.org/news`
Pacifica Radio   `http://www.webactive.com/webactive/pacifica`
ABC RadioNet   `http://www.abcradionet.com`
CBC Radio (Canada)   `http://radioworks.cbc.ca`
Other broadcasters   `http://www.wrn.org/audio.html`
around the world

Where to find a directory of online radio stations (page 146)

The MIT List of Radio Stations   `http://www.wmbr.mit.edu/stations`

CHAPTER 9

Where to find weather information on the Web (page 154)

The Weather Channel   `http://www.weather.com`
Intellicast   `http://www.intellicast.com`
WeatherNet   `http://cirrus.sprl.umich.edu/wxnet`
EarthWatch   `http://www.earthwatch.com`
BBC Weather Centre   `http://www.bbc.co.uk/weather`
(Britain)
Environment Canada   `http://www.on.doe.ca/text/index.html`
The Weather Network   `http://www.theweathernetwork.com`
(Canada)
The Finnish Meteorological `http://www.fmi.fi`
Institute
Meteo France   `http://www.meteo.fr`
German Climate   `http://www.dkrz.de`
Research Center
Weather Underground   `http://underground.org.hk`
of Hong Kong
Japan Weather Association `http://www.jwa.go.jp:80`
The Weather in Israel   `http://weather.macom.co.il/`
Italian Weather links   `http://www.dsi.unive.it/~amartini`

New Zealand	`http://crash.ihug.co.nz/~stormy/`
Weather Outlook	`http://www.gov.sg/metsin/fort.html`
for Singapore	
Central Weather	`http://www.cwb.gov.tw`
Bureau Taiwan	
Thai Weather Forecasts	`http://www.nectec.or.th/bureaux/met-dept/`

Where to find sports news on the Web (page 157)

AFP World SportsReport	`http://www.afp.com/sportsreport`
ESPN SportsZone	`http://espnet.sportszone.com`
Nando SportsServer	`http://www.nando.net/SportServer`
Sports Illustrated Online	`http://pathfinder.com/si/`
TSN (Canada)	`http://arena.tsn.ca`

Where to find links to live audio play-by-play of sports events on the Web (page 162)

| Yahoo!'s directory | `http://events.yahoo.com/Sports/` |
| TimeCast | `http://timecast.com` |

Where to find financial information on the Web (page 163)

CNNfn	`http://cnnfn.com`
Bloomberg Personal Online	`http://www.bloomberg.com`
Quote.com	`http://www.quote.com`

Where to find a directory of online magazines (page 165)

| Ecola | `http://www.ecola.com/news/magazine` |

CHAPTER 10

Where to find links to complete books on the Web (page 173)

The Internet Public Library	`http://www.ipl.org/reading/books`
The On-line Books Page	`http://www.cs.cmu.edu/books.html`
Alex: A Catalogue of Electronic	`gopher://rsl.ox.ac.uk:70/11/`
Texts on the Internet	`lib-corn/hunter`

Where to find links to U.S. Government agencies and departments (page 177)

Government Information Xchange   `http://www.info.gov`

Where to find links to foreign government information (page 179)

The Virtual Tourist   `http://www.vtourist.com/webmap`
The Yahoo! list of government sites   `http://www.yahoo.com/Government/`
`Countries`
Foreign Government Information   `http://www.info.gov/Info/html/`
`foreign_government.htm`
The Electronic Embassy   `http://www.embassy.org`

Where to find links to state and local information on the Web (page 181)

All Aboard   `http://pti.nw.dc.us/`
`AllAboard.htm`
State and Local Government on the Net   `http:// www.piperinfo.com/`
`state/states.html`
The Library of Congress Internet Resource   `http://lcweb.loc.gov/global/`
Page for State and Local Governments   `state/stategov.htm`

Where to find health and medical information on the Web (page 182)

thrive@pathfinder   `http://pathfinder.com/thrive`
Reuters Health Information Services   `http://www.reutershealth.com`
America's HouseCall Network   `http://www.housecall.com`

Where to find travel information on the Web (page 184)

Internet Travel Network   `http://www.itn.net`
TravelWeb   `http://www.travelweb.com`
Trip Link   `http://www.sys1.com/trip`
Epicurious Travel   `http://travel.epicurious.com`
Travelocity   `http://www.travelocity.com`

CHAPTER 11

Where to find collections of shareware and freeware programs on the Web (page 198)

Shareware.com	http://www.shareware.com
Download.com	http://www.download.com
Jumbo	http://www.jumbo.com
Winsite	http://www.winsite.com
ZDNet Software Library	http://www.hotfiles.com
FilePile	http://filepile.com

Where to find collections of Internet tools on the Web (page 202)

Stroud's Consummate List	http://www.stroud.com
TUCOWS	http://www.tucows.com

Where to find computer user groups (page 204)

User Group Connection	http://www.ugconnection.org

CHAPTER 12

Where to find business directories on the Web (page 213)

Big Yellow	http://bigyellow.com
BigBook	http://www.bigbook.com
GTE SuperPages	http://yp.gte.net
AT&T Toll-Free Internet Directory	http://att.net/dir800
Big Yellow Global	http://bigyellow.com/global

Where to buy books through the Web (page 219)

Amazon.com	http://www.amazon.com
Book Stacks Unlimited	http://www.books.com
BookServe	http://www.bookserve.com
The Elliott Bay Bookstore	http://www.elliottbaybook.com/ebbco
The University Bookstore	http://www.bookstore.washington.edu
Cody's	http://www.codysbooks.com
Powell's Books	http://www.powells.com
The Tattered Cover Book Store	http://www.tatteredcover.com
The Australian Online Bookshop	http://www.bookworm.com.au
Blackwell's (Britain)	http://www.blackwell.co.uk/bookshops
Duthie Books (Canada)	http://www.duthie.com

Canada's Internet Bookstore	`http://www.canadabooks.com`
Canada's Virtual Bookstore	`http://cvbookstore.com`
Osiandersche Buchhandlung (Germany)	`http://www.osiander.de`
Fred Hanna's Bookstore (Ireland)	`http://www.adnet.ie/hannas`
The Ireland Bookstore	`http://indigo.ie/~spc`
La Bancarella International Bookstore	`http://www.interware.it/bancarella`
Liberia Rinascita (Italy)	`http://www.rinascita.it/rinascita_ web/rinascita_libr/rinlibringl.html`
Liberias Gandhi (Mexico)	`http://www1.gandhi.com.mx`
New Zealand Books Online	`http://www.nzbooks.co.nz`
The Singapore Bookshop	`http://www.bookshop.canadasia.com.sg`
Antiquarian Booksellers Association of America	`http://www.clark.net/pub/rmharris/ abaa.html`

CHAPTER 13

Where to find plug-in programs (page 240)

Netscape's directory of plug-ins is located at `http://home.netscape.com/ comprod/mirror/navcomponents_download.html`.

Where to find directories of audio services on the Web (page 247)

TimeCast	`http://www.timecast.com`
StreamWorks	`http://www.xingtech.com/content/sw2_content.html`
TrueSpeech	`http://www.dspg.com/cool.htm`
Shockwave Audio	`http://www.macromedia.com/shockwave/epicenter/ index.html`
Internet Wave	`http://www.vocaltec.com/sitesdt.htm`

Where to find links to live audio events on the Web (page 248)

TimeCast	`http://www.timecast.com`
NetGuide	`http://www.netguide.com`
AudioNet	`http://www.audionet.com`

Where to find live audio from congressional hearings and debates (page 249)

Fednet	`http://www.fednet.net`
C-SPAN	`http://www.c-span.org`

Where to find other audio services through the Web (page 252)

Police radio   `http://www.policescanner.com`
Dallas/Fort Worth Air   `http://www.audionet.com/simulflite`
Traffic Control

Where to listen to radio programs through the Web (page 252)

RadioTower   `http://www.radiotower.com`
CBC Radio/CBC Stereo `http://www.radio.cbc.ca`
CBS Radio   `http://www.cbsradio.com`
National Public Radio   `http://www.npr.org`
Monitor Radio   `http://www.csmonitor.com/monitor_radio/`
`monitor_radio.html`

CHAPTER 14

Where to find virtual communities on the Web (page 261)

SeniorNet   `http://www.seniornet.org`
The Well   `http://www.well.com`
Electric Minds `http://www.minds.com`
Minitel   `http://minitel.fr`

Where to find directories of communities on the Web (page 263)

Electric Minds Community Center   `http://www.minds.com/`
Forum One   `http://www.ForumOne.com`

CHAPTER 15

Choosing an e-mail client program (page 269)

Netscape and Microsoft include similar e-mail client programs with their browsers. For additional e-mail management features, try the free or commercial version of Eudora. You can download a free copy of Eudora Light from `http://www.eudora.com`. All three programs have similar feature sets.

How to receive and read e-mail messages (pages 270–283)

If your e-mail client program is not configured to automatically check for mail on a regular schedule, click the Check Mail button in the client's toolbar. New messages appear in the Inbox folder.

To read a message, double-click the description of that message.

How to compose and send e-mail messages (pages 270–283

1. Open the message editor.
2. Type the recipient's e-mail address in the To: field.
3. Type a short description of the message contents in the Subject: field.
4. Type the text of the message in the body of the editor window.
5. Click the Send or Queue button in the toolbar.
6. After all your messages are ready to send, click the Send Mail button in the toolbar.

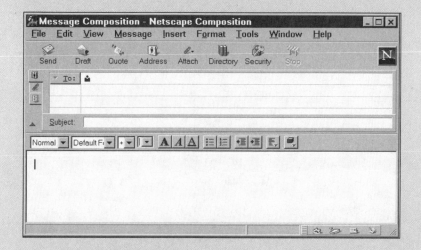

Where to find a directory of Internet mailing lists (page 285)

Liszt   http://www.liszt.com

VISUAL INDEX

Connecting to the Web

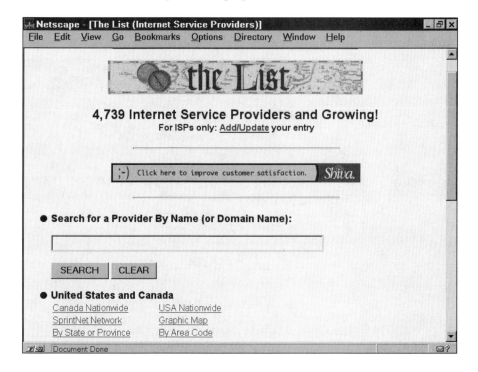

Moving Around the Web

How to repeat a jump from the current page (page 91)
How to use Bookmarks or Favorites to jump to the page described (page 91)

Using Search Engines

How to request a list of links to matching Web sites in Yahoo! (page 103)
How to use AltaVista to request a list of links to Web pages that contain specific keywords (page 106)
Where to find additional directories (page 110)

Using Gopher

How to use Gopher menus to find documents and files (page 117)

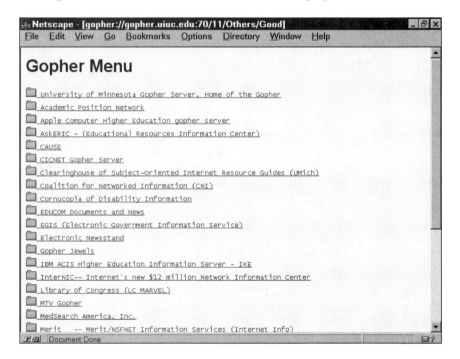

Finding People

How to find addresses, telephone numbers, and e-mail addresses through the Web (page 121)

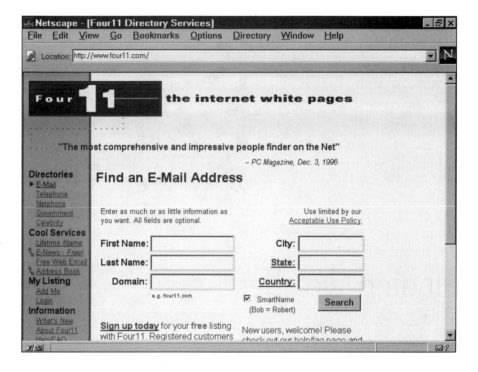

Finding News

Where to find newspapers on the Web (page 129)
Where to find online news services (page 131)
Where to find news from wire services (page 135)
Where to find highlights from many sources (page 141)
Where to find news from radio and television (page 143)

Finding Weather

Where to find weather reports (page 154)

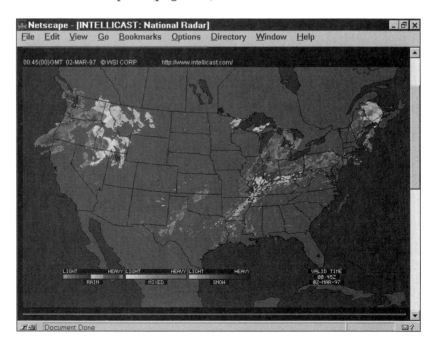

Finding Sports News

Where to find sports on the Web (page 157)

Finding Financial News

Where to find financial news on the Web (page 163)

Finding Specialized Information

How to use library catalogs through the Web (page 173)
. Where to find libraries of online text on the Web (page 176)
Where to find government information (page 177)

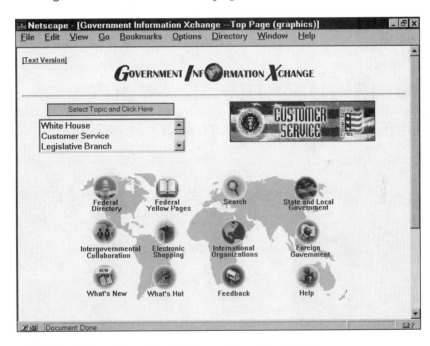

Where to find health and medical information (page 182)
Where to find travel information (page 184)

Finding Computer Resources

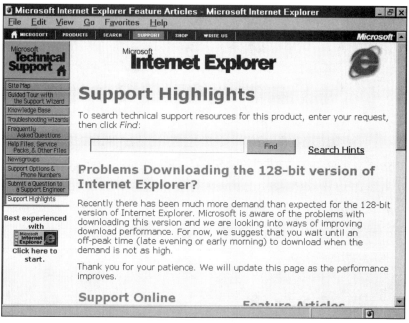

Where to find Internet application programs and utilities (page 198)

Audio on the Web

Online Communities

How to participate in virtual communities (page 260)
Where to find virtual communities (page 263)

INDEX

AOL (America Online)
  basic description of, 59–61
  browsers and, 61–64, 72
  Channels, 60
  chat sessions, 18
  contact information for, 61
  DNS address for, 30
  news sources and, 138
  virtual communities and, 259, 261,
    265
AP (Associated Press), 19, 129–130, 132,
    135–136, 139–140, 159
APP.com Web site, 137
Appearance tab, 112
Apple Computer, 31
applets
  basic description of, 238
  Java, 238–240, 243
Archie McPhee's Web site, 22
Arizona Central Web site, 137
associations, file, 35
asterisk (*), 104
at sign (@), 30
AT&T Toll-Free Internet Directory
    Web site, 214
AT&T World Net, 58
ATM Locator Web site, 8–9
attachments, e-mail, 267, 282
auctions, 227–228
Auction Sales Web site, 228
AudioNet Web site, 249, 250
audio. *See also multimedia; music*
    Web sites
  files, downloading, 245–247
  formats, 247–248
  news sources and, 143–146
  plug-ins and, 237–238, 244–248
  RealAudio and, 25, 143, 146, 163,
    245–249, 254–255
  streaming, 143
  volume, adjusting, 247
Australian Online Bookshop Web site,
    221
AutoPilot Web site, 6, 7

B

backbones, 28–29, 61
backslash (\), 33
Baltimore Sun Web site, 150
BBC Weather Center Web site, 157
BellSouth.net, 58
Bersia Grazing Reserve Web site, 184
Best of Singapore Web site, 88–90
Best of the Web (Web site), 111–112
beta testing, 83, 198
BigBook Web site, 214
Big Yellow Global Web site, 214
Big Yellow Web site, 213
bitcasters, 146
bits per second (bps), 52
Blackwell's on the Internet Web site, 221
Bloomberg News Web site, 164
Bloomingdale's Web site, 215
book buying online, 219–224
Book Stacks Unlimited Web site, 219
bookmarks
  organizing, 92–94
  using, 91–94
bookmarks list, 100
Bookmarks menu, 92
BookServe Web site, 219
Boston.com Web site, 4
Boston Insider Web site, 4
Boston Online Web site, 4–5
bps (bits per second), 52
British Press Association, 19
Browse button, 98
browser(s). *See also plug-ins; specific
browsers*
  basic description of, 26, 69–84
  downloading, 70–71
  finding, 69–72
  free copies of, 71
  history of, 33
  installing, 72–73, 81–83
  links to search tools from, 108–109
  older computers and, 47–48
  using external, with an online service
    account, 64

E

Earthlink TotalAccess, 58
EarthWatch Web site, 156
Ebay Web site, 228
Ebroker Web site, 229
Eccentric Software, 171
Echo Web site, 263
Ecola List Web site, 165
Edit menu, 114, 223, 227
.edu prefix, 30
EINet Galaxy Web site, 114
elected officials, 181
election information, 181–182
Electric Minds Web site, 263
electronic commerce, 215–228
 credit-card transactions, 216–217
 private sales, 229–230
 stock quotes, 40, 164, 228–229
Electronic Embassy Web site, 179–180
Electronic Telegraph Web site, 131
Elliot Bay Book Company Web site, 220
e-mail, 32, 70
 basic description of, 15–16, 267–87
 composing/sending, 274–275,
  278–279, 281–282
 to elected officials, 181
 filters, 279, 286
 how it works, 268–70
 IBM TCP/IP and, 51
 mailing lists, 16–18, 260, 263, 283–286
 online services and, 64
 receiving, 270–271, 275–276, 281
 reminder services and, 230–233
 speed of, 20
Environment Canada Public Weather
 Forecasts Web site, 157
Epicurious Web site, 187, 284
ESPN SportZone Web site, 158
E*Trade Web site, 229
Eudora, 279–283
Evansville Online Web site, 137
Excel, 35, 97–100, 238, 240
Excite search tool, 105, 113, 161, 163,
 186, 198, 224

ExecPC, 202
Expedia Web site, 167–168
Express Mail Web site, 167
Eye on the Web Web site, 115

F

f2f (face to face), 19
family trees, 122
FAQs (Frequently Asked Questions), 205
Fast Search button, 110
Favorites list, 95, 100
 basic description of, 91–92
 organizing, 92–94
Favorites menu, 91, 95
FCC (Federal Communications
 Commission) Web site, 251
FedEx Web site, 166
FedNet Web site, 250–251
FidoNet, 259
file(s)
 associations, 35
 compressed, 73, 82, 197, 199,
  244–245
 copying, to directories, 73, 82
 importing, 97–100
 players, 199
 viewers, 199
File menu, 98, 208
FilePile Web site, 202
financial news, 163–164
Find It Fast! Web site, 108–109
Finger, 51
Finnish Meteorological Institute Web
 site, 157
flags, 21–22
flaming, 60
floppy drives, 49–50
florists, 232
Fodor's Hotel Index Web site, 4
folders. *See also directories*
 basic description of, 33
 copying files to, 73, 82

(continued)

(continued)

Internet Explorer browser *(continued)*
    toolbars, 90–91, 94, 98
    URLs and, 86–87
    versions of, 79–83
    Web site, 81
Internet Health Watch Web site, 183
Internet Mail (Microsoft), 270–274
internetMCI, 58
Internet Pizza Server Web site, 26
Internet Public Library, 177
Internet Travel Network Web site, 187
inventories, 215
investment information, 40–41,
        163–164, 228–229
IP (Internet Protocol) addresses, 30, 210
IRC (Internet Relay Chat), 18, 260
Ireland Bookstore Web site, 222
Irish Times, 19
ISPs (Internet service providers). *See also*
        specific providers
    browsers and, 70, 71
    directory of, 191
    finding, 57–66
    high-speed connections and, 61–62
    local/regional, 57, 59
    national, 57–59
    types of, 57–58
Italian Weather Links Web site, 157
ITAR-TASS Web site, 139–140
ITU (International Telecommunications
        Union), 53
IWAVE (Internet Wave) audio format,
        248

J

Jack White & Company Web site, 229
Japan Weather Association Web site, 157
Java, 124, 238–240, 243, 256
Join button, 210
Jumbo Web site, 201

K

K. Aufhauser & Co. Web site, 229
keywords, 103–106
    Gopher and, 119–120
    multiple searches with, 109–110
    using, basic description of, 103
Krol, Ed, 51
Kyodo News Web site, 141

L

La Bancarella International Bookstore
        Web site, 222
La Grande Ourse Web site, 222
LANs (local area networks), 51, 61
laptop computers, 52
L.A. Trade, 49
LIBCAT: A Guide to Library Resources
        on the Internet Web site, 176
Liberia Rinascita Web site, 222
Liberias Gandhi Web site, 222
libraries, 173–177, 181
Library of Congress Internet Resource
        Page for State and Local
        Government Web site, 181
Libweb Web site, 176
links. *See also URLs (Uniform Resource*
        Locators)
    color of, 78, 87–88
    Internet Explorer preferences for, 78
    using, 87–90, 94–96
LISTSERV, 17–18, 285
The List Web site, 191
Liszt's Web site, 285
live chat, 18. *See also chat*
live events, 162–163, 248–249, 253–255
Lobster Institute Web site, 6, 8
Lobster.net Web site, 6
Location field, 87, 88, 117
LookSmart Web site, 114
Lucida Console font, 74, 78
Lycos search tool, 106–107, 109, 113,
        161, 182, 186, 217

(continued)

IDG BOOKS WORLDWIDE REGISTRATION CARD

Visit our Web site at http://www.idgbooks.com

Title of this book: **Discover the World Wide Web**

My overall rating of this book: ❑ Very good [1] ❑ Good [2] ❑ Satisfactory [3] ❑ Fair [4] ❑ Poor [5]

How I first heard about this book:

❑ Found in bookstore; name: [6]   ❑ Book review: [7]

❑ Advertisement: [8]   ❑ Catalog: [9]

❑ Word of mouth; heard about book from friend, co-worker, etc.: [10]   ❑ Other: [11]

What I liked most about this book:

_____

_____

What I would change, add, delete, etc., in future editions of this book:

_____

_____

Other comments:

_____

Number of computer books I purchase in a year: ❑ 1 [12] ❑ 2-5 [13] ❑ 6-10 [14] ❑ More than 10 [15]

I would characterize my computer skills as: ❑ Beginner [16] ❑ Intermediate [17] ❑ Advanced [18] ❑ Professional [19]

I use ❑ DOS [20] ❑ Windows [21] ❑ OS/2 [22] ❑ Unix [23] ❑ Macintosh [24] ❑ Other: [25]_____

(please specify)

I would be interested in new books on the following subjects:

(please check all that apply, and use the spaces provided to identify specific software)

❑ Word processing: [26]   ❑ Spreadsheets: [27]

❑ Data bases: [28]   ❑ Desktop publishing: [29]

❑ File Utilities: [30]   ❑ Money management: [31]

❑ Networking: [32]   ❑ Programming languages: [33]

❑ Other: [34]

I use a PC at (please check all that apply): ❑ home [35] ❑ work [36] ❑ school [37] ❑ other: [38] _____

The disks I prefer to use are ❑ 5.25 [39] ❑ 3.5 [40] ❑ other: [41]_____

I have a CD ROM: ❑ yes [42] ❑ no [43]

I plan to buy or upgrade computer hardware this year: ❑ yes [44] ❑ no [45]

I plan to buy or upgrade computer software this year: ❑ yes [46] ❑ no [47]

Name: _____ Business title: [48] _____ Type of Business: [49] _____

Address (❑ home [50] ❑ work [51]/Company name: _____)

Street/Suite# _____

City [52]/State [53]/Zipcode [54]: _____ Country [55] _____

❑ **I liked this book!** You may quote me by name in future
IDG Books Worldwide promotional materials.

My daytime phone number is _._____

IDG BOOKS WORLDWIDE

THE WORLD OF
COMPUTER
KNOWLEDGE®

❏ # YES!
Please keep me informed about IDG Books Worldwide's
World of Computer Knowledge. Send me your latest catalog.